EUL VERLAG

Prof. Dr. Wolfgang Chr. Fischer (Editor)

German Hyperinflation 1922/23

A Law and Economics Approach

EUL VERLAG

Bibliografische Information der Deutschen Nationalbibliothek

Die Deutsche Nationalbibliothek verzeichnet diese Publikation in der Deutschen Nationalbibliografie; detaillierte bibliografische Daten sind im Internet über <http://dnb.d-nb.de> abrufbar.

ISBN 978-3-89936-931-1
1. Auflage Juni 2010

JOSEF EUL VERLAG GmbH
Brandsberg 6
53797 Lohmar
Tel.: 0 22 05 / 90 10 6-6
Fax: 0 22 05 / 90 10 6-88
E-Mail: info@eul-verlag.de
http://www.eul-verlag.de

Bei der Herstellung unserer Bücher möchten wir die Umwelt schonen. Dieses Buch ist daher auf säurefreiem, 100% chlorfrei gebleichtem, alterungsbeständigem Papier nach DIN 6738 gedruckt.

AUTHORS

Professor Dr.rer.pol. Wolfgang Christian Fischer (Editor)
Universitätsprofessor (pens.), University of Bremen, Germany, Adjunct Professor of Economics, School of Law, Faculty of Law, Business & The Creative Arts, James Cook University, Townsville, Australia.

Professor Dr. Harrison Alexander Amankwah
BA (Hons) LLB (Hons) (Ghana); LLM (Cornell); SJD (NYU); Adjunct Professor of Law, School of Law, University of South Australia, Adelaide, Australia.

Daniel J. Goulding, BEc
Senior Client Advisor & Head of Derivatives RBS Morgans, Townsville, Australia.

Dr. med. Erich Krausbeck
Neurologist & Psychiatrist, Bad Ems, Germany.

Professor Kenneth Kaoma Mwenda, PhD, LLD
Senior Counsel, Legal Vice-Presidency of the World Bank, Washington, USA.

Dr. jur. Rainhart Schweigert
Lawyer & Tax Lawyer, Bad Ems, Germany.

JAMES COOK UNIVERSITY
AUSTRALIA

Research Monograph
School of Law, Faculty of Law, Business & Creative Arts
James Cook University, Townsville, Australia

Dedication

For my late brother,
Peter Michael Gerhard Fischer
Professor Dr.rer.pol. Wolfgang Chr. Fischer.

For my beloved and adorable daughter,
Alexandra Anika Amankwah
Professor Dr. Harrison Alexander Amankwah.

For my beloved wife,
Charlene Maree O'Dempsey
Daniel J. Goulding BEc.

For my late friend the Visionary of Bad Ems,
Dr.phil. Hans Dadder
Dr.med. Erich Krausbeck.

For my beloved and adorable son,
Joseph T.K. Mwenda II
Professor Kenneth K. Mwenda, PhD, LLD.

For my beloved wife,
Ingrid
Dr.jur. Rainhart Schweigert.

Sweeping up the banknotes from the street after the Hungarian pengő was replaced in 1946

Source: http://en.wikipedia.org/wiki/Hyperinflation

PREFACE

This Research Project about *"German Hyperinflation 1922/1923–A Law and Economics Approach"* aims to contribute to the knowledge and understanding of the significance of inflation and in particular the phenomenon of hyperinflation in numerous ways. Generally this is an unfamiliar territory of law and economics if it comes to hyperinflation with its colossal acceleration of the inflation rate and often this crucial issue had been regarded in the relevant literature of Law and Economics as a quantité négligeable.

At the outset, as editor and as author of this monograph, I would like to express my utter gratitude to the individual researchers, *Professor Dr. Harrison Alexander Amankwah, Mr Daniel J. Goulding BEc, Dr.med. Erich Krausbeck, Professor Dr. Kenneth K. Mwenda and Dr.jur. Rainhart Schweigert,* for their independent contributions. Personal views expressed in the contributions are those of the contributors and not necessarily those of the editor. Nevertheless in accepting this principle there are some issues in a few chapters that are overlapping, but this was unavoidable as the authors approached the topics from different angles.

Additionally, I offer my genuine thanks to *Professor Dr. Stephen Graw,* Head of School of Law, James Cook University, Townsville, Australia, who strongly supported my research work in every way. Furthermore I offer my thanks to *Mrs Shirley Jones,* School Manager, who gave generously of her time and expertise in administrative support.

I am indebted to my academic supervisor, the late *Professor Dr.rer.pol.habil. Fritz W. Meyer,* Head of Department of International Economic Affairs, Faculty of Law and Economics, Rheinische Friedrich-Wilhelms-Universität Bonn, Germany, who inspired me to research the acceleration of inflation during the German hyperinflation many decades ago.

I am very grateful to *Mr Peter Byron MEc,* Statistician, Magnetic Island, Townsville, for his great help in composing several graphs and figures and to *Ms Karen Kuhlmann,* Editorial Office, Eul Verlag, Köln, Germany, for various assistance in preparing the manuscript for its final publication.

Furthermore I would like to express my sincere thanks to Mr *W. Schulz,* Bibliothek des Bundesministeriums der Justiz (Library of the Federal Ministry of Justice), Berlin, who provided me with valuable copies of German legal documents from the archives. In addition I appreciated very much the various helpful advices of *Dr.phil. Dieter Simon,* Lüdenscheid, Germany, in matters related to German historical literature.

Also, I owe a great debt of gratitude to *Mr Bernard Adelt,* Flaxton, Queensland, who translated Chapter 1, Chapter 4, and Excurse Kurt Krausbeck, *Mr Ian Fleming,* Economist, Townsville, *Richard Anthony Lindsay,* Solicitor, Townsville, and *Dr.rer.pol. Milton Spidla,* Toronto, Canada, for their valuable input.

Also I express my gratitude to *Professor Dr. Michael Ottenbacher*, University of Guelph, Canada, for his moral support, particularly in times when I had doubts to complete this research project for various reasons.

Finally I am also indebted to *Mrs Janelle Margaret Fischer,* who revised the manuscript, composed the Index, and carefully prepared it for publication.

Wolfgang Christian Fischer
Editor
Townsville, Australia, May 2010

ABBREVIATIONS

A$	Australian Dollar
US$	American Dollar
KPD	Communist Party of Germany
KZ	Concentration Camp
DM	Deutsche Mark
€	Euro
EU	European Union
GM	"Gold Mark"
USPD	Independent Social Democratic Party of Germany
MRI	Magnetic resonance imaging
M	Mark
NSDAP	Nationalsozialistische Deutsche Arbeiterpartei
RG	Reichsgericht [German Supreme Court]
RGZ	Reichsgerichtsentscheidung [Judgement of the German Supreme Court]
RM	Reichsmark
Gestapo	Secret State Police [Nazi Regime]
SPD	Social Democratic Party of Germany
UN	United Nations
UNCC	United Nations Compensation Commission
WWI	World War I (1914-1918)
WWII	World War II (1939-1945)

CONTENTS

INTRODUCTION

The aim of this research monograph is to explore the establishment of a new economic order in the infant *German Republic* or often called *Weimar Republic (Deutsches Reich)* after *World War I* and its social and economic turbulence. The transformation from the monarchy with *Wilhelm II* as Head of the *German Empire (Deutsches Kaiserreich)* and finally his forced abdication, an enormous loss of soldiers' lives and immeasurable injured casualties in combat as well as the loss of civilian lives through starvation at home, the downfall of the obsolete nobility, and the formation of *Soldiers' and Workers' Councils* at the end of the war created a political, social and economic chaos.

This research monograph is focussing on the longstanding problem of inflation, and in particular on the very interesting hyperinflation. Certainly there is a great amount of literature available on these subjects in Economics, but very little in Law as far as it can be ascertained. Nevertheless there is a remarkable lack of the following highly interesting aspects:

- When inflation turns into a hyperinflation – what factors are crucial?
- What are the outcomes of the hyperinflation – *industrial retrogression*?[1]
- What are the economic and legal procedures to determine a *conversion rate* for a new national currency to stop the hyperinflation?
- What are the legal consequences for contracts, shares, property values etcetera within the hyperinflation and thereafter?

Whenever one is reading something about hyperinflation, in most cases what is analysed is just the tremendous acceleration of the inflation rate and some more general consequences are mentioned, for example that a hyperinflation is a broad tax and causes substantial impoverishment to the detriment of the so-called middle class (whatever that means), but nothing about the redistribution of wealth within a society. Which role the juridical system had played is just not mentioned.

One may consider the hyperinflation as another threat to national economies and the world economy as well; not only to the developing countries (for example in Peru in 1988 under the Government of President *Alan Garcia*, which the editor experienced including a sort of civil war actually right there in Lima and Arequipa, and recently in Zimbabwe), but also to the so-called developed world – or at least a very high inflation rate per annum around 20% (currently China has an estimated inflation rate around 10%). Of course there is an old debate within Economics – in particular Statistics – about the methodology of the measurement of inflation and the composing of various indices. Today with the world facing the impact of rapidly rising oil and energy prices, again the spectre of inflation has emerged as a major issue for governments, politicians and economic managers. It is perhaps timely to consider possible outcomes of inflation, especially every government's

---

[1] Industrial retrogression means a return to a less advanced state, a reversal of development, a decline or deterioration.

nightmare, *Hyperinflation.* Perhaps the best known and documented is the *German hyperinflation* experienced in 1922/23.

Often in literature it is said that the *German hyperinflation* is well documented. However, the colossal accelerating inflationary process reflects a *chaotic system* caught up with numerous factors. Nevertheless some authors consider the *German hyperinflation* monocausal in the sense that the German government tried to finance its spending, either for the war costs, for the war reparations or even for both altogether. In their textbook for economics students *Paul Krugman* and *Robin Wells* (Principles of Economics, 2nd edition 2009) reduce the highly complex phenomenon of *hyperinflation* to governments imposing an inflation tax: "Who ends up paying for the goods and services the government purchases with newly printed money? The people who currently hold money pay. They pay because inflation erodes the purchasing power of their money holdings. In other words, a government imposes an *inflation tax*[2], the reduction in the value of the money held by the public, by printing money to cover its budget deficit and creating inflation" *(Krugman & Wells 2009, 864).* Furthermore they figure out: "A race develops between the government printing presses and the public: the presses churn out money at a faster and faster rate, to try to compensate for the fact that the public is reducing its real money holdings. At some point the inflation rate explodes into hyperinflation, and people are unwilling to hold any money at all (and resort to trading in eggs and lumps of coal). The government is then forced to abandon its use of the inflation tax and shut down the printing presses" *(Krugman & Wells, 865).* Nonetheless the crucial question is still the exploration of *"at some point"* as a part of a complex system?

Within the natural science, in particular in physics, mathematics and biology, *complex systems* are non-linear and very difficult to predict in their progress. Reasonably *Paul Davies*[3] takes an example for a complex system: "Neural anatomy is awesomely complex. The human brain contains some hundred billion neurones and a given neurone may be directly connected to a great many others. It seems probable that some of the interconnections are structured systematically, while others are random. The electrical output signal of a given neurone will depend in a non-linear way on the combined input it receives from its connected partners. These inputs may have both an excitatory and an inhibitory effect. Thus, the character of the output signal from a particular neurone, such as the rate of firing, depends in a very complex way on what is happening elsewhere in the system" *(Davies 1987, 184).*

The *German hyperinflation* is a historical example of a devastating economic development. The issue of this project is to dig out the original ideas of those founders of the first German Republic, which obviously at current times through the discussion of a *"new German Social Democratic Party" (SPD)* or a *"new Australian Labor Party" (ALP)* have been forgotten. The issue is not to find a so-called *"Third Way"*; it is rather purely a fine analysis of the intentions, the instruments used and the achievements of those foundation fathers. This book also includes a presentation in the English language to make Anglo-Saxon scientists and politicians more aware of what *Friedrich Ebert* and his cabinets as well as

---

2 Krugman and Wells deduce the logic of hyperinflation: "High inflation arises when the government must print a large quantity of money, imposing a large inflation tax, to cover a large budget deficit" (Krugman & Wells, 865).

3 British distinguished scientist in theoretical physics & astrophysics.

numerous public office holders at that time had tried to achieve in a hostile environment (the burden of the *Treaty of Versailles*, the leftover power of the abolished nobility, the radicalism of nationalists, communists and anarchists). The infant *German Republic (Deutsches Reich)* had to be set up under the heavy burden of the *Treaty of Versailles (1919)*, signed at the *Paris Peace Conference,* between the Allied and Associated Powers and defeated Germany. The treaty declared Germany guilty of causing the war and among other things imposed immense reparations payments.

This German historical period was extremely controversial, i.e. whether to keep *free market capitalism* (the Emperor period) or to pursue the communists' intentions by abolishing private ownership on land and industrial production facilities. *Friedrich Ebert,* First President of the *German Republic* (1919-1925), and the *German Government (Reichsregierung)* had to establish their policies on the *Erfurter Program of the German Social Democratic Party (Sozialdemokratische Partei Deutschlands - SPD)* from 20th October 1891, which basically had been a Marxist program, and to find a solution of a peaceful transition (without a violent revolution) and integrating all people who were willing to work on a republic with basic human rights and *workers' participation* on economic decisions on various levels.

The economic order was primarily subject to the republican *Weimar Constitution (Verfassung des Deutschen Reichs 1919)* and the following legal framework, shaped by the *German National Assembly,* which had been in session at the city of *Weimar* due to violent unrest in *Berlin* at that time. A major task was the transformation of the previous economic order and the legal framework; based chiefly on the principles of unregulated capitalism with *free market economy*, fairly free international trade and expulsion of workers participation in the management of businesses. The *Council on Economic Affairs of the German Republic (Reichswirtschaftsrat)* was consequently set up, which became an important new legislative institution to transform and regulate the German economy according to the economic thought of revolutionaries and representatives of the labour movement. Based on economic thought about workers participation in the economic decision making process on macro and micro levels at the time, this council had to face various economic problems, for example the great hyperinflation, which was mainly the result of various reasons among others the finance system of military expenditures during World War I and subsequently culminating in 1923 at a very fragile stage of the infant *German Republic.* In the future there was looming the worldwide *Great Depression* (1927-1932). It raises the scepticism whether the founders of the Weimar Republic had been given sufficient time and an adequate amount of means to implement their projected economic order, or was it just an idealistic approach of revolutionaries, which had to be forwarded to future generations? "The inflation did not create an irremediable state of discontent which doomed the Weimar Republic from the outset. Given time, luck and prudence attitudes could have changed and been changed. The tragedy of the Republic was that it ran out of all three of these precious commodities" *(Southern 1979, D1053).* In an excursus three biographies will be presented: The political activities of the contemporary social democratic revolutionaries *Heinrich A. Trinowitz* and *Robert Fischer* (Grandfathers of Wolfgang Chr. Fischer) may illustrate the individual courageousness of social democrats and labour movement representatives at the time of the Early Weimar Republic. In addition some aspects of the political life of the social democratic journalist *Kurt Krausbeck* (Father of Erich Krausbeck) in the succeeding *National Socialist German Workers Party (Nationalsozialistische Deutsche Arbeiterpartei, NSDAP, 1920-1945)* Regime from 1933 to 1945 may demonstrate the very hardship of ordinary Germans during this period.

One may ask the old question of *Theodicy*, which means the vindication of divine providence in the sense of the protective care of God or nature in view of the existence of evil.

Gottfried Wilhelm Leibniz (1646-1716)

The term[4] was coined in 1710 by the German philosopher *Gottfried Leibniz* in his work entitled *"Essais de Théodicée sur la bonté de Dieu, la liberté de l'homme et l'origine du mal"*. Provocatively, *Erich Krausbeck* asserts: "the repeated loss of freedom in favour of integration in an ideology or also in a uniform is a basic need of the herd. Only if the human being developed to a wolf, would it be nearer to the aim of freedom. Wolves live isolated and unite only in winter as a herd for hunting. The people would go to ruin in fear and panic if one gave them freedom?" *Dostoyevsky* had concerned himself intensely with the Théodicée question in his 4-year imprisonment in chains in Siberia. The concept of Théodicée had been used in the 19th century to extend to broader philosophical contexts than the existence of good and evil, as God was used as an analogy to other philosophical problems. Thinkers such as *Georg WF Hegel* tried to argue that there was an absolute truth that reconciled different contradictory truths. *Théodicée* incorporates the old philosophical question why God (for atheists whatever) let it, for example the tremendous misery of hyperinflation, happen to mankind?

[4] The term theodicy comes from the Greek theós ('god') and díkē ('justice'), meaning literally "the justice of God," although a more appropriate phrase may be "to justify God".

Chapter 1 German Taxation Policy and Finances during World War I and beyond (1914 to 1923)

Rainhart Schweigert

At the beginning of 1914 no one in *Germany* could anticipate the great suffering and the utterly negative economic and financial consequences the *First World War* – which began at the end of July 1914 and effectively ended with the ceasefire on the 11th of November 1918 in *Compiègne/France* – would have on subsequent years.

The war death toll in Germany totalled approximately 1.8 million and the war wounded totalled approximately 4.2 million; the *cost of the war* amounted to approximately 194 billion gold marks.[5] The suffering of the civilian population was immeasurable due to exodus, starvation and deprivations. On top of this there were the direct and indirect losses, in particular the loss in production, cessation of territory, care of war victims, inflation during and after the war, as well as the huge reparations payments.[6]

Prior to the *First World War*, the *Territorial States* had the legislative and administrative jurisdiction for direct taxes as well as the authority to raise revenue. From 1871 to 1918 they had to contribute *matricular payments* – that were calculated based on their population – to the *Reich*, who in addition were entitled to all consumption taxes and custom duties. This taxation system already proved to be unrealistic and not financially viable for carrying out the functions and commitments of the *Reich* at the commencement of the *First World War*. In addition, Germany was financially not prepared for the war. *Popitz*, who had joined the *Treasury* in 1917 and in the future *Ministry of Finance* became a high ministry official, as well as acting State Secretary from January 1925 to December 1929, had declared with hindsight in 1928 that the "Reich had entered the greatest struggle in history financially unequipped" and without the "resolve to act".[7]

The tax revenue of the *Reich* and the *States* was totally inadequate; yet a higher tax yield would not have led to a victory by the *German Reich* over the *Western powers* and the *USA*, who had entered the war. The *war expenditure* amounting to 195 billion marks had to be financed largely by loans, although the State Secretary of the Treasury *Helfferich* (1915 to 1916) and others were of the opinion that these costs would have to be paid to Germany by the enemy after their defeat.[8]

The sourcing of the financial resources for the *First World War* was provided in the *German Reich* by the so-called *Julius Tower*, through debt financing and money creation (banknote credits and short-term treasury notes), together with an increase in existing and the creation of new taxes. The *Julius Tower* refers to a fortress tower of the ancient citadel in *Spandau*.

---

[5] dtv-Lexikon München, Bd. 20 S. 86.

[6] Brockhaus-Enzyklopädie, Bd. 24, Brockhaus-Verl. Mannheim.

[7] J. Popitz, Die Finanzpolitik seit 1918 in Zehn Jahren deutsche Geschichte 1918 - 1928, 179 ff.

[8] K. Epstein, M. Enzberger und das Dilemma der deutschen Demokratie, 373/374, Berlin 1962.

The war treasure amounting to 40 million thalers from the *French reparations in 1871*, which was unminted to 120 million marks, was stored there by the treasury.

The *German Reich* financed the war expenditure by short-term banknote indebtedness and by long-term bond issues to the general public. The new war bonds – achieved from 39.1 million citizens in the years 1914 to 1918 – brought in an amount of 98.2 billion marks; half of the war bonds came from medium, small and very small subscribers. From 1916 onwards there was a reduction in the purchasing power because of taxes, notably due to a *War Gain* and *Capital Gains Tax*, as well as an increase in some consumption and transaction taxes. These fiscal measures and the *second war tax reform of 1917* were unable to lead to a consolidation of the Reich's finances.

In order to finance the war expenditure, a *sales tax* (a so-called *Goods Turnover tax*), which was applied across all of Germany, was introduced in 1916 with a taxation rate of 1 in a thousand.[9] The *turnover tax* was repealed a few months before the end of the war on the 26th of July 1918; the general taxation rate was initially 0.5% and it was then increased with an amendment of the law to 1.5% on the 24th of December 1918, to 2% in 1922 and in 1923 it increased to 2.5%. Luxury items were taxed at 15%.[10]

The deliberations over the turnover tax legislation led to the establishment of the *Reich Taxation Court*, pursuant to the legislation of the 26th of July 1918,[11] because uniform judicial decisions were seen as crucially important. It was intended that a *supreme tax court* would be responsible for all matters covered not only by the turnover tax legislation, but indeed for all current and newly created tax legislation introduced by the Reich. The aim was to ensure equality of taxation with a uniform legal system. The resolution for the establishment of the *Reich Taxation Court* was passed by parliament (*Reichstag*) unanimously; the *Reich Taxation Court* which was based in *Munich* (the current *Federal Tax Court* location), commenced sitting before the end of the war, namely from the 1st of October 1918 onwards.[12]

At the conclusion of the armistice agreement in November 1918, the *German Reich* was faced with the almost insoluble task of dealing with the catastrophe on a number of levels. In particular, the integration of the returning soldiers to *Germany* into working life. In contrast to many other countries – who experienced a post-war depression - there was full employment between 1919 and 1923 and in the years 1920/21 even an economic boom.[13] Against this, there were extraordinary costs because of the lost war, above all due to the *Treaty of Versailles* and the reparations imposed by the victorious powers on Germany.

After signing the *Treaty of Versailles* on the 28th of June 1919, Germany had to relinquish 70,579 km of its territory with 7.3 million inhabitants – in particular *Alsace-Lorraine* – as well as its colonies; it lost ¾ of its annual production of zinc and iron ore, over ¼ of its coal production and 1/6 of its grain harvest. In addition, significant deliveries in kind were

---

9 Gesetz v. 26.06.1916 (RGBl. 1916, 639).

10 Rau u.a., Kommentar zum UmsatzsteuerG, Einf. vor § 1 (Rz. 3, 6, 8, 11), 2009 Köln.

11 RGBl. 1918, 959; Popitz, StuW 1928, 974.

12 H. Leidel, Die Begründung der Reichsfinanzverwaltung, Bundesminister der Finanzen, Bonn 1964.

13 Voss, R., Johannes Popitz, Jurist, Politiker, Staatsdenker (1884-1945).

required, as well as the handing over of almost all of the merchant fleet and the liquidation of German property and wealth abroad.[14]

In Article 231 of the *Treaty of Versailles*, Germany and its allies were accused of being solely responsible for the war and this was justification for the reparations and other imposed obligations. Many Germans, as well as all democratic parties – as can be discovered in many newspaper articles from 1919 – rejected the *Versailles Diktat* and the great economic difficulties that arose from it.

According to the *Treaty of Versailles*, reparation payments by Germany – the amount was supposed to be determined by a *Reparations Commission* – had to be made to the allies and associated powers. The reparations debt, which was calculated and demanded by the *Commission*, amounted to 223 billion Reichsmark - it was to be paid off by instalments until 1963 – was repudiated by the *German Reich*. Through the so-called *London Ultimatum* of the 5th of May 1921, the reparations debt was set at 132 billion gold mark and at 26% of the value of German exports.[15]

The debt of the *Reich* amounted to approximately 156 billion mark at the end of the war; to this were added the reparations payments. When comparing this with the *Reich's debt* of approximately 5 billion mark during 1913, the last year of peace, then the huge extent of Germany's financial plight is evident. According to the speech made by the Minister of Finance *Erzberger* in the *National Assembly* on the 30th of October 1919, the Reich's debt was as follows:[16]

31st of March 1915	16,715,000,000 Mark
31st of March 1916	38,855,000,000 Mark
31st of March 1917	69,023,000,000 Mark
31st of March 1918	105,251,000,000 Mark
31st of March 1919	156,092,000,000 Mark

Comparing the pre-war year of 1913 with the post-war year of 1919, the *Reich's debt* had increased 30-fold.

Whilst the total expenditure of the *Reich* in 1913 amounted to 2.4 billion mark, by 1919 it amounted to 7 times this sum, to 17.5 billion mark. The yearly interest amounted to 10 billion mark, therefore four times the total budget before the war. 4.3 billion mark had to be paid to disabled servicemen and surviving dependents, payments to the unemployed, assistance for housing, and compensation for Germans, who had lost private property during the war or from the ceded territories following the *Treaty of Versailles*.[17]

---

[14] Brockhaus-Enzyklopädie „Versailler Vertrag", Bd. 23, Mannheim.

[15] Terhalle, F., Geschichte der deutsch-öffentlichen Finanzwirtschaft vom Beginn des 19. Jahrhunderts bis zum Schluss des 2. Weltkriegs im Handbuch der Finanzwissenschaften, Bd. 1, Tübingen 1952, 294 ff.

[16] Rede zur Neuordnung des deutschen Finanzwesens vom Reichsminister der Finanzen, S. 82, Berlin 1919, Verlag Hobbing.

[17] K. Epstein, a.a.O., S. 83.

The accrued tax liabilities of 156 billion mark by 1919 could be attributed to the *Central Bank's* unsound fiscal policy and the removal of the exchange rate by legislation passed on the 4th of August 1914 (RGBL.326, 327). Until 1914 the money supply was backed by gold reserves that were introduced by the *Reich Central Bank* in 1873. However the *Central Bank* had from August 1914 onwards treated treasury bonds and treasury note trade bills as equal and used these trade bills together with gold to support the currency. With this action, therefore, the issuing bank was "released from the golden brake of the credit machine" (according to *Joseph Schumpeter*). No limits were therefore set on the creation of money by the *Central Bank*.[18]

Following the *November Revolution of 1918* – which led to the collapse of the monarchist regimes in *Germany* – the *National Assembly*, which had been elected on the 19th of January 1919, assembled in *Weimar*. Notably, the *Weimar Constitution* was created to take effect on the 11th of August 1919, with the result that Germany became a republic.

Due to the fiscal emergency, demands were made by many during the *Weimar Constitution* proceedings to preserve and broaden the legislative and tax sovereignty enjoyed by the Reich.[19] In January 1919, *Preuss* referred to this "the nature of the relationship must change and the financial system must be weighted towards the Reich and the Reich must have precedence".[20]

The *Weimar Constitution* gave the Reich exclusive lawmaking power, *tax sovereignty* and the *administration of customs and excise duties* (article 6 number 6, article 83). This guaranteed for the first time in German history an *unrestricted uniform customs service* under a centralised administration, and this was maintained during later upheavals within the State right up to the present day.

Once the constitution came into force on the 21st of June 1919, *Matthias Erzberger* – who was the *Vice Chancellor* at the same time – was appointed by *President Ebert* into the difficult portfolio of *Minister for Finance.* In his first speech, in front of the *National Assembly in Weimar* on the 8th of July 1919, he described the war as "devastating on our finances" and went on to elaborate:

> "There is now only one task for us all: to rebuild what the disastrous war has destroyed, to create a new foundation for the immense obligations that the war and its unfortunate outcome has imposed on us ... The first task for reconstruction is fundamental financial reform."[21]

With his own single-mindedness, energy, persuasiveness and diligence and after only a relatively short incumbency of 9 months (21st of June 1919 to the 12th of March 1920), *Erzberger* carried out the most comprehensive financial reform in the Reich until then and

---

[18] a.a.O., S. 84.

[19] Von der Reichsschatzkammer zum Bundesfinanzministerium, herausgegeben vom Bundesminister der Finanzen, Köln S. 99, 101.

[20] Hagen Preuss in Denkschrift zum Verfassungsentwurf v. 03.01.1919, S. 9, Deutscher Reichsanzeiger Nr. 15 v. 20.01.1919.

[21] Rede zur Neuordnung des Finanzwesens, a.a.O., S. 3, 4.

established the *Reich Fiscal Authority*. He managed to ensure that the following 16 acts which dealt with tax, finance and the consolidation of the Reich budget were passed:

1. Fiscal Authority Act (Gesetz über die Reichsfinanzverwaltung) (10/09/1919)
2. The Extraordinary War Tax Act for 1919 (Gesetz über die außerordentliche Kriegsabgabe für das Jahr 1919) (10/09/1919)
3. War Tax from Capital Gains Act (Gesetz über die Kriegsabgaben vom Vermögenszuwachs) (10/09/1919)
4. Death Duties Act (Erbschaftsteuergesetz) (10/09/1919)
5. Duty on Matches Act (Zündwarensteuergesetz) (10/09/1919)
6. Tax on Playing Cards Act (Spielkartensteuergesetz) (10/09/1919)
7. Tobacco Goods Tax Act (Tabakwarensteuergesetz) (12/09/1919)
8. Acquisition of Land Tax Act (Grunderwerbsteuergesetz) (12/09/1919)
9. Reich Tax Code (Reichsabgabenordnung) (13/12/1919)
10. Turnover Tax Act (Umsatzsteuergesetz) (24/12/1919)
11. Reich Emergency Contribution Act (Gesetz über das Reichsnotopfer) (31/12/1919)
12. Tax Pardon Act (Gesetz über Steuernachsicht) (03/01/1920)
13. Income Tax Act (Einkommensteuergesetz) (29/03/1920)
14. Capital Gains Tax Act (Kapitalertragssteuergesetz) (30/03/1920)
15. Corporations Tax Act (Körperschaftsteuergesetz) (30/03/1920)
16. Distribution of Revenue between the Reich, States and Local Government Act (Landesteuergesetz über den Finanzausgleich zwischen Reich, Ländern und Gemeinden) (30/03/20)

Admittedly *Erzberger* could rely on the preliminary work by his predecessors *Schiffer* and *Demburg*, with contributions from outstanding public servants in the former Ministry of Finance, such as *Enno Becker, Herbert Dorn, Rolf Grabower, Stefan Moesle and Johannes Popitz*. Yet, it is to his credit that he managed to get these bills passed against opposition by politicians on the left and right of the political spectrum and many sections of the public. For this reason, there was no reorganisation of the *Reich* budget, but instead a fundamental restructuring of the administration of finance and tax laws was achieved. The introduction of the administration for Reich taxes and the creation of the *Tax Code* had according to *Hettlage* "to be credited as one of the greatest reforms of German administrative history".[22]

The *tax code* which was passed on the 13th of December 1919, was a particularly important part of the uniform tax system, namely the codification of the general tax laws into uniform legislation across the Reich. What was missing until then was a blanket law that contained basic clauses for all tax laws for the taxation and the administration of finance. The Reich uniform tax code had created the foundations for uniform and equitable taxation subject to the law and through the "orderliness" of the taxation process and the setting up of an appeal procedure introduced legal certainty for the tax payer.[23]

The policy of tax equity was enshrined in § 1 of the tax code, so that taxes were imposed on "those to whom the facts apply and under the law the obligation is established". Previously article 134 of the *Weimar constitution* had determined: "All citizens without

[22] Hettlage, Die Finanzverwaltung in Jeserich, Deutsche Verwaltungsgeschichte, Bd. 4, 182.
[23] Hübschmann, Kommentar zur Abgabenordnung, Einf. A, S. 5.

distinction will contribute in proportion to their resources to public expenditure, subject to the legislation". With these provisions the principle of universality of taxation, which had been demanded by the social masses at the end of the German Empire, was combined with the ability to pay and this principle of taxation equality and equity still prevails today.

An additional significant achievement by *Minister of Finance Erzberger* was the simplification of tax administration. In his fifth speech on financial reform before parliament (*Reichstag*) on the 3rd of December 1919 he declared: "What I have tried to achieve with all my energy from the first days of my appointment was a tax system for the Reich. The old system was flawed because the Reich had too few taxes and it was unable to administer these taxes independently".[24] With the *Fiscal Authority Act* of the 10th of September 1919 (RGBl. S. 1991) the consolidation of 25 German tax administrations was achieved after difficult negotiations with the representatives of the States, who viewed the tax administration of taxes by the Reich as a serious intervention into their rights. At the same time, the creation of a tax administration, with uniform skills, was achieved. For the first time, the Reich was responsible for taxation on a state or local government level.

In addition, *Erzberger's financial reform* included the transfer of income tax powers to the Reich. On the first day of the new government, on the 13th of February 1919, *Chancellor Scheidemann* announced this measure as the most important link towards uniform and socially equitable tax legislation. Only after the takeover of this, the largest direct tax, was the Reich in a position to achieve a relatively high tax income. By these means, the relationship with the States was fundamentally changed. The payment of matricular contributions to the Reich by the States was eliminated. Conversely the *States* became "*boarders of the Reich*", as they became dependent on remittances of tax revenue from the Reich and until 1923 their share of income and corporations tax was two thirds, of turnover tax one tenth; further they shared in the newly created taxes such as acquisition of land tax and death duties.[25]

The goal was to calculate income tax based on the *principle of capacity to pay*. Accordingly those on high incomes were taxed at a higher rate (*progressive tax*). For example, previously the top tax rate in *Prussia* was 4%; the rate under the new income tax act was increased dramatically, namely from 10% to 60%, hence the top rate increased fifteen-fold. The rate of 60% applied to incomes above 50,000 mark. Social Democrat members of parliament even asked for a top tax rate of 80%.

Previously the local councils were entitled to levy surcharges on top of income tax, which in practice had led to very high tax variations; for example there were some councils, who had levied a surcharge of up to 300%. As well, the income tax rate varied amongst the states. *Erzberger* stressed this in a speech before parliament regarding the restructuring of the German financial system:

> "The German taxpayer will in future not have to worry about working out whether he will get away with cheaper taxes, regardless of whether he lives in

---

[24] Rede zur Neuordnung des Finanzwesens, a.a.O., 111.

[25] H. Dieckmann, Johannes Popitz, Entwicklungen und Wirksamkeit in der Zeit der Weimarer Republik, Berlin 1960, S. 30.

Berlin, Brunewald, Coburg or on Lake Constance. The obligations have to be mutual and the same, regardless of the tax payer's abode."[26]

In contrast to the taxation on individuals, companies, especially companies listed on the stock exchange, were taxed under the *Corporations Law Act* of the 30th of March 1920. So that the *Reich*, states and local councils could jointly share in the most lucrative taxes, the final act of Erzberger's financial reform regulated this under *The Land Tax Act* of the 30th of March 1920.[27]

In order to prevent the feared outflow of capital from Germany abroad a *capital flow law* was passed.

In the years that followed, trotting inflation during 1919 to 1922 turned into *galloping inflation* by 1923. The rapid monetary devaluation should have been overcome with new tax legislation and amendments to the taxation laws. So in April 1922, during the term of the Minister for Finance *Hemes*, fourteen new taxation laws (*Wealth and Capital Growth Tax, law for mandatory loans, an increase in turnover tax and other taxes*) were passed (RGBL 335 ff.). Nevertheless, the new and amended taxation laws were unable to put a stop to the constant increase in inflation, which worsened to *hyperinflation* from autumn 1922 onwards. Rather than introducing monetary reform, the government and parliament took social problems into account, in order to use the excuse of insolvency to avoid reparations payments or at least to mitigate them.[28]

Due to the worsening inflation the Reich budget got more than ever out of balance. The ordinary and extraordinary expenditure of the public administration not covered by income amounted in 1920 to 123.4 billion mark, in 1921 to 160.7 billion mark and in 1922 to approximately 7 billion mark. *Minister for Finance Wirth* stressed in his speech before parliament on the 6th of July 1921 that given a permanent market slump every financial and tax policy was reduced to *ad absurdum*.[29]

Despite the constantly worsening monetary devaluation the principle still applied as before: "*Mark equals mark*".

This principle was abandoned with an important decision that was handed down by the *Supreme Court in Civil Matters* on the 28th of November 1923 (RGZ 107, 78 ff.). With this judgement, the *highest German civil court* gave the creditor the right to refuse the discharge of mortgages entered into from before the first war, when payment was made at face value. The court gave the judiciary the power to upvalue a mortgage appropriately and in good faith (§ 242 BGB).

In the years following 1919 a serious devaluation of German financial assets occurred. The exchange rate for one dollar amounted to 4.20 mark in July 1914 and in July 1922 to 20,000 mark; in August 1923 the dollar exceeded the million mark level and shortly afterwards the billion mark level. On the 15th of November 1923 one dollar cost 4.2 billion mark. In the

---

[26] Zitiert in Von der Reichsschatzkammer ..., S. 104.
[27] P. Kirchhof, Matthias Enzberger, Patriot u. Visionär, Hohenheim 2007.
[28] S. Haffner, Von Bismarck zu Hitler, 186 ff., Johannes Popitz, München 1989, 52 ff.
[29] 132. Sitzung des Reichstages, Steu.Ber., S. 4469.

period from January 1913 to November the inflation rate based on *wholesale prices* was 1 over 750 billion.[30] Eventually, the *expenditure by the Reich* had to be covered *by 99.6% debt.*

The monetary evaluation turned out to be positive for the owners of real property, but devastating for the owners of financial assets. The monetary economy practically came to a standstill in Germany. A further weakening of the German Reich's position occurred because of the *London Ultimatum* of the 15th of June 1921 when the valuable industrial territory in Upper Silesia had to be ceded to Poland.

As reparations were either not paid or only partly paid, *France* had gradually sent soldiers into the German cities of *Düsseldorf, Duisburg, Oberhausen* and *Mühlheim.* On the 11th of January 1923 powerful *French military units* occupied the *Ruhr district*, which was at the time the most important and for the economic viability of Germany indispensible industrial region. *France* tried to separate this territory with military means, economically and then politically from the *German Reich.* Germany responded with passive resistance: all production in the Ruhr district was stopped.[31] As a result, the *Reich Treasury* had to pay huge damages to the workers, as well as the industrial firms in the Ruhr district.

In June 1923 only 19% of expenditure was covered by income from the Reich. Legislation for the consideration of the monetary devaluation in relation to the tax laws, for the safeguarding of bread supply (Bread Supply Levy Act of the 23rd of June 1923) (Brotversorgungsabgabe), as well as "Sacrifice for the Rhine and the Ruhr" (Opfer für Rhein und Ruhr) and the contributions by employers and states, could not delay the advancing destruction of the State's finances. Dramatic measures were taken against delinquent and fraudulent taxpayers. Belated tax payments were charged interest on arrears of 30% per month and for tax avoidance fines of up to twenty times the lower tax amount were imposed. The cities moved to *printing emergency money* – that was supposed to replace the money issued by the *Central Bank* – in large quantities and uncontrolled and brought it into circulation. The unstable emergency money was valued in November 1923 at 320 trillion mark. *Popitz* described the following situation:

> "A person going inside the Tax Office in those days would not forget the amazing sight. Paper money lay in baskets and boxes, on shelves and on the cash desk in unruly lots. After all, it was no longer possible to establish the authenticity and validity of the (as it was) privately printed paper."[32]

The rapidly intensifying inflation led to a devaluation of all income paid in cash, in particular employees' wages. The wage paid to the worker was worth considerably less the next day or even worth nothing. Therefore disturbances within the populace – which on the 27th of July 1923 led to a *proclamation of a state of emergency in all of the Reich* – occurred everywhere. In the autumn of 1923 the *German Reich* stood at the very edge of its economic and political existence.

A short time after his appointment – on the 13th of August 1923 – the *Minister for Finance Hilferding* had attempted to acquire foreign currency, in order to keep feeding the

---

[30] Popitz a.a.O., S. 84.
[31] Haffner a.a.O., S. 188.
[32] Popitz a.a.O., S. 402.

population as well as to run public amenities such as the railway. After "containment of the foreign exchange market" he was hoping to bring about the movement in the dollar rate of exchange, so that he could make improvements to the wages and price policy. The government ceased the struggle on the Ruhr, or more specifically the passive resistance in the *Ruhr district*, on the 26th of July 1923. The reparation creditors *England* and the *USA* pressured *France* to end their occupation of the Ruhr district, which occurred soon after.

The *Minister for Finance Luther*, who was in office from the 6th of October 1923, managed to stabilise the currency and balance the Reich budget. His predecessor *Hilferding* had presented the cabinet a closed currency plan on the 10th of September 1923. The central idea was the creation of an independent gold bank; his plan contained the correct and realised concept of gold basis.[33]

The *enabling act* of the 13th October 1923 and the "Regulation for the Establishment of the *German Rentenmark*" (Rentenmarkverordnung/RGBl. 943) brought about the reform of the currency. The *Rentenmark* was redeemable for interest-bearing, gold-backed government bonds, which were backed by a mortgage on all agricultural land. The devalued paper mark was converted on the 20th of November 1923 at the rate of 1 billion to 1 rentenmark. The *German Central Rentenbank* was entitled to issue up to 2.4 billion rentenmark banknotes. This bank was established to reform the currency and remained as a Bank of Issue until October 1924; the *rentenmark* was then replaced by the *Reichsmark*.

In 1924 it became possible – not least through the *Dawes Plan* and the considerable reduction in reparation payments – to stabilise the finances of the Reich, as well as to bring tax revenue and expenditure by the Reich in a financially viable position. *Luther* is considered to be the *Minister for Finance* who "overcame inflation". Apart from the success of the currency reform, this positive result was due to the radical reduction in expenditure, three positive and effective tax emergency regulations (end of 1923 and the beginning of 1924), the resumption of production and exports, and in particular the will, spirit and commitment by the *German population* – who 5 years after the end of the war had ended, agitated for a positive restructuring of their lives and country.

Still to mention is that in the *Weimar Republic* (1919–1933) the *Minister for Finance* was replaced fifteen times and seven times in the here depicted period of 1919 to 1923, so that not one minister was able to push through a long-term funded plan for the consolidation of the State's finances, a proper functioning taxation system as well as undertake a realistic and just overhaul of the taxation laws. From February 1919 until December 1924 the *Reich Ministers for Finance were Schiffer*, *Demburg*, *Erzberger*, *Wirth*, *Hermes*, *Hilferding* and *Luther*. Despite their relatively brief tenure, the above named ministers made many positive decisions – as described – on behalf of the German Reich in the difficult years after the *First World War*.

---

[33] Im Gedenken an Reichsfinanzminister Rudolf Hilferding in Blickpunkt Finanzen, Bd. 6, herausgegeben vom Bundesministerium der Finanzen, Bonn 1971.

Chapter 2 Treaty of Versailles and the League of Nations

H. Alex Amankwah

2.1 Introduction

A curious twist of irony in the evolution of international law and international relations in the early 20th century was that a 'family' feud between European princes should wield the potential to engulf the whole world in a war. In *The Causes of World War One Duffy* remarked:

> "The First World War has sometimes been labelled, with reason, 'a family affair'. This is derived from the reality that – many of the European monarchies (including those of Russia, Germany and Austria-Hungary) – were interrelated.
> The British monarch *George V's* predecessor, *Edward VII* was the German Kaiser's uncle via his wife's sister, uncle of the Russian Tsar as well. His niece Alexandra was the Tsar's wife. Edward's daughter Maud was the Norwegian Queen and his niece Ena Queen of Spain; Marie a further niece was to become Queen of Romania.
> Despite these familial relations … European politics was all about power and influence, of protection and encirclement."[34]

This situation, he opines, explains in part the tangled web of alliances which mushroomed soon after the inauguration of the newly united German Empire. And while the assassination of *Archduke Franz Ferdinand*, heir to the Austria-Hungary throne ignited the conflagration which burned out of control to consume the entire world leading to the First World War, the real reasons for the war were far more complex and hidden than apparent due to the tangled web of alliances that linked European nations together. Alliances created a sense of family and belonging and consequently security. They operated as insurance against risk – aggression, menace or annihilation by or from more prosperous or powerful and larger polities.

The Treaty of Versailles 1919 was the product of the truce wrenched from defeated Germany by the Allied and Associated Powers (USA, UK, France, Italy and Japan) at the end of the First World War. Treatment or analysis of the treaty is meaningless without an excursus of the antecedents of the war. That task invariably will involve an expose on the causes of the war.

The League of Nations came into existence along the lines of *President Woodrow Wilson's* formulation of a peace plan, the so-called Fourteen Points for Peace plan which formed the platform of peace negotiation with Germany. That institution was rooted in the philosophy that wars occur where a mechanism for the peaceful resolution of disputes in international relations was non-existent, and that: "A general association of nations must be

---

[34] Duffy, M "The Causes of World War One" available at http://www.firstworldwar.com/origins/causes.htm.

formed under specific covenants for the purpose of affording mutual guarantees of political independence and territorial integrity to great and small states alike."[35]

The idea of the prevalence of universal peace among nations was not a novel one. It had been espoused by the German philosopher *Emmanuel Kant* in his time.[36] *President Wilson* himself might have been influenced by the then British Foreign Minister Edward Gray's musing on the concept.[37]

2.2 The League of Nations

For the purposes of this research the League's relevance will be confined to its role as the enforcer of the Treaty of Versailles, the culmination of the peace negotiations *(The Paris Peace Conference)* which the Allied and associated Powers concluded with the *Central Powers* (Germany, Bulgaria and Turkey).

The League was established under Part 1 of the Treaty of Versailles. Its constitution- the Covenant – was drafted by a special commission. It was adopted by the Paris Peace Conference as its act and deed in April 1919. It enunciated the principles of collective security of member states (Art 16) and the settlement of disputes through arbitration or Adjudication (Arts 12, 13, 15) and mandated the imposition of economic sanctions on any country that resorted to war as a means of settling a dispute with any other nation (Art 16).

Although the founding fathers were motivated by the desire to outlaw war as a means of resolving international dispute, the League's Covenant merely provided for a mandatory cooling off period of three months, thus only ensuring that in times of dispute the disputant nations did not precipitate a war by rushing into combat at the least provocation. By making war a last resort (Art 12), the Covenant preserved the right to resort to war as a legitimate remedy at international law. The most glaring weakness of the Covenant therefore was its inability to proscribe war as an instrument of state policy.

---

[35] Speech given at the Paris Peace Conference, 1919. See MacMillan, M Peacemakers: The Paris Peace Conference of 1919 and Its Attempt to End War London: John Murray Publishers (2001); Nicholson, H Peacemaking, 1919, Being Reminiscences of the Paris Peace Conference Boston: Houghton Mifflin Co (1933).

[36] See his Perpetual Peace: A Philosophical Sketch (1795) available at http://www.mtholyoka.edu.acad/intrel/kant/kant1.htm).

[37] See Egerton, G Great Britain and the Creation of the League of Nations: Strategy, Politics and International Organization: 1914-1919 Chapel Hill University of North Carolina Press (1978). See also Walters, F A History of the League of Nations Vols I & II London: Oxford University Press (1952); Kennedy, D "The Move to Institutions (1987) 8 Cardozo LR 841; Gill,G The League of Nations form 1929-1946 New York: Avery Publishing Group (1996), Northedge, FS The League of Nations: Its Life and Times London: Holmes & Meir (1986); Bassett, J The League of nations: A Chapter in World Politics (1930); Kuehl, W and Dunne, L Keeping the Covenant: American Internationalists and the League of Nations 1920-1939 (1997).

2.3 Development of the Modern State System

The state system which the Peace of Westphalia spawned forth was neither secular nor democratic.[38] States continued to be religion-based – Catholic, Protestant and Calvinist – and coincided with territorial sovereignty. The principle was symbolized and encapsulated in the maxim: *cuius religio eius religio.*[39]

Political and territorial sovereigns constituted Christendom under the over-arching surveillance of the *Holy Roman Empire.* One of its enduring legacies however was the annihilation of the principle that religion offered justification for war, which had been the pretext for many European wars notably the *Thirty Years War* in which Germany and many of the major European powers participated and the *Eighty Years War* in whish Spain attempted to crush the Dutch Revolt.

Papal influence over states waned with greater assertion of independence by states and their quest for collective security through group solidarity and formation of alliances as it became increasingly evident that the state symbolized by feudalistic and monarchical despotism was both otiose and obsolete in the face of an evolving new world order. Territories and populations long considered personal possessions of feudal princes and therefore transferable at will became and formed the basis of nation states with the rise of nationalism and the concomitant notion of national self-determination. This phenomenon was given recognition in the *Final Act of Vienna,* (1815) following the defeat of *Napoleon Bonaparte.*

Collective security arrangements served as a fortification against the forces of revolution which swept across Europe in the 19th century. These were accomplished usually through treaties of alliance.[40]

European alliances in the decades preceding the First World War consisted of a series of arrangements between two or more states in which each undertook to assist the other or others in time of need. Between1879 and 1914 at the outbreak of the First World War there were at least eight different types of alliances:

(1) *The Dual Alliance (1879)*
This was an alliance between Germany and Austria-Hungary the object of which was the protection of the parties from Russia.

(2) *The Austro-Serbia Alliance (1881)*
This alliance between Austria-Hungary and Serbia had as its sole purpose the prevention of Russian control of Serbia.

(3) *The Triple Alliance (1882)*
This was an agreement between Germany, Austria-Hungary and Italy designed to ensure that Italy would assist Germany or Austria-Hungary if France attacked any of them.

---

[38] Treaties of Münster and Osnabrück (1648).
[39] See Gross, L "the Peace of Westphalia" (1948) 42 Am Jorn'l I L 20.
[40] Hall, S Public International Law Sydney: LexisNexis Butterworths (2003) at 4-5.

Two years later, Italy signed a secret treaty with France in which Italy undertook to remain neutral in any conflict between France and Germany thus rendering the Triple Alliance worthless.

(4) *The Reinsurance Treaty (1887)*
This was a treaty between Germany and Russia to ensure the neutrality of the parties if either were to be at war with a third party. However if that third party were to be France, Russia would not be obliged to provide Germany any assistance

(5) *Franco-Russian Alliance (1894)*
This alliance between France and Russia sought to protect Russia from Germany and Austria-Hungary.

(6) *Entente Cordiale (1904)*
This was not a formal agreement but a situation in which the parties, France and Britain were under a moral obligation to assist each other in time of war. This was the basis of Britain's entry into the war against Germany when Germany attacked Belgium as a prelude to its attack on France. Britain had signed a treaty (The Treaty of London 1839) to guarantee Belgium's neutrality which Britain considered violated by Germany attack on her. And since Germany's real aim was France, Britain felt compelled to go to France's assistance.

(7) *Anglo-Russian Entente (1907)*
This again was an understanding between Britain and Russia that each would assist the other in time of need, usually and aggression by a third party against each of them.

(8) *The Triple Entente (1914)*
This was merely an arrangement (understanding not really an agreement) between Britain, France and Russia whereby each party undertook not to sign a separate peace agreement without the others. This was aimed at Germany's menacing posture on the eve of the First World War.[41]

2.4 Antecedents of the First World War

In any attempt to delineate the causes of the war, a caveat must be entered at the outset: early historian and chroniclers based their conclusions on memoirs and official releases from some countries that were involved in the conflict or were actual participants. These countries tendered to minimize their culpability in contributing to the war. There is also the issue of bias due to the ideological inclination or orientation or nationalism on the part of the writers. Some sources were found to have been deliberately doctored. And, sometimes different conclusions have been arrived at by historians with the same cultural background.[42]

---

[41] Gleaned from http://www.firstworldwar.com/origins/causes.htm.

[42] See generally Luigi, A The Origins of the War of 1914 Vols I-III transl. IM Massey London: Oxford University Press (1952); Hillgruber, A Germany and the Two World Wars Cambridge, Mass Harvard University Press (1981); Mayer, A The Persistence of the Old Regime: Europe to the Great War New York: Croom Helm (1981); Turner, L Origins of

The causes of the war are multifarious, and while one cause could explain a couple of pertinent issues only the aggregation furnishes the clue to an appreciation of the real underlying current that brought matters to a head. They range from ideological causes through colonialism and imperialism, the structure and design of Europe, the arms race to precursor skirmishes and wars.

Ideological causes

Charles Darwin's theory of natural selection sometimes abbreviated as 'survival of the fittest which fuelled unbridled competition among national, social and ethnic groups and led to the enthronement of the philosophy of social Darwinism found expression on the international arena also. In the context of Europe on the eve of the First World War, the theory served to exacerbate antagonism between various nationality groups especially those grounded in Slavic and Germanic culture. Since one was perceived as superior to the other, stretched to its logical conclusion, this would mandate the extirpation of the inferior culture. The idea was extended to even the colonial exploits of some of the European powers and was used by Britain for example to justify her policy of 'strategic exclusion' according to which potential adversaries were kept at bay.[43]

The domestic belief systems were not immune to the infestation of the theory either as manifested in the belief of the Social Democratic Party that Germany had not been accorded the respect and dignity it rightfully deserved by the rest of Europe.[44]

In France, belligerency was relished and perceived as a weapon to be seized and wielded by a superior entity to teach an inferior one lessons in good behaviourism.[45]

Colonialism and Imperialism

The rivalry between the major European powers for colonial possessions in Africa, Asia and the Pacific is a notorious chapter of world history. Not content to dominate Europe, European nations extended their rule to foreign territories in search of natural resources to feed industry at home. While Spain, Portugal, Britain and France were early candidates in the race for control of resources, markets, territories and humans, Germany on the other hand was a late starter due initially to Chancellor Otto von Bismarck's policy of deference to French colonial aspirations and interests, which was in reality a strategy to divert the attention of France from European political development. This approach he believed, perhaps erroneously would assure the primacy of German leadership in continental Europe. Successor German Chancellor saw the fallacy in Bismarck's logic and were therefore galvanized to reverse that policy and to go in search of colonies for Germany and succeeded in the acquisition of Namibia in East Africa, Cameroon and Togo in West Africa and New Guinea in the South Pacific.[46]

---

the First World War New York: Norton & Co (1970); Barnes, HE The Genesis of the War: An Introduction to the Problem of War Guilt New York Alfred Knopf (1929).

[43] See Fay, S The Origins of the War New York: Macmillan & Co (1929) at 385.

[44] Balfour, M The Kaiser and His Times New York: Houghton Mifflin (1964) at 434.

[45] Ibid.

[46] Taylor, AJ Bismarck the Man and Statesman New York: Vintage Books (1967) at 113.

Lenin much later perceived the First World War as the apogee of imperialism and attributed it to the rivalry and among European nations consequential upon extremely centralized commercial monopolies which propelled competition for markets and raw materials.[47]

Architecture and Design of Europe
Post-Congress of Vienna Europe was marked by conflict between the advocates of change and progress and proponents of the status quo. Propelling this conflict was the phenomenon of nationalism and the philosophy of self-determination. Behind the great revolutions in 19th century Europe was the realization that groups had been coerced into unions where they remained outfits and essentially foreigners. For example *Bismarck's* unification of Germany between 1864 and 1871 was the result of wars designed to forge a united Prussia. In Italy two warriors, *Cavour and Garibaldi* similarly accomplished Italian unification in 1866.

The emergence of two more powers on the European continent fractured the extant axis of power until that time dominated by Britain, France, Spain and Russia.

The Arms Race
Perhaps there is some validity to the assertion that to wield superior military capability is to possess also the power of deterrence because it guarantees stability, power equilibrium and security in a complex political environment. Perhaps for that reason European powers vied with each other for military superiority, Germany's effort to expand its navy simply galvanized Britain to undo Germany in naval matters. Britain was the unrivalled and undisputed European naval power and so when Germany inaugurated its own naval build-up, Britain took steps to counter German efforts which culminated in the construction of the revolutionary battleship *Dreadnought.*[48]

Allied to the arms race was the prevailing war mobilization system with its rigidity and the doctrines of 'the primacy of the offensive' and 'war by time table.' Once initiated mobilization was difficult to change or called off.

2.5 Precursor Conflicts

The Great War was preceded by several 'regional' conflicts and served as prelude to what was to come.

The Crimean War (1854-56)
This was a war between Russia and the combined forces of Britain, France and the Ottoman Empire. Russian defeat in this war presaged a radical shift in European diplomacy. After this war Austria-Hungary entered into an alliance with Germany while Germany threw her support behind the Slavic cause in the Balkans. Russian backing of the Slavs established some vital elements (Germany's declaration of war on Serbia meant declaration of war on Russia also) in the conditions that led to the Great War.

---

[47] Lenin, V Imperialism: The Highest Stage of Capitalism Moscow: Progress Publishers (1978).
[48]Steiner, Z Britain and the Origins of the First World War London: Macmillan Press (1977); Ferguson, N The Pity of War New York: Basic Books (1999) at 82.

Franco-Prussian War (1870-1871)
Again as with the Crimean War some of the elements of the First World War were discernible in the outcomes of this war. This war made possible the inauguration of a 'new' Germany – expanded, prosperous, industrial and therefore arguably greater military potential – which the existing European nations at once coveted and considered a threat. German annexation of Alsace-Lorraine served as smouldering amber. The French would exact revenge and would not rest until their land was recovered from German occupation.

Summing Up
Early narratives of the causes of the First World War, with a few notable exceptions tendered to be biased depending on whether the writer's nation was a participant or on the victorious or the vanquished side. Later writers tended generally to be more circumspect and apportion blame and responsibility evenly. Mayer for example queries why Germany should be blamed for doing what all the powerful nations of the time engaged in – armament, and acquisition of colonial territories.[49]

A recent writer placed the blame squarely on the Austria-Hungarian nobility not on Germany.[50] Still another recent author apportions the blame equally on Germany and Austria-Hungary, and none whatsoever on the other participating nations.[51] For *Ferguson* however Britain's diplomatic posturing should not escape the blame stricture.[52]

Without a doubt, Germany assumed enormous risks in her decision to back the Austria-Hungarian regime in that nation's quest of avenging the assassination of Archduke Franz Ferdinand. As events spiralled out of control and Germany occupied Luxemburg as a first stage in the invasion of Belgium, little did Germany envision that a consequence of the complex web of alliances forged between the major European nations would be Britain's invocation of an obscure treaty of neutrality between her and Belgium to enter the foray.[53]

Nor did the Kaiser help his own cause by deflecting German war efforts on the western front onto Russia upon realizing that the hitherto prevaricating British government of *David Lloyd George* would enter the war if Germany attacked France. In the event retreat was as difficult as going forward.

2.6 The Treaty of Versailles

After four years of internecine belligerency between the *Central Powers* and the *Allied* and Associated Powers a truce came into effect on 11th of November 1918 and formerly brought hostilities to an end. It was to take another six months of intense negotiations

---

[49]Mayer, A The Persistence of the Old Regime: Europe to the Great War New York: Croom Helm (1981).
[50]Williamson, SR Austria-Hungary and the Coming of the First World War St Martin's London: Press (1991).
[51]Fromkin, D Europe's Last Summer: Who Started the Great War in 1914? New York: Alfred Knopf (2004).
[52]Ferguson, N The Pity of War New York: Basic Books (1999).
[53]Treaty of London, 1839.

between the Allied Powers themselves to conclude a peace treaty. The length of time taken by the process of reaching an agreement on the form and text of the treaty is a measure of the differences in the aims of the victorious side regarding the nature and quality of the treated to be meted out to the losing side. For while the USA and to some extent the UK emphasized moderation and a political and economic rehabilitation of Germany, France, he nation which lost the most in the war due to the extent of devastation she suffered focused entirely on revenge and retribution. France wanted Germany demobilized to the point where it would be difficult for her to rearm and constitute a threat again to other European nations. The compromise arrived at in the circumstances is controversial and difficult to assess objectively. Germany for many years was under an international obligation to make reparation payments which merely exacerbated the nation's economic hardships which together with other factors led to social unrest and political chaos. Some argue that the chain of events triggered by the Treaty of Versailles inevitably sowed the seeds of the Second World War that is Germany's determination to free itself from the yoke of the treaty and restore her national pride and dignity.[54]

In international law, this treaty represents the unequal type. One party, Germany and her allies took no part in the negotiation process. Germany was not invited to the negotiation table nor did she take part in the crafting of the treaty.[55]

At the end of the *Paris Peace Conference* five treaties emerged in relation to the defeated nations. The principal treaty – *The Treaty of Versailles* – may be divided into several segments each of which dealt with specific issue- The League of Nations; Territorial settlements and changes; Disarmament; Reparation and Responsibility for the war; Judicial and Justice and Economics. Necessary were the adjustment of territorial claims and the return of territories forcibly wrenched from other nations and respect for territorial integrity and sovereignty of existing states and the creation of new ones.

Part II, III, and IV dealt with the territorial issues. These included the surrender of all colonial territories to the League of Nations to be administered as Mandates; the return of Alsace-Lorraine annexed by Germany in the Franco-German War to France; cession of Eupen-Malmedy to Belgium: Memel to Lithuania: the Hultschin district to Czechoslovakia; Poznania, parts of East Prussia and Upper Silesia to Poland; Danzig was to become a free city; and plebiscites were to be held in Northern Schleswig to settle the Danish-German frontier issue and the occupation and special status for the Saar under French control and

[54]See Toynbee, AJ Major Peace Treaties of Modern History, Vol 2 London: Oxford University Press (1967). American attitude to the Treaty of Versailles was one of ambivalence; on the one hand the U S viewed it as oppressive; on the other hand it was seen as an European issue to which America could afford to be indifferent. Perhaps it was on account of these attitudes that the US which ironically dictated the treaty rejected it. In the U S Senate Mr Henry Cabot Lodge led the assault on the treaty which culminated in the Senate's refusal to recommend ratification of the treaty. In the end the US did not join the League of Nations thus ensuring its damnation and eventual demise right from the start.
[55]See Harris, DJ Cases and Materials on International Law 6th ed (2004) at802-808. Under the current Geneva Convention of the Law of Treaties 1969 duress, coercion or the application of pressure on a party to elicit consent to a treaty invalidates the treaty as it negates consent: Art 51. See also Zasloff, J "Abolishing Coercion: The Jurisprudence of American Foreign Policy in the 1920's" (1993) 102 Yale LJ 20.

occupation of a demilitarized Rhineland. French occupation of German territory, Rhineland was one of the downsides of the treaty. The occupation simply deepened old wounds as it amounted to humiliation and reduction in the size of Germany.

While German territory was dismembered, Germany was banned from entering into any form of political association with Austria with which she shared a common historical origin, language and culture. This reveals a certain level of hypocrisy in the application of the principle of self-determination which President Wilson insisted should be rigorously enforce in the settlement of European territorial claims, for, while Slav culture and language assisted in the settlement of the territorial issues in the Balkan it was either negated or applied against Germany

Part V dealt with German disarmament. Limitations were place on German military capability and preparedness for belligerency. The German army was limited to one thousand men without tanks, heavy artillery, poison-gas, air-craft and the right to conscription. The navy was similarly limited to five-teen thousand men without sub-marines and vessel under ten thousand tons in weight.

Part VII provided for the return of *Kaiser Wilhelm II* who had taken refuge in the Netherlands to be tried by an international tribunal to be manned by judges from the Allied and Associated Powers (each power to appoint one judge) for committing "a supreme offence against international morality and the sanctity of treaties." He did not have to come back as he died in exile.

Part VIII dealt with responsibility for the war and reparation for damage cause by it. This is one of the most controversial aspects of the treaty. Germany was adjudged to be solely culpable for a war in which the whole world, sovereign nations and their colonial cohorts took part. Germany was held responsible 'for causing all the loss and damage to which the Allied and Associated Governments and their nationals have been subjected to as a consequence …" (Art 231). The quantum of reparation payable was not agreed on initially. This meant Germany gave the Allied and Associated Powers a blank cheque. The figure was later pegged at six and half million pounds. The amount was however progressively reduced by the Dawes and Young Plans of 1924 and 1929 respectively and was finally written off in 1932. This was perhaps the most profound provision of the treaty and it would later cause dissension and political turmoil in Germany.[56]

[56]See generally, The Treaty of Versailles and After: Annotations of the Text of the Treaty, Washington DC: Government Printing Office (1944); Sforza, S Diplomatic Europe Since the Treaty of Versailles New Haven, Conn: Yale University Press (1928); Bretton, H Streseman and the Revision of Versailles Stanford, Cal: Stanford University Press (1953); Davis, W A History of France from the Earliest Times to the Treaty of Versailles New York: Hough Mifflin (1919); Aldcroft, D "The Versailles Legacy" (1997) History Review 1; Newton, D "The Lansdowne "Peace Letter" of 1917 and the Prospect of Peace by Negotiation with Germany" (2002) Australian Journ Inten'l Pol & Hist. 15; Muller, S "Democracy in Germany" (1994) 123 Daedalus.

2.7 Effects of the Treaty on Germany

Given that the war had a catastrophic effect on the German economy; brought about a horrific down-turn in the supply of labour – it was estimated that the war claimed two million lives; caused food shortages and near starvation of the civilian population – the "*Turnip Winter*" episode encapsulated a situation where humans consumed animal feed; created a traumatized and demoralized citizenry; led to the abdication of the monarch, a hitherto vital nation institution; resulted in the creation of a chaotic condition for the inauguration of representative form of governance in place of monarchical absolutism; and arguably therefore launched the conditions for a volatile political and social climate, the timing of the proclamation of the Weimar Constitution was anything but felicitous.

Returning soldiers remained dangerously armed – a consequence of the haphazard decommissioning of troops following the Allied Powers' blockade of Germany's northern ports– and unemployed. They formed marauding gangs of menacing proportions to an already sensitized civilian populace. These former soldiers *(Freikorps)* together with workers sympathetic to the communist order in Russia became natural allies and organized themselves into soldiers' and workers' councils *(Spartacists)* ready to take on any government of the day.

2.8 Birth of the Weimar Republic

The Weimar Republic came into being with the proclamation of the *Weimar Constitution in November 1919*. The constitution was named after the sleepy town of *Weimar* (the town where the renowned poets *von Goethe* and *von Schiller* had lived). This was the place where the German Parliament *(Reichstag)* had retreated owing to the civil strife which had engulfed Berlin the capital city and previous seat of government. In this Parliament the *Social Democratic Party* led by *Friedrich Ebert* was the most prominent. The previous Chancellor, *Max von Baden* who manoeuvred the abdication of King Kaiser Wilhelm II had transferred his powers to Ebert to enable normal functioning of government in abnormal times. The legality of the transfer of power to Ebert remains a disputed issue. The times were neither benign nor felicitous and Ebert inherited numerous economic, social and political problems that a beleaguered nation faced as a consequence of the war. The problems were to prove intractable and presaged a catastrophic failure for Ebert's effort to stabilize the nation through democratic and constitutional processes. These processes were designed to meet one of *President Wilson's* conditions for peace embodied in his *Fourteen Point Peace Plan* – the democratic transformation of Germany. It was envisaged that a form of constitutional monarchy fashioned after the British model would satisfy that condition. However, the abdication of the Kaiser was to overtake events. Some argue that the infant republic was doomed *ab initio* to calamity and ultimate ruination.[57]

[57]See discussion below.

2.9 The Constitution of the Weimar Republic

The Weimar Constitution which ordained the Weimar Republic was a direct German response to one of *President Wilson's* conditions for Germany's return to the comity of nations – the democratization of her political institutions. *Wilson* asserted then:

> "She (Germany says that she has abolished all the old forms of government by which little secret councils of men, sitting nobody knew exactly where determined the fortunes of a great nation and incidentally tried to determine the fortunes of mankind; but we want her to prove that her constitution is changed and that it is going to stay changed; and then who can say 'No' to a great people 60 million strong if they want to come in on equal terms with the rest of us and do justice in international affairs?"[58]

The constitution resonated themes of a modern constitution with emphasis of government under law, the rule of law, human rights and limited executive. It reflects and replicates familiar modern day constitutional of detailed provisions that leave little or no room for ambiguities.

The Republic status of the nation
The constitution proclaimed Germany a republic – a change from monarchy to representative form of government (Arts 1-19). The German state *(Reich)* and its constituent provinces *(Länder)* were defined and the relationship between them defined with rights and the responsibilities that attached to those rights (Arts 20-40).

Machinery of government
The modality for the election of parliament *(Reichstag)*, the positions of the president *(Reichspräsident)* who represented the whole German nation and the chancellor *(Reichskanzler)* the leader of government business were spelt out (Arts 41-59). The president's emergency powers were subsumed under Art 48. The constitution established a council of state *(Reichsrat)* made up of the representatives of all the provincial governments (Arts 60-67). It outlined the law making process and mechanism of the state (Arts 68-77). Provision was made for the state's administrative set up (Art 78-101). Law and justice was covered by the constitution (Art102-108)

Basic rights of citizens
The basic rights *(Grundrechte)* and obligations *(Grundpflichten)* of citizens were defined in a way reminiscence of a modern day constitution (Arts 104-118) and encompassed individual and personal liberties – inviolability of the human person and home; freedom from arbitrary arrest; freedom of speech and expression; freedom of association and communication; equality of all citizens before the law; the abolishment of all privileges etc.

Economic well-being of Germans
The constitution provides for the economic welfare and security (economic justice) and a dignified life-style for all German nationals (Arts 151-165). This was embodied in the philosophy of social democracy, a state of affairs in which worker and employers together

[58] Speech on the League of Nations, September 8, 1919.

played equal role in regulating wages and working conditions of workers. This guaranteed the economic status of Germans. This it was thought would ensure the support of labour for business and government. It would underwrite the German welfare system which aimed at the prevention of crippling individual poverty. The right to private property was guaranteed, thus obviating the necessity for citizens clamouring for a Russian-style socialism and state monopoly of wealth. Leninism-Marxism it will be recalled flourished on the notion that there was a perpetual state of war between those who owned the means of production and those who supplied the labour that propelled industry. By guaranteeing the right of private property the risk of people hankering after the Russian social system just across Germany's borders was arguably minimised.[59]

Although the constitution was regaled with liberal and democratic resonance appropriate to a modern polity it proved too malleable and within a decade succumbed to one of the most heinous form of government humanity has ever experienced. A post-mortem analysis of the constitution has unearthed some of its fundamental flaws. These include the provisions on proportional representation that made the rise of splinter parties possible. These favoured political extremism at the expense of moderation and tolerance. The provisions on the allocation of presidential powers, it has been observed made the president look like a Kaiser substitute especially the notorious *Article 48* the so-called *Notverordnung* (emergency decree provision) which gave the president unlimited powers if it was "in the public interest" to suspend civil liberties and govern by decree. This was to arm *Adolf Hitler* with the mechanism and the means to unparallel dictatorship in Western European history. Finally the provisions on the distribution of powers between the state and provincial governments had the effect of making some provinces disproportionately more powerful than the Reich itself, thus creating a "state within a state" situation in some cases.[60]

---

[59]See generally, Abraham, D The Collapse of the Weimar Republic 2nd ed New Jersey: Holmes & Meir Publishers (1986); Berghahn, V Modern Germany Cambidge UK: Cambridge University Press (1982); Bookbinder, P Weimar Germany: The Republic of the Reasonable Manchester UK: Manchester University Press (1996); Broszat, M Hitler and the Collapse of the Weimar Republic Leamington Spa, New York: Berg Publishers (1987); Craig, G Germany 1866-1945 Oxford History of Modern Europe Oxford: Oxford University Press (1980); Feuchtwagner, E From Weimar to Hitler: Germany London: Macmillan Publishers (1993); Grey, P Weimar Culture; The Outsider as Insider New York: Harper & Row (1968); Kaes, A, Jay, M and Dimendberg, E The Weimar Republic: Sourcebook Berkeley CA: Berkeley University Press (1994); Kolb, E The Weimar Republic PS Falla (trans) London: Unwin Hyman Publishers (1988); Nicholls, A Weimar and the Rise of Hitler New York: St Martin's Press (2000); Peukert, D The Weimar Republic: The Crisis of Classical Modernity New York: Hii & Wang (1992); Rosenberg, A, A History of the German Republic London: Methuen (1936); Wheeler-Bennett, J The Nemesis of Power: German Army in Politics 1919-1945 New York: Palgrave Macmillan Publishing Co (2005) ; Shirer, W The Rise and Fall of the Third Reich New York: Simon & Schuter (1960).

[60]Shirer, W The Rise and Fall of the Third Reich New York: Simon & Schuter (1960) at 1.

2.10 Reasons for the Collapse of the Weimar Republic

There is a never-ending argumentation between historians that perhaps the Weimar experiment was destined for failure due to opposition to it not only from extremists but also from the ranks of moderates on both sides of the political divide; and, in the absence the absence of an established democratic tradition in Germany the experiment in constitutional governance mired as it was in gargantuan chaos was unlikely to succeed. To begin with, it lacked legitimacy as it was identified as the one which supervised German surrender in the face of undisputed evidence that the nation had been devastated militarily and economically and could not go on fighting the war. The naval blockade of the country meant that vital life sustaining imports could not get into the country. The cost of living had escalated several folds; and the incidence of desertion of soldiers from the armed forces painted a picture of gloom and despair of a demoralized community.

Historians however attribute three salient reasons to the failure of Weimar namely: economic, institutional anomalies and the role of individual Germans.

Economic factors:
The enormous financial obligations which the *Treaty of Versailles* imposed on Germany by way of reparation for war damages as the price for cessation of hostilities fell on the fledgling republic to honour. Massive unemployment, hyper-inflation and Germany's heavy dependence on American loans were all sufficient factors to break the back of even a sound economy in normal times. Most Germans regarded the treaty as punitive as Germany was according to some of the terms forced to relinquish control of its resource-pregnant territories to the victors especially France. And, as credit for government expenditure dwindled, the new government was forced to finance its deficits through artificial liquidity – printing more money and thus merely causing *hyperinflation.* The government also alienated the support of industry leaders who linked it and the Treaty of Versailles with labour unions and the Social Democrats. It was no wonder, therefore that when *Adolf Hitler* emerged on the political arena he was mobbed initially by industry leaders who regarded him as the Messiah.

Institutional anomalies:
It has been pointed out that Pre-1919 Germany lacked an established democratic tradition. The Weimar Constitution created the positions of president who was elected by popular vote (Art 41) and chancellor who was appointed by the president (Art 53). However, the chancellor could only be removed from office by parliament on a "Motion of No Confidence" being carried (Art 54). The constitution also gave the president emergency powers to use if "Public order and security are seriously disturbed or threatened (Art 48). The power was to be employed in the governance of the nation on several occasions without the support of parliament.

Proportional representation (Art 61) it was noted only resulted in the rise of splinter political parties whose only loyalty was to their membership rather than to the nation and extreme factionalism.

By providing that in time of death, incapacity or resignation of the president, the chancellor would assume that office (Art 48) the stage was set for the slide into dictatorship of the type which Germany experienced after the death of *Paul von Hindenburg,* with Hitler's ascendancy, the inevitable consequence of his assumption of the role of president. This was followed by the persecution, murder, torture and liquidation of political opponents; the curtailment of civil liberties; government by decrees and the virtual demise of the rule of law.

Specific individuals:
For the period pertinent and critical to this essay the one individual whose actions and decisions are often investigated and analysed by writers, historian and commentators is *Paul von Hindenburg* who was Chief of Staff of the Supreme Army Command at the time of German capitulation. He supervised the installation of a so-called democratic and representative form of government of the type President Wilson demanded as a pre-condition to peace. With a new chancellor, *Prince Max von Baden,* he steered the ship of state through turbulent straits and became the president in 1925. He was the embodiment of the old autocratic political institutions of the 1871 German Empire and therefore an unlikely candidate to promote democratic governance and institutions and the rule of law. He held this position until he was past eighty and some narratives state that he was senile some of the time. Not tutored in democratic traditions, he laid the foundation for rule by decrees and governed without parliamentary support, a situation which began with the enactment of a law designed to reform the finances of the German Reich in 1930. This was followed by the Reich Fire Decree of the same year. It was only a matter of time before Hitler stepped into his shoes as president of the Reich to complete the cataclysmic slide into unprecedented dictatorship.[61]

2.11 Conclusion

In this chapter an effort is made to essay the place of the *Treaty of Versailles* in the early stages of the *Weimar Republic.* As the genesis of the treaty was the *First World War*, an overview of that war is undertaken. It was surmised that perhaps Germany alone ought not to be singled out as the sole culprit to shoulder all the blame regarding the causes of the war.

The *League of Nations* was an adjunct of the *Treaty of Versailles* and, also necessitated by it due to the desire of the Founding Fathers of the League to eliminate war as an instrument of national policy in international relations. To that end the League was mandated to supervise the observance and enforcement of the treaty. Its coverage in the essay is therefore confined to its role in that regard only. It is noted however that the League failed in the realization of its principal objective, because only two decades after its inauguration mankind was confronted with yet another war.

The *Weimar Constitution* and the Weimar Republic which the constitution brought into existence are discussed. The inherent flaws in the constitution are indicated and the factors which inhibited a successful and efficacious management of the infant republic are similarly outlined. *Thomas Jefferson's* famous assertion that the move from despotism to liberty does not come in a featherbed was borne out by the series of political and constitutional events leading up to the rise of the *Third Reich.*

---

[61]See Shirer supra.

Chapter 3 Legal Aspects of Payment of War Reparations

Kenneth K. Mwenda

3.1 Introduction

During World War I, one of the warring blocs was the *Allied Powers,* comprising countries opposed to the *Central Powers.* The Allied Powers included *France, the British Empire and the Russian Empire*, formally enjoined together by the *Treaty of London,* signed on September 5, 1914 *(see: Tucker, 1999).* Other Allies, linked by treaty to one or more of the Allied Powers, included *Portugal, Japan, and Italy,* but not the *US,* albeit its participation in the war from April 1917 *(see: Tucker, 1999).* The US and other countries opposed to the Central Powers were known as the *Associated Powers (Ellis, 1993).* The coalition of countries known as the *Central Powers,* later defeated by the Allied Powers, comprised the *German Empire and Austria-Hungary*, including the *'central' European states* that were at war from August 1914 against France, Britain and Russia *(see: Ellis, 1993).*

This chapter examines the legal aspects of payment of war reparations by Germany after *World War I.* The chapter is an exploratory and evaluative study, arguing, among other things, that there is growing evidence today to suggest that customary international law, like certain treaties, recognizes the principle of reparation payments. This chapter is not an indictment of any particular jurisdiction or legal system and neither does it aim at offending any vested interests of some among the readership. Suffice it to say, the issue of Germany's obligations to pay up war reparations relating to World War I is still alive today. And in examining this issue, we will also detail out some important historical perspectives on the topic before proceeding to draw analogies with claims for reparation payments relating to the holocaust and the slave trade.

After Germany's defeat in *World War II,* an international conference decided in 1953 that Germany would pay the remaining debt only after the country was reunified *(Keylor, 1998).* Nonetheless, as a show of continued self-effacement, West Germany paid off the principal by 1980. In 1995, after reunification, the new German government announced it would resume payments of the reparations. Germany is expected to finish paying off the Americans in 2010 *(see: Findley and Rothney, 2006).* But before delving into intricacies of the legal aspects of Germany's obligations to pay up war reparations relating to World War I, we will take a more reasoned look at some of the historical developments in Germany in order to set the discussion in context. In this chapter, the term 'reparations' refers to aspects of compensation to be paid by a culpable or defeated state to other states for damage resulting from a war caused by or instigated by the compensating state. Generally, war reparations are understood as referring to the monetary compensation intended to cover damage or injury occasioned during a war. As such, the term 'war reparations' refers mainly to money or goods changing hands, rather than such property transfers as the annexation of land. Examples of war reparations relating to World War I have included: (a) *Russia* agreeing to pay reparations to the *Central Powers* when Russia exited the war in the *Treaty of Brest-Litovsk* (which was repudiated by the *Bolshevik government* eight months later); (b) *Germany* agreeing to pay reparations of 132 billion gold marks to the *Triple Entente* in the

Treaty of Versailles; and (c) Bulgaria paying reparations of 2.25 billion gold francs (90 million pounds) to the *Entente*, in accordance with the *Treaty of Neuilly (see: Bottigliero, 2004).*

Following below are some historical perspectives to set the discussion in context.

3.2 How it all started

After World War I, reparations to the *Allied Powers* were required of Germany under the *Treaty of Versailles 1919.* But were the claims against Germany unusual or unjustified? The policy of demanding reparations from the losing side of a battle can be traced all the way back to 264-241 BC, when *Rome* imposed large indemnities on *Carthage* after the *First and Second Punic Wars (van Horn, 2007).* One of the most significant cases of war reparations in history was following the *Franco-Prussian War* in 1870-1871 *(van Horn, 2007).* According to the *Treaty of Frankfurt*, France was obliged to pay a war indemnity of 5 billion gold francs over the course of 5 years. To enforce this condition, German trooper remained in France until the last instalment was made *(van Horn, 2007).* Van Horn *(2007)* observes:

> "More frequently, however, as seen in the effects of the Treaty of Brest-Litovsk between Germany and Russia in 1917, was that a government which came to power following the aftermath of a war eventually repudiated the reparations agreement. The harsh terms Germany imposed on Russia in 1917 encouraged the victors of 1918 to punish Germany heavily in the 1919 Treaty of Versailles. Not only was Germany stripped of territory and almost all of its military might, it was also forced to agree to pay the enormous sum of £6.6 Billion in war reparations, chiefly to Britain, France and Belgium."

Article 231 of the Treaty of Versailles 1919 provided the legal pedigree upon which Germany was bound to pay war reparations to the Allied Powers. According to Article 231,

> "The Allied and Associated Governments affirm and Germany accepts the responsibility of Germany and her allies for causing all the loss and damage to which the Allied and Associated Governments and their nationals have been subjected as a consequence of the war imposed upon them by the aggression of Germany and her allies."

In much of the literature on war reparations, Article 231 of the *Treaty of Versailles 1919* is commonly known as the 'Guilt Clause' or the 'War Guilt Clause' *(see, for example: Marks, 1976: 13).* Under Article 231, Germany was 'forced', or rather made, to take complete responsibility for starting World War I. And the United Kingdom and France played a primary role in perpetuating World War I. The United States, on the other hand, did play a minor role. However, the original amount of US$33 billion meted out against Germany, as reparation payment for causing World War I, was later reduced by the *Dawes Plan* and the *Young Plan,* respectively, and then subsequently cancelled after 1933 *(see: Schuker, 1976 and McKercher, 1991).* In a 1923 article, written by one German commentator, that commentator explained the experience of many Germans during the reparations payment period *(see: Bookrags, 2008).*

> "It is impossible to envisage the amount of problems the Treaty of Versailles has brought to us. As soon as our leaders signed the Treaty reluctantly, chaos had triggered in Germany. We had no ruler because the Kaiser had abdicated his throne and fled to Holland. Promptly after that *Friedrich Ebert* became the new leader of Republic of Germany. After consulting the army commander, *Hindenburg* about the military war situation he decided to sign the Treaty instantly so that we wouldn't suffer anymore."

The commentator goes on to say *(see: Bookrags, 2008)*:

> "As soon as the new Weimar Republic had formed, it received opposition from both Left and Right Wings. The Right-wing blamed Ebert for accepting the Terms of the Treaty and they didn't like the democratic government that replaced the autocratic system, which was to their liking… In March 1920, *Dr. Wolfgang Kapp* (a right-wing journalist) led 5000 *Freikorps* into Berlin in a rebellion with the aim of overthrowing Ebert's government. It looked as if this would have been successful because our army refused to fire at the Freikorps. However it did not work because:
> (a) The industrial workers in Berlin went on a General Strike. This event forced the capital to a halt with no access to transport, power, water or food. The strike call received massive support. Unfortunately many civilians in our capital suffered severely with no resources to survive.
> (b) The Freikorps had the support of only a minority of the extreme right. Most of the leading Freikorps refused to join Kapp Putsch."

The post-World War I German reparations scheme was, of course, complex, and included features designed to impede the ability of German exports to compete effectively with domestic producers in Allied nations *(Trachtenberg 1980: 3)*. But that simply meant that the recipient governments took some reparations payments in forms other than cash. In terms of costs on Germany, the impact of the *Treaty of Versailles* 1919 was phenomenal. As the 1923 commentator observed *(see: Bookrags, 2008)*:

> "Germany's economy started falling since there were no goods to trade and to solve this problem the government started printing more money. This caused more problems like:
> (a) Hyperinflation – printing money is reducing the value of Marks. They are worthless now.
> (b) Everybody is losing their savings.
> (c) All the prices are increasing immensely. People can't afford food, medicines or any other necessities."

Under the *1924 Dawes Plan,* a committee of experts, presided over by *Charles Dawes,* prepared a plan of new arrangements for Germany to pay reparations to the Allies after World War I *(see: Schuker, 1976)*. The total amount of reparations was not determined, but payments were to begin at 1 billion gold marks in the first year and rise to 2.5 billion by 1928. This plan, which also provided for the reorganization of the Reichsbank and for an initial foreign loan of 800 million marks to Germany, was later replaced by the more lenient *Young Plan (see: McKercher, 1991).*

Under the *1929 Young Plan,* a committee was set up to renegotiate obligations of Germany to pay the World War I reparations *(see: McKercher, 1991).* The committee tasked to carry out the renegotiations was chaired by a US lawyer, Mr. Owen D. Young, and meetings were held in Paris. The Young Plan, a revision of the Dawes Plan, reduced the amount due from Germany to $26.3 billion, to be paid over 59 years, and ended foreign controls on German economic life *(see: McKercher, 1991).* And the Young Plan went into effect in 1930, but the world depression affected Germany's ability to pay. When *Adolf Hitler* came to power in 1933, he repudiated treaty obligations arising under the Treaty of Versailles 1919, including the obligations of Germany to pay the Allied Powers war reparations.

3.3 German opposition and the emergence of the 'Liberty Law'

Although the Young Plan had effectively reduced Germany's reparation obligations, the plan did not sit well with many in the political domain of Germany *(see: McKercher, 1991).* Many conservative groups that had been outspoken from the outset seized the opportunity to start criticizing the Young Plan in a more coordinated manner. A coalition was formed of various conservative groups under the leadership of *Alfred Hugenberg,* the head of the German National People's Party *(see: McKercher, 1991).* Adolf Hitler and the National Socialist German Workers Party also joined this coalition. The National Socialist German Workers Party was a group that had previously been dismissed by the more mainstream conservative parties as simply an extremist fringe.

One of the goals of the coalition that Hitler had joined was to enact the *Freiheitsgesetz ('Liberty Law').* This law would renounce all reparations under the Treaty of Versailles 1919 and make it a criminal offense for any German official to cooperate in the collection of such payments *(McKercher, 1991).* The law would also renounce Germany's acknowledgement of 'war guilt' under Treaty of Versailles 1919, including any foreign occupation of German territory pursuant to the Treaty of Versailles 1919. Interesting, as it so happened then, under the terms of the German constitution, if ten percent of the eligible voters in the country signed a petition in favour of a proposed law, the Reichstag had to put the matter to a vote. But, if the *Reichstag* voted against the law, the proposal would automatically be put to a national referendum. And if fifty percent of the people voted in favour of it, it would become a law.

And so, the *Liberty Law* proposal was officially put forth on October 16 1929. The Nazis and other groups held large public rallies to collect signatures. The German Government opposed the Liberty Law and staged demonstrations against it. However, the coalition succeeded in collecting enough names to put the proposal before the Reichstag *(see McKercher, 1991).* And the Reichstag voted the bill down by a 318-82 margin. In the subsequent popular vote on December 22, the Liberty Law referendum only received 13.8 percent of the votes in its favour. While the *Liberty Law* was not enacted in 1929, the campaign for it was a major factor in bringing *Hitler* and the Nazis into the political mainstream. Hitler later enacted by decree most of the proposals of the Liberty Law after achieving power.

We now turn to examine if at all, aside from Article 231 of the Treaty of Versailles 1919 as well as the *Dawes Plan* of 1924 and the *Young Plan* of 1929, customary international law did place some obligations on Germany to pay up reparations for World War I to the Allied Powers.

3.4 Customary international law and war reparations

Whereas *Article 231 of the Treaty of Versailles 1919* promulgates the position under conventional international law by stating that the 'Allied and Associated Governments affirm and Germany accepts the responsibility of Germany and her allies for causing all the loss and damage to which the Allied and Associated Governments and their nationals have been subjected as a consequence of the war imposed upon them by the aggression of Germany and her allies', the position under customary international law was still evolving, albeit some isolated evidence of State practice and *opinio juris*. However, more recently, the International Commission of Jurists, making a legal submission on Fiji's Promotion of Reconciliation, Tolerance and Unity Bill 2005, observed that Fiji had an obligation under customary international law to provide reparations for victims of gross human violations *(International Commission of Jurists, 2005: 3)*. It would therefore appear that the issue of reparation payments has now gained wide international support through increased State practice and *opinio juris* to crystallize into customary international law. As van Horn observes *(van Horn, 2007)*, after the first Gulf War the practice of paying war reparations gained the solidity of a customary international law, with the founding of the *United Nations Compensation Commission (UNCC)*. The first Gulf War, which took place sometime between 1980 and 1988, was a conflict between *Iraq and Iran (see: Benvenisti, 2004)*.

The establishment of the *UNCC* after the first Gulf War provided a forum for states, corporations as well as individuals to file claims for war reparations. The UNCC prioritized claims filed by individuals ahead of those filed by corporations and states. Since the founding of the *UNCC* there have been many attempts to codify the war reparations process, as seen, for example, in Article 79 of the Statutes of the International Criminal Court and the *United Nations (UN)* Basic Principles on the Right to a Remedy and Reparations for Victims (*i.e.* General Assembly Resolution 60/147 of December 16, 2005). But can norms of customary international law have retroactive effect and apply to incidents that took place before such norms were formally recognized? Or should we, instead, treat these pronouncements of customary international law as mere declarations of customary norms that already exist?

American legal scholar, *Lon Fuller,* in his book, *The Morality of Law (see: Yu and Guernsey, 2008)*, identified eight elements of law which are recognized by many States as necessary for a society aspiring to institute the rule of law, and that these elements are as follows: (i) Laws must exist and those laws should be obeyed by all, including government officials; (ii) Laws must be published; (iii) Laws must be prospective in nature so that the effect of the law may only take place after the law has been passed (for example, the court cannot convict a person of a crime committed before a criminal statute prohibiting the conduct was passed); (iv) Laws should be written with reasonable clarity to avoid unfair enforcement; (v) Law must avoid contradictions; (vi) Law must not command the impossible; (vii) Law must stay constant through time to allow the formalization of rules (however, law also must allow for timely revision when the underlying social and political circumstances have changed); and, (viii) Official action should be consistent with the declared rule.

Of the eight precepts of the rule of law spelt out above, the precept listed as the third; that is, laws must be prospective in nature so that the effect of the law may only take place after the law has been passed, shows that in civilized nations were governments claim to uphold the most basic tenets of the rule of law, the retroactive application of a law to cover events that occurred before that law was enacted is very much discouraged. In short, a rule of customary international law that was not in existence when a particular action of a subject of international law took place cannot be made applicable to cover that action. However, we must proceed with caution here because there is a stark difference between stating that a particular norm of customary international law did not exist and stating that a particular State was a persistent objector to the customary norm in issue. Indeed, in the latter case, the existence of customary international law is not in dispute. The issue rather is whether that particular custom is opposable to the persistent objector *(see: Brownlie, 1996: 10).*

Also, a treaty can be entered into to provide for payment of reparations pertaining to events or incidents that could have occurred in the past. To illustrate, the Reparations Agreement between *Israel and West Germany* was signed on September 10, 1952, and entered in force on March 27, 1953 *(see: Honig, 1954).* According to the Agreement, West Germany was to pay Israel for the slave labor and persecution of Jews during the *Holocaust*, and to compensate for Jewish property that was unfairly appropriated by the Nazis *(see: Honig, 1954).*

3.5 What about reparation payments to African States by the West for slave trade?

In 2001, at a United Nations-sponsored *World Conference against Racism, African States* demanded an apology, amongst other stipulations, from ex-colonial European States for their past involvement in the slave trade *(see: Leaphart, 2002: 157).* But, some critics of the movement for reparations for slave trade have argued that slavery was not illegal in the US prior to the Thirteenth Amendment to the US Constitution (being ratified in 1865). Yet, these critics forget that the US is not immune from international law. As such, it would be irresponsible, intellectually speaking, for one to argue that within the US there is currently no legal basis for compensating the descendants of slaves for crimes committed against their ancestors since, as highlighted above, there was allegedly a lacuna in US municipal law that made it difficult for slavery to be treated as a crime.

Other critics of the movement for reparation for slave trade continue to argue that the current US Government did not exist prior to June 21, 1788 when the *US Constitution* was ratified, and that the current US Government simply inherited the institution of slavery. On that basis alone, these critics argue that the US Government cannot be held legally liable for the enslavement of Africans by Europeans prior to that time. The critics contend further that figuring out who was enslaved and by whom, in order to fairly apply reparations from the US Government only to those who were enslaved under US laws, would be an insurmountable task. Further, anti-reparations advocates maintain that reparation payments based on race alone would be perceived by nearly everyone forced to make payments as a monstrous injustice, embittering many and inevitably setting back race relations. And these critics insist that the apologetic feelings that many whites hold because of slavery and past civil rights injustices would, to a significant extent, be replaced by anger.

That said, it has already been shown in this chapter that, although historically many claims of reparation payments were based on treaty obligations, customary international law, especially today, does make provision for reparation payments. It would, however, be folly to attempt to argue unintelligibly that during the times of slave trade there was no customary international law prohibiting such forms of trade. Also, even if there was a lacuna in US municipal law, for example, it could still be argued that, from the perspective of dualism, public international law did fill that gap. Indeed, the term *jus cogens* refers to a fundamental principle of public international law, pointing to rules of customary international law which cannot be set aside by treaty or acquiescence but only by the formation of a subsequent customary rule of contrary effect *(Brownlie, 1996: 513-514)*. In 1969, this principle was buttressed by the codification of Article 53 of the Vienna Convention on the Law of Treaties 1969. The said Article 53 provides for the general inviolability of peremptory norms, except where such norms are overridden by a norm of equal force *(see: Brownlie, 1996: 513-514)*. And it is our contention that the international crime of slave trade falls, irrefutably, within the domain of *jus cogens (see: Brownlie, 1996: 513)*. On that basis, we argue that when slave trade was taking place, customary international law had already recognized fully that such forms of trade were contrary to public international law and that no State can now claim that it had objected persistently to the prohibition of slave trade since such objection has never been sustainable or permissible under customary international law. But, then, does the violation of *jus cogens* here by the West automatically invite a cause for payment of reparations by the West to Africa? What lessons can be learned from the Reparations Agreement between Israel and West Germany 1953? And just how different is slave trade from the holocaust? Or, should Africans be seen simply as Africans and less human such that their lives don't really matter after all?

On March 26, 2007, the *Archbishop of Canterbury* observed that the *Church of England* should consider paying reparations for its role in the slave trade *(Ekklesia News Brief, 2007)*. However, some cynics have often maintained that if slave trade reparations were to be paid, then we ought to ask ourselves: by who, to whom and on what terms? *(Worldpress.org, 2007)* In spite of these scepticisms, the Archbishop of Canterbury's comments have come after acts of remembrance commemorating the bicentenary of the British Act of Parliament which brought to an end Britain's role in the transatlantic slave trade. The Archbishop's statement followed a vote in 2006 by the Church of England's General Synod to apologize for the Church's part in the slave trade *(Ekklesia News Brief, 2007)*. However, the British Government has stubbornly resisted to offer an apology, for fear of opening itself to claims of reparations. *(Ekklesia News Brief, 2007)*

But *Dr Rowan Williams,* the Archbishop of Canterbury, indicates that Anglicans need to acknowledge that they belong to an institution partly shaped 'by terrible things that our forebears did' *(see: Ekklesia News Brief, 2007)*. He observes further that the church had to 'work at' the question of reparations, but adds that the issue is complex and it is unclear who should receive such payments *(see: Ekklesia News Brief, 2007)*.

The Anglican Church, which owned slaves on its Caribbean plantations, did not free them until 1833 – that is, 26 years after the abolition of the slave trade in the British Empire *(Ekklesia News Brief, 2007)*. Yet, the British Government paid the Anglican Church significant compensation for the loss of its slave labour *(see: Ekklesia News Brief, 2007).* Many organizations that received compensation from the British Government in the 1830's were, according to Dr. Williams, still 'living off the historical legacy' of slavery *(see: Ekklesia News Brief, 2007).* Dr. William's comments, made a day after the 200th anniversary of the advent of UK legislation abolishing the slave trade,

> "...could be seen as a challenge to other institutions that profited from slave labour, such as banks, universities and galleries, to consider paying reparations... London Mayor Ken Livingstone has offered an apology for the capital's role in the slave trade, and...the Archbishop of York, Dr John Sentamu has called on Britain to make a formal apology. ...the leader of the World Council of Churches – which brings together Christians from many of the world's major denominations and traditions – asked Prime Minister Tony Blair to change his mind and make an apology for Britain's involvement in the slave trade. ...the prime minister, Tony Blair, said the UK's role was a 'matter of deep sorrow and regret'. However, his statement fell short of demands from campaigners." *(Ekklesia News Brief, 2007)*

However, if guilty can be brought to bear on the conscience of the church, and yet many view the church as a repository of decent moral and ethical values, in spite of some of its historical shortcomings, what about the secular States that formally institutionalized slave trade? Indeed, do secular States espouse any better moral or ethical values than the church? Several debates have taken place to address the issue of reparation payments for slave trade by the West. And a number of theoretical, legal, ideological and pragmatic constructs have been advanced by several publicists and lobbyists *(see, for example: Thomas, 1997: 804-805; Chang, 1997: 222)*, including the view that slave trade should be understood as a form of genocide *(see: Laremont, 1999)* and thus bringing liability on the West for infringing and offending the principle of *jus cogens* under customary international law. Laremont argues forcefully that *(Laremont, 1999)*:

> "Reparations have been paid for the harm inflicted on a class or race of people. For example, since World War II, Germany has paid at least 88 billion Deutsche Marks in reparations to the state of Israel and will pay another 20 billion Deutsche Marks by the year 2005. The United States Government has paid \$1.2 billion or \$20,000 per person for each Japanese American illegally imprisoned in American concentration camps during World War II. Further, the American government has issued an apology for the illegal imprisonment of the Japanese in America."

So, why has it taken so long for the American Government to issue an apology to the African and African-American people for the atrocities of slave trade and slavery committed on their ancestors? Are African and African-American people lesser humans? Laremont observes:

> "Presently, the Chinese have discussed the possibility of suing the government of Japan for the atrocities committed during the capture of the city of Nanking, which resulted in the systematic murder of more than 300,000 Chinese by Japanese soldiers during World War II. 'Comfort

women' from Korea who were forced into prostitution during World War II by the Japanese have similarly organized to sue the government of Japan for reparations. A legal suit for reparations to a race of peoples has been recognized in international, German, and American law. States may be held liable for damages caused to a class or race of peoples. The case of reparations paid to Japanese Americans by the American government and the case of reparations paid to Israel by Germany establish those precedents. The question before us is whether the African slavery reparations movement should pursue legal paths or political paths for the satisfaction of their claims." *(Laremont, 1999)*

Whichever path the African slavery reparations movement takes, the ultimate success lies, in part, on whether the Western powers can admit responsibility and thereby act with a certain sense of civility and magnanimity that confirms their self-imagined notions of self-righteousness. We have seen, for example, that although international law does not provide explicitly for the repudiation of contractual debt obligations incurred by underdeveloped States, on the ground that such debts are 'odious' in nature *(see: Frankenberg and Knieper, 1984: 12)*, many Western States, as lenders, are somewhat reluctant to extinguish in totality such debts. So, will there be a change of heart this time around in the West so as to advance from that hard heart they are commonly known for to a more contrite and humane one?

3.6 Conclusion

This chapter has examined the legal aspects of payment of reparations by Germany after World War I, providing some important historical perspectives while drawing analogies and comparisons with claims for reparation relating to the holocaust and the slave trade. The chapter observed that the issue of Germany's payment of war reparations has not yet abated, and that after Germany's defeat in World War II an international conference decided in 1953 that Germany would pay the remaining debt only after the country had reunified. And, in 1995, after reunification, the new German government announced it would resume payments of the reparations.

The chapter established that there is increasing evidence to suggest that customary international law does recognize the principle of reparation payments. For a claimant to succeed in a claim of reparation payments, he or she need not necessarily show that he or she is relying on a particular treaty in making that claim. Although many cases show that claimants have relied on conventional international law, or rather treaties, so to speak, the International Commission of Jurists, making a legal submission on Fiji's Promotion of Reconciliation, Tolerance and Unity Bill 2005, observed, as we have noted already, that Fiji had an obligation under customary international law to provide reparations for victims of gross human violations. Such a pronouncement supports the view that customary international law does, indeed, recognize the principle of reparation payments. And the Reparations Agreement between Israel and West Germany, as alluded to earlier, is seen as a practical guide and precedent for the development of treaty obligations on which African States and their sympathizers can additionally base their claims for reparation payments for slave trade.

Chapter 4 The Psychopathology of the Money

Erich Krausbeck

As a psychiatrist I am told by economics professors that fifty percent of economics is psychology. This is not completely understood by a *psychiatrist* because the assumption is that economics and trade are subject to the law of the market and the desire for profit. It is therefore not immediately clear to the doctor of psychiatry that money transactions are subject to emotional and even to neuropsychological laws.

As however all participants in the economic process are independent from one another and because of this have to get along, the question must be asked how people relate to one another in the market place. It is evident to everyone that a high demand for a share increases its value. The higher the amount that is bid for a share, then it follows that it will be traded for a higher price. When there is no demand for a share then it is available for a cheap price, even when the value behind the share - possibly in the form of manufacturing - has not changed. The true value behind a share fluctuates depending on how the participants in the market evaluate it. The stock market speculator and publicist *Kostolany* believes that a speculator is someone who buys things that no one else wants. It is therefore absolutely possible to have a difference of opinion about the value of a share. Needless to say, the speculator hopes that there will be wide interest and a high demand for his shares over time. It is the same with money. If the demand for money is high then credit becomes more expensive. By the same token a reasonable interest rate will be paid for your money when your partner in business wants to make sure that you lend it to him. These are processes which more or less take place without difficulty and as a matter of course. Obviously it is possible to increase the demand for a share by promoting it and pushing up its value. Promoters of shares have been known to apologise to the buying public for shares that were heavily promoted, but later crashed.

But can inflation be caused by emotions whipped up by fear and demand? Inflation will in all likelihood occur when there are large amounts of money available but there are only a limited number of goods on offer. Sometimes there is only a sense of an inflationary trend, because the products which affect us personally appear to increase in price before our very eyes and these are of greater concern to us than other prices, which move more in the background. After the introduction of the *Euro* in *Europe* there was a belief in some *European Community Countries* that prices had increased, whereas the inflationary feeling by the consumer was obviously higher than the official inflation rate.

However the *Hyperinflation of 1923 in Germany*, Austria and Hungary appears to be a different phenomenon. In that year, prices increased at an unstoppable pace with the result that the price of a consumer item increased from just one mark to a billion mark by the end of 1923. How can we possibly explain the rationale behind the constant upward push in prices by business, especially as this occurred simultaneously and was across the board? Should an individual merchant charge prices that are exorbitant, and then there is no chance of finding a customer who will pay such a high price for a product in the same market that can be purchased around the corner at a much lower price. However, in

Germany in 1923 there was a uniform increase in prices. It was a straight forward increase that became quite contagious.

To give account of my own family's situation, the hotel trade in *Baden-Baden* was bad and after the *First World War* the health spas went through difficult times. The monarchy had been annihilated and the world war had to be paid for. Social structures had fundamentally changed and enquiries for expensive hotels in health spas had visibly declined. There were some hotelier families, who had converted their hotel to a military hospital during the world war and this had ensured the economic viability of the property. The Krausbeck family had not done this. This is because there was an assumption that after the war the spa hotel would be occupied once again. But after the First World War the mood was revolutionary and the splendour of the *Belle-Epoque* was over. In the end, the need was too great and the Kaiserin Elisabeth Hotel in Baden-Baden was sold during the period of inflation. Even though a family member was a banker, the impact from this inflation was underestimated and the amount of money realised from the sale of the hotel literally melted away. Incidentally, the hotel became after the Second World War the seat of the newly created radio station in the French zone; the "*Südwestfunk*" broadcast from the Elisabeth Hotel in Baden-Baden. The value of the property was undoubtedly retained, but the amount of money realised from the sale had become worthless.

The question is what induces a merchant to constantly push prices upwards in exactly the same way as other traders, so that in the end the unit price of low value items has changed from a few pfennigs to billions of marks. It must be assumed that there was an unconscious feeling of uncertainty combined with collective fear – the devil takes the hindmost.

In 1995 *Giacomo Rizzolatti* and his colleague discovered *mirror neurons* in the brain of monkeys *(Rizzolatti G, Fadiga L, Gallese V, Fogassi L 1996, 131-141)*. This deals with the structure of the brain and the connection of neurons, which naturally were anatomically known previously, but this role had not been assigned to it. The scientists discovered when conducting tests upon macaque monkeys that the nerve cells of the cerebrum in the animal react with another animal who moves its paw. The first monkey watches his counterpart eat and the nerves in his brain are activated, even though the monkey sitting opposite has only moved its paw to its mouth.

Monkeys in a Toy Shop

It was discovered in the course of these tests that motorised actions are imitated at the same time in the observer. It is not any different with humans. If someone opposite me puts out his hand for a handshake then I have to control myself with great difficulty not to imitate this action and to greet him the same way. How could a couple walk side by side without adopting the same steps as their partner? Prussian military parades would have never existed without the spontaneous ability of humans to march and even belt out a marching song at the same time. Subsequently brain researchers could prove that not only was it possible for mechanical actions to be transmitted from person to person, but feelings and moods too. We develop a response with each other and can "ape" the experience.

Magnetic resonance imaging creates pictures of the brain, as if a salami sausage had been sliced open, so that we could examine it closely slice by slice and identify the contents of the sausage. In a functional *MRI* it is even possible to determine which nerve cell groups have been activated. With mirror neurons it was possible to determine that the actions of the motor areas of the cerebral cortex could lead to an activation of the pre-motor cortex of the other partner. Subsequently it was possible to prove this phenomenon in humans too. Emotional responses of one person are mirrored in the person opposite too. In addition, we humans constantly sense the feelings and actions of others. The frontal brain areas and the amygdale belong to these centres. The region to the right, between the temporal lobe and the parietal lobe, the temporoparietal junction, has no other function than to read the thoughts of other people and to understand others.

With this sensational discovery the feeling of empathy could be explained in neuropsychological and anatomical terms for the first time. This capacity for empathy is the foundation of our social life. We constantly delve into the thinking and actions of others. The concept "*Theory of Mind*" describes a similar phenomenon. Communication without this ability does not appear to be possible. With this ability we can recognise the intentions of the other person. In conversation with someone we have the ability to recognise whether their spoken words correspond with their feelings. We can then sense whether it is genuine or not.

When a cabaret artist steps on stage, he must establish contact with the audience. He must not only be present on stage, but must be on the same wavelength as the audience. The cabaret performer *Henning Venske* went on stage at the famous Long Night of The Cabaret and all he said was: "We arrived by train!" This was immediately acknowledged with tumultuous applause. With these simple words he had unleashed more from the audience of 500 people than he thought possible. At the time there was a lot of talk in the media about the delay of trains. It had at the time been a constant headline in the newspaper. The fact that the train had arrived late was not the end of the world for the parties involved, but at the very least it was annoying. It was simply the topic of the day. With a single blow the expectant audience had clearly formed an emotional attachment to this hitherto unknown stranger. The audience responded with hearty applause and laughter to the pertinent remarks by the guest artist, because they knew, suspected and sensed that there was more behind it, and the announcement that he had arrived by train, was most probably just the beginning of a long and emotional story. It did not turn out not quite so bad after all, that is for *German Railways*, but the contact with the audience had been established and the entertainer had found an emotional entrée to the audience, and as they say – to his audience. Language therefore conveys more than a linguist can extract from words. At the right moment a specific feeling is addressed and a sympathetic, perhaps better connection is established between people. Despite an audience of 500 at this soirée an emotional bond was established with the first few words and laughter. This for example would not have happened had those words been spoken on a train platform. On the cabaret stage the sentence "We arrived by train" had been the direct entrée to the thoughts and stream of feelings by the audience. It is clear that certain expectations (the cabaret evening), combined with a certain talent for mime (that is the art of the actor) together with visual signals created by the appearance of the guest artist and a controversial joke that broke the tension created an immediate connection with the audience. The sudden realisation of this connection released joy and laughter. And those who sat next to each other or in between were unable to escape this. The *mirror neurons* in their brains got stimulated by the laughter of their neighbours. The vibrant turmoil in the room and the collective laughter was so exhilarating, that it was impossible to resist the joy and laughter. It is by no means an unpleasant experience. It was for everyone in the hall a group experience and this does connect. If we humans with our mirror neurons were not programmed to imitate the things that others do in a similar situation, then there would be no joint applause at a concert and definitely no joint laughter by the audience at a performance. The comedian's job would be unthinkable. Everything that relies on communication in human society would be unthinkable. If we did not have this ability, described as the Theory of Mind, then every morning there would be a massive collision of people at the central railway station in Frankfurt. However, we have the ability to understand intentions and anticipate actions by others without being fully aware of it. In fact we are in a position to move comfortably through the diagonally moving stream of commuters in a detached and casual manner. Naturally this has disadvantages and it can create problems. It is possible to imagine that panic is reliant on a similar response by fellow human beings. If an individual should have a so-called *panic attack,* then other people will perhaps try and help sympathetically by attempting to comfort the person who is paralysed by fear. However, if an alarm goes off that resonates with all people in the same way, such as the sound of a siren or the smell of fire, then panic can rapidly overtake other people in the room and trigger an irrational panic reaction. In this case, the ability to think rationally is largely switched off.

The *mirror neurons* are therefore functions that imitate motor skill actions by a partner in conversation. It is possible for two people to walk side by side deep in conversation and despite this concentrate on their discussion. The stroll in the forest by the German Chancellor *Helmut Kohl* with the Soviet President *Michael Gorbachev*, where in 1989 the reunification of Germany was discussed and an agreement reached, would not have been possible had both men not been able to walk uniformly and automatically side by side and at the same concentrate on the international political task at hand. Fortunately they succeeded.

But not only are motor skills successfully imitated, but feelings and perceptions are imitated too, whether intentionally or unintentionally. Every nurse knows that a patient with an unpleasant or painful itch of the skin (pruritus) will trigger the same itch and even the same type of scratching in fellow patients in the same hospital ward. This cannot be avoided, because the same structures of the brain are activated in the other person via the mirror neurons.

The social fabric is not always made up of laughter and walks but we also assess and experience life. Fear and hope are part of life. In the times of inflation every businessman had to be careful not to become impoverished, which unfortunately happened to the Krausbeck family and their hotel in Baden-Baden. Simply by the mechanism of *mirror neurons* is it possible to explain the uniform and steady increase in prices over several months. There was no government regulation or rational reason for this. Had prices stopped increasing on a specific day, then that would have been the end of inflation.

Society though could not accomplish this in its own right. The sense of being left behind and to be the loser had for all, and therefore for everyone, an existential meaning. It is impossible to withdraw from society which is touched by these collective thoughts of fear. Further, no one stands up during a play and calls out to the actors that they should be performing something else, because it is too boring. Even if a play is boring, the interaction amongst the theatre audience is explained via the *mirror neurons*. Their motor reactions are the same; they do not move, sit quietly and concentrate on the events on stage or nod off. They would be incapable of getting up in order to disrupt the event.

It has been established during the past 10 years that we have a *social brain*. The individual does not think in isolation. He thinks in association with other people and the social brain behaves in a group precisely as it should behave in a group. Not all people are the same. However, many types of behaviour are identical in group situations. On mornings we avoid bumping into other commuters at the railway station, in the restaurant we talk in hushed tones and in contrast at a sports stadium we are absolutely combative and boisterous. The phenomenon of fear can be downright infectious. In 2009 the world experienced a collective fear of swine flu. It was nothing less than a psychic epidemic, which abated during the winter period again. In the meantime, the matter has been forgotten and no pigs create fear any longer. That is the way it is when I sense what my neighbour feels and I then only feel secure if there is a sense of security in my surroundings too. My brain is socially trained in such a way as to strengthen behaviour, so that I remain socially integrated and abstain from actions that isolate me socially.

The *social brain* is certainly only one aspect of our emotional life. There are great many other emotions and illnesses. A person with autistic tendencies manoeuvres because of this around the edge of society. However, this is the exception. We think collectively and act collectively. Our brains are interconnected, so that as a rule we understand each other. Psychic epidemics would not be conceivable without this functional connection and they can be attributed to mirror neurons. The escape by the French from the north of France when the German troops drew near in 1940 was a psychic epidemic. Once the Germans reached Bordeaux they all went home again. The big inflation of 1923 was a mass phenomenon which grew out of the collective behaviour by merchants, who collectively were certain that all other merchants would match their prices during the same week. However, the matching of prices during the period of hyperinflation took place in anticipation of expected price increases and led to the collective rapidly moving increase in prices, because in effect they were all concerned about missing the boat.

With the discovery of *mirror neurons* the group dynamics phenomenon was elevated from the realm of *behavioural disorders* to the realm of *psychology*. We humans have no choice other than to feel, think and to act within a social unit. We are unable to remove ourselves from it, because if the person opposite me scratches his head, then in my brain the premotor cortex for my hand and arm is activated, whether I want to or not, and at the same time the sensory centres picks up on the itch by the person opposite and an unpleasant sensation is produced in me, whether I want to or not. And if the person opposite has a contagious disease or appears to have fleas, then I will not be able to remove myself so quickly from that unpleasant sensation again. The discovery of the social brain allowed a different status to be applied to many a behavioural type within a social setting. In retrospect many a phenomenon can be classified now and until recently it was perhaps only possible to define them in an unsatisfactory way. The question of public opinion is evident not only in the collective unconsciousness coined by *Carl Gustav Jung* and in group dynamics. As a society our absolutely conscious thought processes are performed with our *social brains.* What connects us therefore is not only what is genetically predisposed – for example the collective fear of snakes – but instead the ideas, whether conscious or unconscious that we bring to the society in which we move. During the *Age of Enlightenment* the individual became aware of liberty. With the discovery of the *social brain,* he must be aware that he assumes responsibility for the actions of others because of the things that he says and does. He is at the same time subject to the feelings, behaviour and views of others. There is no restriction on freedom, but instead there is an extension of the notion of freedom on all of *social thinking,* in which the individual participates as a vital constituent part.

The question why a *Voltaire*, a *Robespierre*, a *Frederick The Great* or a *Catherine the Great* would have discussed the concept of individual freedom during the *Age of Enlightenment,* or debated the relationship of the individual with *God* or with authority, could be explained by the fact that these strong historical figures would not have imagined themselves to be bound to a social way of thinking with their *social brains.* Only now, with the available technology of a functional *MRI* is it possible to get a better insight into the function of our brains. To refer to brains in the plural is increasingly justified, because with a single brain, such as that of a *Robinson Crusoe*, no further cultural development would be possible. It is collective thinking with all its advantages and risks that has been shaped by the human experience and this makes a cultural narrative possible.

Chapter 5 Hyperinflation 1922/1923

Wolfgang Chr. Fischer

5.1 History of Economic Thought about Inflation at the Turn of the 20th Century

> *"The history of economic thought has a twofold function; to explain the past and to help us to understand the present. By examining the economic theories of the past we can learn to see the problems of earlier times, as it were, through the eyes of their contemporaries. By comparing them with the theories of the present we can realize better the implications and the limitations of the knowledge of our own day." (Robbins 1937, p.xi).*

Inflation has an extensive notation within the *History of Economic Thought*. Going back even to the *Medieval Ages* and the *Scholasticism* some aspects of inflation were a matter of concern. *St. Thomas Aquinas*, the most important of the scholastic writers, attempted to reconcile the religious teachings of the *Catholic Church* with the slowly increasing economic activity of the time.

St. Thomas Aquinas (1227–1274)

In his time the medieval *Catholic Church* was concerned that increasing economic activities would turn the minds and hearts of humans from religious and ethical affairs and toward materialism *(Landreth & Colander 2002, 37)*. St. Thomas Aquinas and other scholastics were less interested in analysing the formation of prices in an economy including the role that prices play in the allocation of scarce resources, but more focused on the ethical aspects of prices, that is discussing issues of equity and justice. The basic question was whether religious doctrine forbade merchants to sell goods for more than they paid or for trades people to charge more for their services than their labour costs – in other words the religious and moral area under discussion was whether taking profits and interest were sinful acts? "Thus, the scholastic concept of just price is seen alternatively as a forerunner of the *Ricardian-Marxian* labour theory of value,...and the notion implicit in classical-neoclassical theory that competitive markets yield ideal just prices" *(Landreth & Colander 2002, 38)*.

In *Adam Smith's* famous book *"An Inquiry into the Nature and Causes of the Wealth of Nations" (1776)* he affirmed that markets are the *invisible hands* to produce the best outcome from economic interactions. Smith was concerned about the new economic order, which should be replacing the state intervention within the economic order of mercantilism at his time in England. He drew his major policy conclusion from his stated facts that human beings are rational, have astute powers of judgment and are driven by *self-interest.* If they are left alone each individual will follow its self-interest, and in promoting self-interest support the interests of society. Therefore governments should not interfere by imposing regulations and can consequently follow a policy of *laissez faire.* Smith conceded that markets often fail to produce ideal social results, but current reality convinced him that the results of government intervention were less acceptable than those flowing from free markets *(Landreth & Colander 2002, 38). Adam Smith* advocated *laissez faire,* but he was also aware that markets do not always produce the best outcome for the society. However, inflation in a broader sense was a matter of less concern, only price inflation could be seen as a matter of interest. However, the classical economists were very exact in defining economic terms, because they were constructing a language on which an emerging science was being built. "Among their first contributions was to make explicit the distinction between 'real' and 'nominal' prices. A good's real price, or *value,* was defined as the effort required to produce it, while its nominal, or *money,* price was said to be its cost in money alone (fixed in terms of gold or some other precious metal)" *(Bryan 1997, 1).* Therefore the value of goods is attached by the laws of nature and the effort of labour, but their nominal price fluctuates with the availability of the precious metal, and the laws of the *Sovereign,* that define a nation's money *(Bryan 1997, 1).* "The real price of everything…is the toil and trouble of acquiring it. The same real price is always of the same value; but on account of the variations in the value of gold and silver, the same nominal price is sometimes of very different values"*(Smith 1776).*

Adam Smith
Professor of Moral Philosophy at University of Glasgow (1723-1790)

Karl Marx and his collaborator *Friedrich Engels* contrary to the often expressed public opinion that both had written about how a socialist or communist economy should be built – had only a few ideas about a communist society, which were published in *The Communist Manifesto* in 1848.

"Das kommunistische Manifest" Karl Marx & Friedrich Engels
(1848) (The Communist Manifesto) 'Proletarians of the World, Unite!'

The Communist Manifesto (Some selected elements of a *Classless Society*):

- Abolition of property in land and application of all rents of land to public purposes;
- Abolition of all right of inheritance;
- Equal liability of all to labour;
- Free education for all children in public schools;
- Abolition of children's factory labour in its present form.

Karl Marx analysed in his famous book *Das Kapital – Kritik der politischen Ökonomie (The Capital) 1867,* a treatise against the laissez faire of *Adam Smith* and *David Ricardo,* the underlying principles and mechanism of capitalism in detail, embedded in a precise study of the economic and social history of mankind and the antagonism of the integration of the new working class into the newly formed industrial society, but analysing the phenomenon of inflation was not a concern. On the whole *Karl Marx* was a protagonist of a communist society, which would bring an end to all the misery of the class struggle. "And just as for post-millennial Christians, man, led by *God's* prophets and saints, would establish a *Kingdom of God on Earth* (and, for pre-millennials, *Jesus* would have many human assistants in establishing such a Kingdom), so for *Marx* and other schools of communists, mankind, led by a vanguard of secular saints, would establish a *secularized kingdom of heaven on earth*" *(Rothbard 2006, 317).*

Karl Marx (1818-1883)

Friedrich Engels (1820-1895)

Karl Marx asserted that the central driving force of capitalism was in the exploitation and alienation of labour. The ultimate source of capitalist profits and surplus was the unpaid labour of wage labourers. Employers could appropriate the new output value because of their ownership of the productive capital assets, protected by the state. By producing output as capital for the employers, the workers constantly reproduced the condition of capitalism by their labour *(Marx 1867).* He explained the objective "*laws of motion*" of the *capitalist system* as a whole, its origins and future. He aims to reveal the causes and dynamics of the accumulation of capital, the growth of wage labour, the transformation of the workplace, the concentration of capital (the expropriation of the expropriators), competition, the banking and credit system, the tendency of the rate of profit to decline, land-rents and in conclusion "The worker becomes all the poorer the more wealth he produces, the more his production increases in power and range. The worker becomes an ever cheaper commodity the more commodities he creates" *(Marx 1867, Vol. 1). Karl Marx* had experienced the expansion of markets; the accumulation of capital, and that in reality the cash nexus stripped away all previous religious and political illusions, but only to replace them with another kind of illusion, the 'commodity fetishism'. *Karl Marx* predicted that in capitalism, improvements in technology and rising levels of productivity increase the amount of material wealth in society while simultaneously diminishing the economic value of this wealth, thereby lowering the rate of profit. This is a tendency that leads to the paradox, characteristic of crises in capitalism, of 'poverty in the midst of plenty', or more precisely, crises of overproduction in the midst of underconsumption *(Marx 1867).*

Although *Karl Marx* and *Friedrich Engels* were not focused on the matter of 'inflation' in the broader sense, their analysis of the *Laissez faire* market concept and the 'laws' of capitalism laid the foundation of critical discussions about the economic and social order to be placed in a rapid growing industrialization with periods of mostly 'free trade'. It was left to later economists to study the phenomenon of 'inflation' once inflation had become an essential economic problem.

The integration of the working class into the emerging industrial state was a matter of concern to the so-called *Kathedersozialisten* (mock name) *(Socialists of the Chair) Verein für Socialpolitik (Association for Social Policy).* This was a group of national economists who gathered in 1872 in *Eisenach*, Germany, to look for solutions to this essential social question. The *Verein für Socialpolitik (Association for Social Policy)* had an important influence on the social legislation of the *German Empire (1871-1918).*

Gustav von Schmoller (1838-1917)

Gustav von Schmoller, Professor in Halle (1864-72), Strasbourg (1872-82), and Berlin (1882-1913) *was* the leading economist of *Imperial Germany.* He was the leader of the *Kathedersozialisten* and founder and long-time chairman of the *Verein für Socialpolitik*

The idea that changes in the quantity of money affect only the money price of goods, not their value, was championed by many of the early classical economists, most notably *David Hume.* This theory was more rigorously developed in the early twentieth century by American economist *Irving Fisher*, and has come to be known as the 'quantity theory of money' *(Bryan 1997).* "To these early economists, the word *money* almost always referred to a metallic coin. But the first generation of economists following *Adam Smith* in the nineteenth century was very interested in paper money, since this form of payment had become popular in the burgeoning American colonies. The colonies offered a large variety of paper currencies, virtually all of which were conspicuous by their 'overproduction' and their subsequent rapid loss of purchasing power. The Continental Congress issued a paper note to help finance the *American Revolution*, and these 'bills of credit' became a circulating medium. In 1775, Congress issued $6 million of the new currency and urged the states to impose taxes for its ultimate redemption. The taxes were never raised, however, and larger continental issues were authorized. By the end of 1779, Congress had expanded the number of continental bills of credit more than 40-fold, and, to make matters worse, the states had issued their own paper monies in a similar magnitude. In 1781, a dollar in paper was worth less than two cents in gold coin" *(Bryan 1997).*

"Inflation is the process of making addition to currencies not based on a commensurate increase in the production of goods" - *Federal Reserve Bulletin 1919 (Bryan 1997).* During the first several decades of the twentieth century the effects on the increase of the price level became more obvious for economists, because they could be certain of the 'excessiveness' of the circulating medium only by its effect on the price level, the notions of an inflated currency and prices became inextricably linked *(Bryan 1997)*. "Linking *inflation* to the price level proved to be another important turning point for the world. With the publication of *John Maynard Keynes' General Theory* in 1936, an assault on the quantity theory of money commenced, and it dominated macroeconomic thought for the next forty years. "By appealing to the belief that resources could be regularly and persistently underemployed, an idea given support by the worldwide depression of the time, *Keynesian* theory challenged the necessary connection between the quantity of money and the general price level. Moreover, it suggested that aggregate price increases could originate from factors other than money. In addition to separating the price level from the money stock, the Keynesian revolution in economics appears to have separated the word *inflation* from a condition of money and redefined it as a description of prices. In this way, inflation became synonymous with any price increase. Indeed, Keynes spoke about different "types" of inflation, including income, profit, commodity, and capital inflation" *(Bryan 1997)*.

John Maynard Keynes (1883-1946)

Keynes takes a tough attitude in his *Economic Consequences of the Peace (1919)*, condemning inflation in the harshest possible way *(Humphrey 1981, 4)*. *Keynes* came to the conclusion: "*Lenin* is said to have declared that the best way to destroy the capitalist system was to debauch the currency. By a continuing process of inflation, governments can confiscate, secretly and unobserved, an important part of the wealth of their citizens. By this method they not only confiscate, but they confiscate arbitrarily; and, while the process impoverishes many, it actually enriches some. He agrees with Lenin that inflation has the potentiality of destroying the basis of capitalist society. Lenin was certainly right. There is no subtler, no surer means of overturning the existing basis of society than to debauch the currency" *(Humphrey 1981, 4)*. *Keynes*' concern with the dangers of inflation influenced his policy advice in the post-war boom of 1920 when an outburst of inflation threatened the British economy. "*Keynes*' advocacy of tight money in this episode clearly rested on his fear of the damage that continuing rapid inflation could inflict on society and the capitalist system. He stated as much in a memorandum written shortly after his meeting with the Chancellor of the Exchequer. He feared that persistent inflation would generate social unrest and strike at the whole basis of contract, of security, and of the capitalist system generally, eventually leading to socialistic control over industry *(Humphrey 1981, 5)*.

At the turn of the 20th century the *American Institutionalist School,* commonly associated with *Thorstein Bunde Veblen (1857-1929)* and *Wesley Clair Mitchell (1874-1948),* was for a short period dominant in the *United States.* The *American Institutionalist School* was developed in the late 1880s in the *United States* and was heavily influenced by the *German Historical School* and the *English Historicists.* They asserted that much in the economic world was not immutable but rather conditioned by the influence of an always changing history - whether acting on the individual directly, or indirectly through the institutions and society which surround him *(Stavro 2006, 26)*. It was then *John Kenneth Galbraith,* who presented in his famous book

The Affluent Society (1958) a harsh critic of the American's private wealth and materialism in the sense of 'private wealth versus public poverty'.

John Kenneth Galbraith (1908-2006)

Galbraith argued that the free market economy was a myth and that the 1000 largest American corporations dominated both the nation's economy and social life. Giant corporations essentially operated free of competition, often turning out frivolous goods for an ever increasingly consumer-minded society, while the capitalistic economy ignored more pressing social needs *(Stavro 2006, 26)*. He tried to advocate for a substantial support of the poor and he favoured intervention by the government to rein in corporate power, while using more tax money to better social needs, such as improving education and protecting the environment *(Stavro 2006, 26)*.

It is worth mentioning that in the current world-wide financial crisis, which is connected with the gigantic granting of credit, the money creation by banks and the acceptance of *fiat money,* that is notes which are not worth as much as paper or metal, but are said by the government to have a value, *Karl Marx's* observations on the financial crisis of 1857, on the *'Roving Cavaliers of Credit'* was recently quoted by *Steve Keen:* "Talk about centralisation! The credit system, which has its focus in the so-called national banks and the big money-lenders and usurers surrounding them, constitutes enormous centralisation, and gives this class of parasites the fabulous power, not only to periodically despoil industrial capitalists, but also to interfere in actual production in a most dangerous manner - and this gang knows nothing about production and has nothing to do with it" *(Keen 2009)*. *Steve Keen* comes to the reasoning "that we should never have fallen for the insane notion that the financial system should be self-regulating. All that did was give the Cavaliers a licence to run amok, with the consequences we are now experiencing yet again - 150 years after *Marx* described the crisis that led him to write *Das Kapital*" *(Keen 2009)*.

5.2 Inflationary Process

> *"Cheap money is a stimulant, also an intoxicant. If the dose is large enough, a substantial temporary effect can be brought about, but headaches follow. If the matter really were that simple, everybody could be an economist, and only the perversity of central banks would keep us from endless prosperity. Merchants and manufacturers will not be induced to increase borrowings, since interest on money borrowed is only one small factor in total costs. But if merchants and manufacturers will not use cheap money, speculators will". (Benjamin Anderson, Chief Economist of Chase National Bank, New York Times, April 1930)*

Hyperinflation is very high inflation that is a sustained increase in the aggregate price level. Although the threshold is arbitrary, economists generally reserve the term *hyperinflation* to describe episodes where the monthly inflation rate is greater than 50 percent. At a monthly rate of 50 percent, it corresponds to an annual rate of approximately 13,000 percent. Simply a hyperinflation is an uncontrollable inflation with extremely high monthly rates. Additionally, hyperinflation is a very *complex phenomenon*, which has its roots in not merely macroeconomic factors but also in behavioural factors of human beings. Unfortunately the arrow of time is irreversible for the period of the *German Hyperinflation* 1922/1923, or in other words, one can not revisit the past, that is one can not observe the actual *German Hyperinflation 1922/1923* as a *complicated system* at its time. Furthermore, the highly complex process of hyperinflation that is for example in the initial state of the process the substantial variety of factors influencing each other, one can not regard as mono-causal and simply deterministic. *Paul Davies* had described the basic problem involved in his work *The Cosmic Blueprint (London 1987)* from the viewpoint of a theoretical physicist:

> "The traditional approach to complicated, irregular systems is to model them by approximation to regular systems. The more irregular the real system is, the less satisfactory this modelling becomes...When it comes to very highly organized systems, such as a living cell, the task of modelling by approximation to simple, continuous and smoothly varying quantities is hopeless. It is for this reason that attempts by sociologists and economists to imitate physicists and describe their subject matter by simple mathematical equations is rarely convincing." *(Davies 1987, p.22)*

In addition *Davies* criticised the traditional modelling in four major central themes:

> "Generally speaking, complex systems fail to meet the requirements of traditional modelling in four ways. The first concerns their formation. Complexity often appears abruptly rather than by slow and continuous evolution. Secondly, complex systems often (though not always) have a very large number of components (degrees of freedom). Thirdly, they are rarely closed systems; indeed, it is usually their very openness to a complex environment that drives them. Finally, such systems are predominantly 'non-linear' *(Davies 1987, p.22).*

Michel Baranger analysed *chaos* and *complexity* in the following way: "Lacking a precise definition, we can try to convey the meaning of complexity by enumerating what seem to be the most typical properties: Some of these properties are shared by many non-biological systems as well:

- Complex systems contain many constituents interacting nonlinearly.
- The constituents of a complex system are interdependent.
- A complex system possesses a structure spanning several scales.
- A complex system is capable of emerging behaviour
- Complexity involves an interplay between chaos and non-chaos.
- Complexity involves an interplay between cooperation and competition
- Complexity involves an interplay between cooperation and competition. Once again this is an interplay between scales." *(Baranger 2008,11)*

The American *artificial intelligence* researcher *Marvin Minsky* argued rightly:

> "Many scientists look on chemistry and physics as ideal models of what psychology should be like. After all, the atoms in the brain are subject to the same all-inclusive laws that govern every other form of matter. Then can we also explain what our brains actually do entirely in terms of those same basic principles? The answer is no, simply because even if we understand how each of our billions of brain cells work separately, this would not tell us how the brain works as an agency. The 'laws of thought' depend not only upon the properties of those brain cells, but also on how they are connected. And these connections are established not by the basic, 'general' laws of physics, but by the particular arrangements of the millions of bits of information in our inherited genes. To be sure, 'general' laws apply to everything. But, for that very reason, they can rarely explain anything in particular." *Minsky, Marvin (1987) The Society of Mind, New York, p. 26, quoted by Paul Davies (1987) p. 193.*

In a *hyperinflation* there are many agents, for example public authorities, business, consumers, which contribute in an unpredictable way – in a *complex system* – to establish the full momentum of an inflation, and like the consumers as part of the group of agents, the "rational" behaviour will be replaced by actions of non-consistency.

For example, consumer behaviour has been investigated in many aspects in modern times, in particular through market research and marketing analyses. However, how consumers react if an economic situation occurs with high inflation, even in a hyperinflation, this is an almost unoccupied scientific area in economics and law. Most likely consumers do not react in a reasonable rational way, more likely the majority of consumers will follow the old motto *"Save our Souls"*.

It should not be forgotten that the very existence of *Consumer Affairs* as a concern is an admission of the failure of *consumer sovereignty*, which means in short that consumers in the economy determine the production of goods and services by casting money 'votes'. Traditional rational consumers (so-called *'homo economicus'*) consistently make optimum decisions, as they are perfectly informed about the prices and all characteristics of all products and services for sale. The theory behind this *'homo economicus'* sets the conditions under which the consumer maximises his satisfaction from a given budget and is able to identify whether one parcel of goods and services is preferable to another. These assumptions of consumer behaviour lead to the *'Law of demand'*, stating that the quantity of products and services purchased is inversely related only to the price. Of course, this holds only in theory. In the course of time it has been beyond doubt that the old fashioned – and related – concept of *Caveat Emptor* (sold as seen) has been denied for decades. It is indisputable that market failure relating to the lack of sufficient information about price, quality, durability, availability, time and environmental performance of consumer goods and services exists. Consumer organizations in *OECD countries* agree that consumers do not have the collective power to make relevant changes in the marketplace. Consumers are not sovereign, this being a fiction as income is unevenly distributed; there is a lack of sufficient information about price, availability and quality performance of goods and services; and the widespread rise of marketing and the associated use of sophisticated techniques in selling products and services. The notion of the equality of bargaining positions is also most unlikely.

Within economics since the 18th century, especially during the period of the classics and the so-called marginal benefit theory, it was persistently assumed that consumers made rational purchasing decisions as a result of underlying rational behaviour. Since the 20th century this has been challenged by, amongst others, the studies of *Thorstein Veblen (1857-1929)* and his famous book *"Theory of the leisure class"*, and *George Katona* and his numerous publications on consumer behaviour. It has since become obvious that besides economic factors like price, quality, durability, availability, time and environmental aspects, sociological and psychological factors are crucial. Even with respect to numerous empirical studies trying to explain consumer behaviour, it seems to be an endless task to reveal the open and honest expression of people's values, beliefs and emotional reactions *(Bainbridge & Jones, 1992, 11)*. In the present chaotic world, uncertainty about the future is endemic *(Ormerod, 1994)* and consumer behaviour cannot be adequately described by the rational expectations theory of pure economics.

Maynes asserts that *John Kenneth Galbraith (The Affluent Society)* stands almost alone among economists in stressing the role of advertising in creating and managing the preferences of consumers *(Maynes, 1976, 263)*. In attacking the accepted doctrines of economics, *Galbraith* stresses two major themes:
(1) Producers, not consumers, are sovereign. Through successful advertising and salesmanship, producers/sellers 'manage' the preferences of consumers. Thus, it is producers, not consumers, who ultimately determine the volume and composition of output.
(2) Many of the wants being satisfied in our economy are non-urgent, even frivolous. This follows from the notion that many wants are contrived by sellers and are not original with consumers themselves *(Maynes, 1976, 264)*.
If conceded that *Galbraith* is right, the imbalance between corporate sellers and consumers could be seen in the following way: "The individual private consumer is typically an amateur dealing with a highly skilled professional, and will, also typically, lack the skill, knowledge, awareness or even the incentive (in respect to small transactions) to attempt to act as would the professional" *(Terry, 1988, 123)*. Furthermore, it might be said that consumers are not interested in goods as such, but in their properties or characteristics. Thus, the individual's constrained choice involves both the space of characteristics and the space of goods, linked through the consumption technology. Individual preferences determine the relative weights given to the various characteristics in making choices, and thus different individuals may choose different goods or collections of goods even though they face a common consumption technology *(Lancaster, Kelvin, 1991, 4)*.

Consumer behaviour may be defined as the decision process and physical activity individuals engage in when evaluating, acquiring, using or disposing of goods and services (*Lawson 1996, 4*). *Consumer behaviour* involves a *mental decision process* as well as physical activity. Therefore the act of purchase is just one part of the decision process, and remains part of a system of mental and physical activities that occur during a period of time. Some of these activities precede the actual buying, while others follow it (*Lawson 1996, 6)*. It is noteworthy that factors affecting individuals in their daily lives also influence their purchase activities. Internal influences, such as learning and motives, as well as external factors, such as social expectations and constraints, affect consumer behaviour (*Lawson 1996, 7)*.

Furthermore consumer behaviour is enfold in culture, that is everything socially learned and shared by the members of a society as ideas, customs, beliefs and habits (*Lawson 1996, 74*).

Michel Baranger described in his contribution to *Chaos and Complexity* "There are many possible definitions of the word fractal. A very loose and general definition is this: a fractal is a geometric figure that does not become simpler when you analyse it into smaller and smaller parts. The famous *Mandelbrot set,* which is highly popular in the picture books and in the museums, is a less trivial fractal, but its definition is still amazingly simple, given the resulting complexity" *(Baranger 2008, 5).* The *Mandelbrot Set* of *Benoît Mandelbrot* follows the simple formula $y=x^2+c$ and has to be repeated according to a certain rule. The Mandelbrot set is a famous example of a *fractal,* which is generally "a rough or fragmented geometric shape that can be split into parts, each of which is (at least approximately) a reduced-size copy of the whole," a property called self-similarity *(Fractal, Wikipedia 2009).*

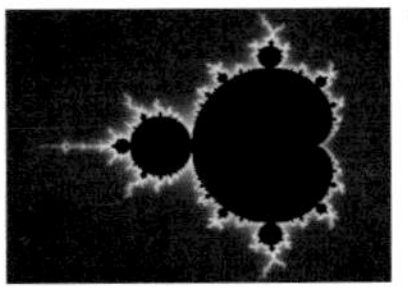

Benoît Mandelbrot Set

Because they appear similar at all levels of magnification, fractals are often considered to be *infinitely complex* (in informal terms). Natural objects that approximate fractals to a degree include clouds, mountain ranges, lightning bolts, coastlines, snow flakes, even various vegetables (cauliflower and broccoli). However, not all *self-similar objects* are *fractals* – for example, the real line (a straight *Euclidean line*) is formally self-similar but fails to have other fractal characteristics; for instance, it is regular enough to be described in Euclidean terms*(Fractal, Wikipedia 2009).* "More than 40 years ago *Benoit Mandelbrot* described the fractal structure of cotton prices and the emanating properties of fat tails and volatility clustering and *Hyman Minsky* proposed a theory for endogenous speculative bubble formation. More recently *Robert Shiller* and *Alan Greenspan* made the irrational exuberance paradigm fashionable. These all fit in the framework of *Complexity Economics,* which describes the properties that emerge from interacting agents" (*Sornette 2009).*

The fairly new thought of *Complexity Economics*[62] is in general the application of the *complexity science* to the dilemmas of Economics.[63] *Complexity, chaos, catastrophe and cybernetics* are

[62] See Appendix 6, Comparison with Traditional Economics, http://en.wikipedia.org/wiki/Complexity_economics.

[63] See further details of Complexity Economics:
The Santa Fe Institute (SFI) is a non-profit research institute located in Santa Fe (New Mexico, United States) and dedicated to the study of complex systems. The Santa Fe Institute was founded in 1984 by George Cowan, David Pines, Sterling Colgate, Murray Gell-Mann (American physicist who received the 1969 Nobel Prize in physics for his work on the theory of elementary particles), Nick Metropolis, Herb Anderson, Peter A. Carruthers, and Richard Slansky.
Beinhocker, Eric D. The Origin of Wealth: Evolution, Complexity, and the Radical Remaking of Economics. Boston, Massachusetts: Harvard Business School Press, 2006.

embedded in this new mode of economic thought, which "rejects traditional assumptions that imply that the economy is a closed system that eventually reaches equilibrium. Instead, it views economies as open complex adaptive systems with endogenous evolution. Complex systems do not necessarily settle to equilibrium – even ideal deterministic models may exhibit chaos, which is distinct from both random (nondeterministic) and analytic behavior" *(Complexity Economics 2010)*. "In the light of the new concepts introduced, economic systems shall no more be considered as 'naturally' inclined to achieve equilibrium states. On the contrary, economic systems - like most complex and self-organized systems - are *intrinsically evolutionary systems*, which tend to develop, prevailingly toward levels of higher internal organization; though the possibility of *involution processes - or even of catastrophic events - remains immanent" (Complexity Economics 2010)*. The *hyperinflation* may well be seen as one of these catastrophic events. Furthermore the episode of the tremendous acceleration of the inflation in Germany in 1923 could be classified as a *sensitive dependence on initial conditions*, which had changed substantially at that time.

It would be worthwhile to implement the inflationary process of a hyperinflation into the *Chaos Theory*. *Chaos Theory* studies the behaviour of those systems which appear random to the naked eye, but are in fact deterministic from a mathematical perspective in that the current state of the system fixes the system at later intervals. The *inherent randomness* is attributable to a concept called sensitive dependence on initial conditions whereby relatively minor variations in the initial variables can have a significant impact on future behaviour. The signature of time-chaos is something called *sensitivity to initial conditions*. "It says that, if you have two sets of initial conditions or two points in phase space, extremely close to each other, the two ensuing trajectories, though close to each other at the beginning, will eventually diverge exponentially away from each other. *Edward Lorenz*, the discoverer of sensitivity to initial conditions, also called it "the butterfly effect" because, thanks to sensitivity to initial conditions, it is possible for a butterfly, by flapping its wings on some Caribbean island today, to change completely the weather pattern in Europe a month from now." *(Baranger 2008, 6)* This interpretation underscores the difficulty associated with forecasting of chaotic systems. This difficulty has been seized upon by a number of scientists who have argued that chaos is detrimental to determinism, and the hyperinflation in Economics, in particular its accelerated process of the price level and the decay of the value of money relative to the previous purchasing power, certainly fulfil some criteria of the Chaos & Complexity Theory.

In a *hyperinflation* the interacting agents are continuously influencing each other. "In scientific literature it is said that such a system is subject to non-linear dynamics. Modeling such a system in full detail is practically impossible to do" *(Sornette 2009, 1-2)*. 'Recent research, however, has provided new tools to analyze complex non-linear systems without having to go through the simulation of all underlying interactions. When interacting agents are playing in a hierarchical network structure very specific emerging patterns arise. Let us clarify this with an example. After a concert the audience expresses its appreciation with applause. In the beginning, everybody is handclapping according to their own rhythm. The sound is like random noise. There is no imminence of collective behavior. This can be compared to financial markets operating in a steady-state where prices follow a random walk. All of a sudden something curious happens. All randomness disappears; the audience organizes itself in a synchronized regular beat, each pair of hands is clapping in unison. There is no master of ceremony at play. This collective behaviour emanates endogenously. It is a pattern arising from the underlying interactions. This can be compared to a crash.

There is a steady build-up of tension in the system (like with an earthquake or a sand pile) and without any exogenous trigger a massive failure of the system occurs" *(Sornette 2009, 1-2)*. Similar argues the historian *Ferguson* "Such systems can appear to operate quite stably for some time; they seem to be in equilibrium but are, in fact, constantly adapting. But there comes a moment when complex systems 'go critical.' A very small trigger can set off a 'phase transition' from a benign equilibrium to a crisis" *(Ferguson 2010, 2)*.

Why was there a tremendous *acceleration of the inflation* in a very short time in Germany?[64] Generally, the traditional explanation reduces the causes of *hyperinflation* completely to the financing of WW1 by means of war bonds, and the reparation payments, as well as on financing of national debts and public expenditures of the German Government after WW1.[65] "In 1922-23 Germany suffered the most famous hyperinflation of all time, and the only one to have afflicted a major industrial power this century. Both during and after the First World War the inflation was an instrument of government policy. Inflation, Keynes observes, is a form of *"taxation by currency depreciation." (J.M. Keynes, A Tract on Monetary Reform, London, 1924, p.9, p.41)* The rise in prices puts real commodities at the disposal of the note-issuer, who offers paper money in exchange. The inflation resulted from excessive monetary expansion via budget deficits." *(Southern 1979, p.D1030)*

John Maynard Keynes intervention at the *Peace Conference in Paris* where his main interest had been in "trying to prevent Germany's compensation payments being set so high it would traumatize innocent German people, damage the nation's ability to pay and sharply limit her ability to buy exports from other countries - thus hurting not just Germany's own economy but that of the wider world" *(Keynes-Wikipedia)*.[66] The following diagram represents the decay of the value of the German currency: One can clearly observe a "strong upward curvature characterising a 'super-exponential' behaviour or a faster than exponential growth" *(see also Johansen & Sornette 2001)*. The collapse of the German currency *Mark* seemed to be inevitable and a new behaviour would be on the agenda that is the introduction of a new currency the *Rentenmark* by the end of 1923 and in August 1924 the *Reichsmark*.

However there is no generally accepted hypothesis why this acceleration of the *inflation* into a *hyperinflation*, particularly since August 1923, took place.[67]

---

[64] See also Chapter 6.3.

[65] Carl-Ludwig Holtfrerich, Deutsche Inflation 1914-1923, http://de.wikipedia.org/wiki/Deutsche_Inflation_1914_bis_1923.

[66] Keynes himself and the Treasury were largely excluded from formal high-level talks concerning reparations. Their place was taken by the Heavenly Twins - the Judge Lord Sumner and the Banker Lord Cunliffe whose nickname derived from the "astronomically" high war compensation they wanted to demand from Germany. Keynes was forced to try to exert influence mostly from behind the scenes, but was unfortunately not successful.

[67](Davies 1987, p.203) "...I intended that the gaps left by the inadequacies of reductionist thinking should be filled by additional scientific theories that concern the collective and organizational properties of complex systems, and not by appeal to mystical or transcendent principles...."

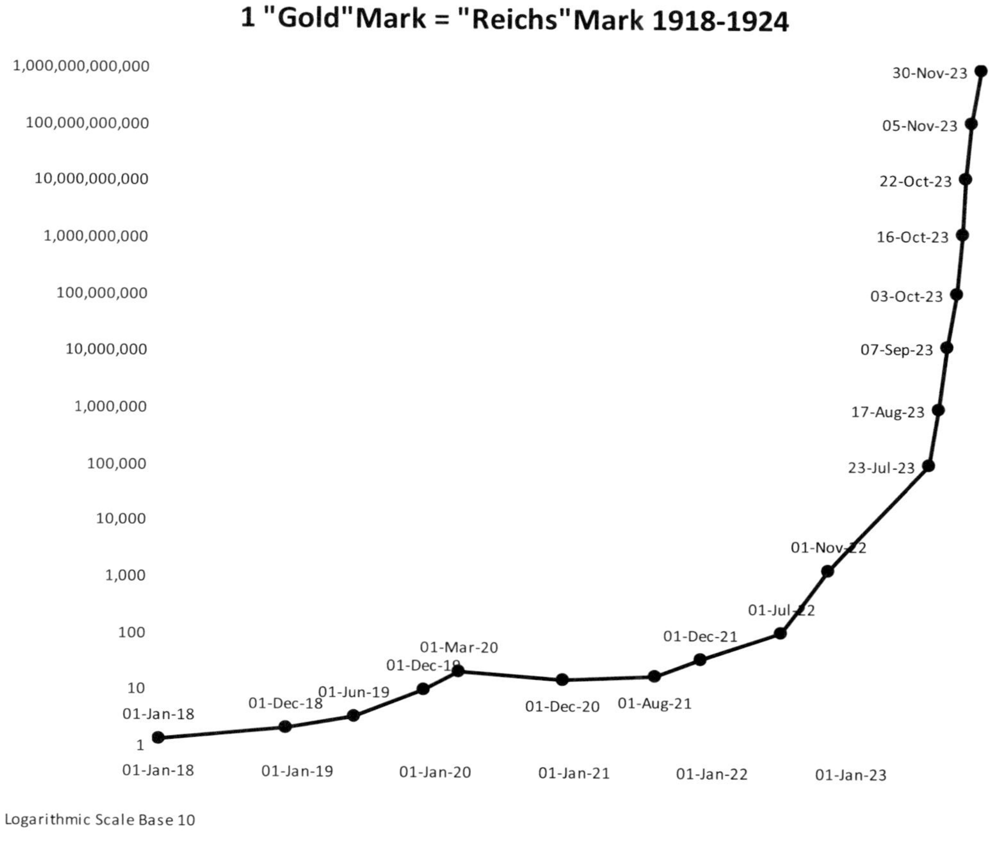

Note: 1 "Gold"Mark value in grammes of fine gold (1913) = 0.35842g;
"Reichs"Mark = Currency not tied to the goldstandard in 1918 to 1924.

Source: Law about the Revaluation of Mortgages and other Claims (Revaluation Act 1925), issued the 16th of July, 1925 (Aufwertungsgesetz, Reichsgesetzblatt, Teil I, 1925, p.133-135) and Author's calculations.

Until the outbreak of WW1 the *Mark* was convertible into gold, but then the convertibility was suspended to allow unrestricted expansion of the note issue. "Inconvertible paper currency (paper marks) was made legal tender by legislative fiat. The legal tender legislation established the rule that paper marks were compulsorily acceptable at their face value. The rule that payment in paper marks at their nominal value was a good legal discharge of debts was enshrined in the rule *'A mark is worth a Mark'* (*Mark gleich Mark*)." *(Southern 1979, p. D1030)*[68]

This principle embodied the *nominalist view* that money has no intrinsic worth but is simply that which the state declares from time to time to be a good legal discharge of money contracts. The traditional explanation has been given by *Southern* in a shortened version and containing only the main point of the inflationary process leading to hyperinflation. "After the war a number of factors pre-disposed Germany to hyperinflation. The government had to pay both the huge internal debt contracted to pay for the war and massive reparations imposed by the Allies on Germany. These outgoings were too great to meet from taxation. The economy was weakened by the havoc of war and the loss of territories containing many of its most valuable resources and industries. This reduced the economy's taxable basis. The government lacked legitimacy in the eyes of wide sections of the population. The system therefore appeared weak and unstable, which reduced confidence in the currency. Experience of rising prices convinced people of the folly of saving and prudence of debts. They therefore spent money more rapidly thus increasing the velocity of circulation. The *Reichsbank*, convinced that inflation was the result – not the cause – of a credit-shortage, lent money to industry at rates which lagged far behind inflation" *(Southern 1979, p.D1030)*.

100 Mark in 1908 (by way of gold backing)

---

[68] (Southern 1979, p.D1030)

The compulsory value of the paper mark was based on the following laws:

- Bank Law of 1909 which made Reichsbank notes legal means of payment: 1 June 1909, Reichsgesetzblatt (=RGB1) 515;
- Coin Law of 1914, which made coins exchangeable only for bank notes and Treasury certificates: 4 August 1914, RGB1 326;
- Banknotes Law of 1914, which suspended the Reichsbank's obligation to redeem its notes in gold and obliged the Reichsbank to redeem Treasury certificates in banknotes to an unlimited extent: 4 August 1914, RGB1 347;
- Bundesrat Decree of 1914, which suspended all gold-payment clauses in contracts: September 23, 1914, RGB1 417.

Respective tenfolding of the US Dollar rate in Mark since the outbreak of WW1

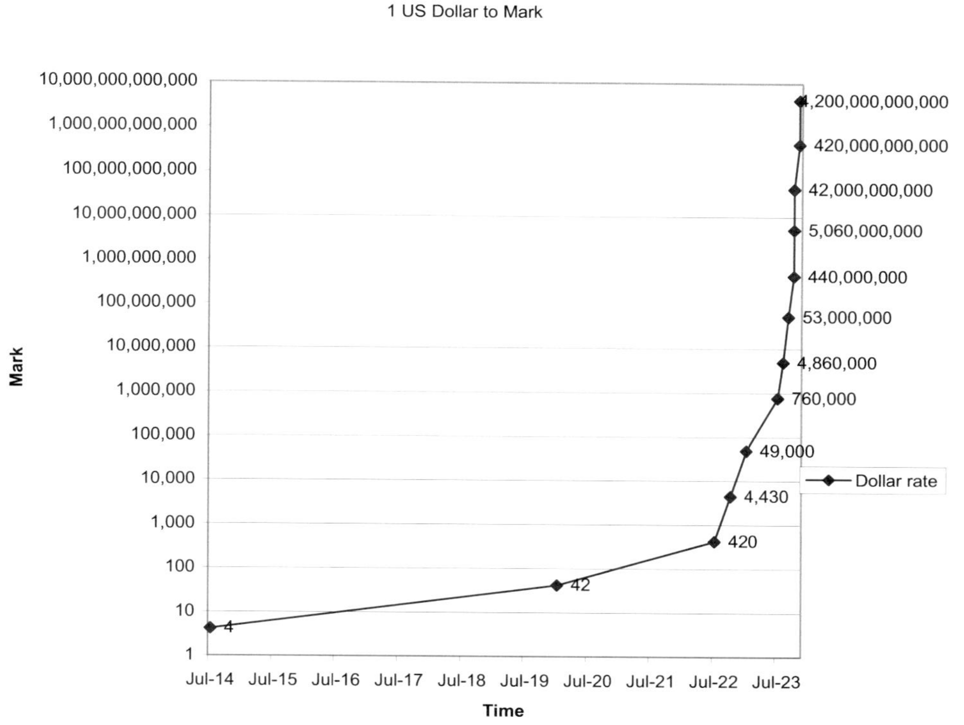

Source: Carl-Ludwig Holtfrerich, Deutsche Inflation 1914-1923, http://de.wikipedia.org/wiki/Deutsche_Inflation_1914_bis_1923

An explanation of increasing the price level generally offers the *quantity equation* of *Irving Fisher*. This formula can be transformed to:

$$PriceLevel = \frac{MoneySupply \bullet CurrencyCirculationVelocity}{TransactionNumber}$$

- The price level rises, therefore, among other things if the money supply rises (if the central bank puts in circulation, e.g., more money), currency circulation velocity and transaction number, however, unchanged remain.
- The currency circulation velocity rises; however, money supply and transaction number remain unchanged. ·
- The transaction number decreases (e.g., by disturbance of the economic cycle by disasters if suddenly the ability of delivery of goods and services diminished, but the demand remains), however, money supply and currency circulation velocity remain unchanged (*Hyperinflation; http://de.wikipedia.org/wiki/Hyperinflation*).

Thomas Sargent breaking new ground on the subject of rational expectation argued "it is not the base supply of money that determines inflation but the velocity of its circulation, which in turn is a function of expectations" *(Ferguson 2010, 11).*

"The ratio of the German price index in November 1923 to the price index in August 1922 – just fifteen months earlier – was 1.02×10^{10}. This huge number amounts to a monthly inflation rate of 322 percent. On average, prices quadrupled each month during the sixteen months of hyperinflation. In October 1923, German prices rose at the rate of 41 percent per day" *(Salemi 2007).*

Money Stacks in the Berlin Reichsbank (German Reserve Bank)
October 1923

Salemi argues with regard to the causes of hyperinflation that "no one-time shock, no matter how severe, can explain sustained (i.e., continuously rapid) price growth" *(Salemi 2007).* Furthermore the world war itself did not cause the hyperinflations in Germany. The destruction of resources during the war can explain why prices in Germany would be higher after them than before. But the war itself cannot explain why prices would continuously rise at rapid rates during the hyperinflation periods. "Hyperinflations are caused by extremely rapid growth in the supply of "paper" money. They occur when the monetary and fiscal authorities of a nation regularly issue large quantities of money to pay for a large stream of government expenditures. In effect, inflation is a form of taxation where the government gains at the expense of those who hold money whose value is declining. Hyperinflations are, therefore, very large taxation schemes" *(Salemi 2007).*[69] In addition *Salemi* concludes that: "During the German hyperinflation the number of German marks in circulation increased by a factor of 7.32×10^9. This number is smaller than for the growth in prices. In hyperinflations prices typically grow more rapidly than the money stock because people attempt to lower the amount of purchasing power that they keep in the form of money. They attempt to avoid the inflation tax by holding more of their wealth in the form of physical commodities. As they buy these commodities, prices rise higher and inflation accelerates" (*Salemi 2007).* The involved agents in a hyperinflation embattled economy are trying to spend the money they receive quickly in order to avoid the inflation tax; the government responds to higher inflation with even higher rates of money issue – the *inflationary process* had begun to accelerate tremendously. However, this accelerating inflationary process reflects a *chaotic system* caught up with numerous factors. Nevertheless some authors consider the *German hyperinflation* monocausal in the sense that the German

[69] See for further details also: Salemi, Michael. "Hyperinflation, Exchange Depreciation, and the Demand for Money in Post World War I Germany", Ph.D. diss., University of Minnesota, 1976.

government tried to finance its spending, either for the war costs, or for the war reparations or even for both altogether.

Sennholz argues that immediately after the war the German government, under the leadership of the *Social Democratic Party (SPD)*, embarked upon heavy expenditures for health, education, and welfare *(Sennholz 1979, 79-83)*. "While government expenditures rose by leaps and bounds, the revenue suffered a gradual decline until, in October 1923, only 0.8 percent of government expenses were covered by tax revenues. For the period from 1914 to 1923 scarcely fifteen percent of the expenses were covered by means of taxes. In the final phase of the inflation the German government experienced a complete atrophy of the fiscal system." *(Sennholz 1979, 79-83)* On the other hand one has to bear in mind, that the former *German Government under the Emperor Wilhelm II* had been dependent in its revenues on the various state contributions *(Matrikularbeitraege)* from the Kingdom of Bavaria, the Kingdom of Hessen, and the dominant Kingdom of Prussia etcetera. The *German Government under the Emperor Wilhelm II* had very little access to a tax base in its own right, which was introduced after *WW1* by the new German Government.

From time to time it is argued that Germany had to inflate its currency to pay the war reparations required under the *Treaty of Versailles*[70], but this is ambiguous. "The German currency was relatively stable at about 60 Marks per US Dollar during the first half of 1921. But the *'London Ultimatum' in May 1921*[71] demanded reparations in gold or foreign currency to be paid in annual installments of 2 billion gold marks plus 26 percent of the value of Germany's exports. The first payment was paid when due in August 1921. That was the beginning of an increasingly rapid devaluation of the Mark which fell to less than one third of a cent by November 1921 (approx. 330 Marks per US Dollar). The total reparations demanded was 132 billion gold marks which was far more than the total German gold or foreign exchange. An attempt was made by Germany to buy foreign exchange, but that was paid in treasury bills and commercial debts for Marks which only increased the speed of devaluation" *(Wikipedia, London Ultimatum 1921)*.

Ten Million Mark *Fifty Milliard (Billion) Mark*

German Reserve Bank (Reichsbank) 1923

In January 1923 French and Belgian troops occupied the industrial region of Germany in the *Ruhr area* to ensure that the reparations were paid in goods, such as coal from the Ruhr and other industrial zones of Germany, because the Mark was practically worthless. The German government under *Chancellor Wilhelm Cuno* exclaimed the *'Ruhr battle'* and to keep

70 See Chapter 2.

71 See Chapter 3.

the strikers in high spirits, appropriate financial help was paid to them *(Holtfrerich, Wikipedia, Deutsche Inflation 1914-1923)*. Subsequently the unemployment rose, the wages fell into the bottomless pit and the *Communists Party (KPD)* got more and more inflow. Meanwhile, the government-carrying labor unions were so minimized that they had to be financed by the government. When *Gustav Stresemann* became Chancellor, he terminated in September 1923 the *Ruhr Battle* due to the crucial fear of a putsch *(Holtfrerich, Wikipedia, Deutsche Inflation 1914-1923)*. Nonetheless war reparations accounted only for about one third of the German deficit from 1920 to 1923 *(Wikipedia, London Ultimatum 1921)*.[72] The *London Ultimatum 1921* itself does not explain the monstrous acceleration of the inflationary process in a very short time in 1923. That Germany was faced with reparations after 1921 that could not be paid except at ruinous economic cost has been argued all along but Ferguson on the contrary "argues that Germany could have easily paid reparations had there been the political will" *(Wikipedia, Ferguson)*.

In a hyperinflation the trend to switch to the *'shadow economy'* is well known: "Hyperinflation reduces an economy's efficiency by driving agents away from monetary transactions and toward barter. In a normal economy great efficiency is gained by using money in exchange. During hyperinflations people prefer to be paid in commodities in order to avoid the inflation tax. If they are paid in money, they spend that money as quickly as possible. In Germany workers were paid twice per day and would shop at midday to avoid further depreciation of their earnings. Hyperinflation is a wasteful game of 'hot potato' where individuals use up valuable resources trying to avoid holding on to paper money" *(Salemi 2007)*.

German Stamps 1923; 200 Million & 20 Milliard (Billion)

Still the question is not answered why the economic agents react in a similar way in their economic disposition during a period of hyperinflation with an *accelerating inflationary process* in the very crucial time of July 1923 till December 1923, when the hyperinflation was ended by issuing a new currency the *"Rentenmark"* and in August 1924 the new currency *"Reichsmark"?* The exorbitant acceleration of the inflationary process, apart from the already given hyperinflation, can be judged as very important for other research as well as for this very unsettled area in economics. One attempt to explain within the *Complexity Economics* the reactions of the agents in this short period may be *mass hysteria* and *the Bandwagon effect.*[73]

Mass hysteria - also called collective hysteria, mass psychogenic illness, or collective obsessional behavior - is the sociopsychological phenomenon of the manifestation of the same or similar hysterical symptoms by more than one person. A common manifestation of mass hysteria occurs when a group of people believe they are suffering from a similar

72See also: Wikipedia, Harold James (historian) "Role of Banks in the Interwar Economy, Cambridge University Press 1991.

73See Chapter 4.

disease or ailment. The features of *mass hysteria* include no plausible cause found, ambiguous symptoms, rapid escalation of cases - often spread by line of sight - and rapid remission of symptoms. Mass hysteria consists of actions of ordinary people in indefinite shape. Hysterical reaction can be seen as a wild uncontrollable emotion or excitement *(Mass hysteria, Wikipedia).*

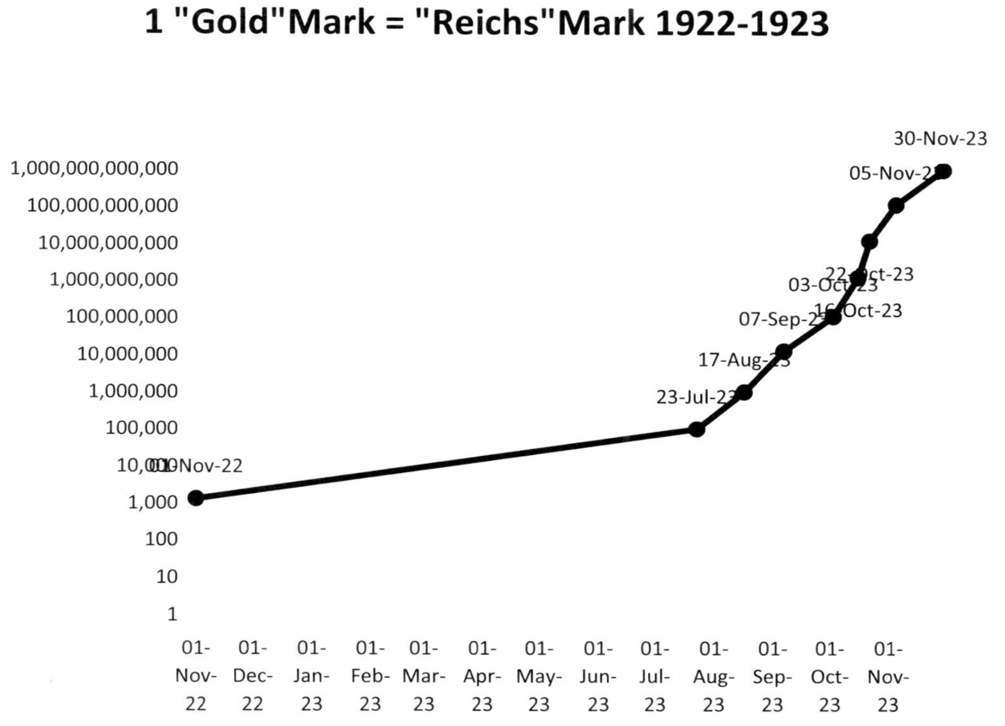

Note: 1 "Gold"Mark value in grammes of fine gold (1913) = 0.35842g;
"Reichs"Mark = Currency not tied to the goldstandard in 1918 to 1924.

Source: Law about the Revaluation of Mortgages and other Claims (Revaluation Act 1925), issued the 16th of July, 1925 (Aufwertungsgesetz, Reichsgesetzblatt, Teil I, 1925, p.133-135) and Author's calculations.

The *Bandwagon effect,* also known as social proof and closely related to opportunism, is the observation that people often do and believe things because many other people do and believe the same things. The effect is often pejoratively called *herding instinct,* particularly when applied to adolescents. People tend to follow the crowd without examining the merits of a particular thing *(Bandwagon effect, Wikipedia).* The *bandwagon effect* is well-documented in *behavioral psychology* and has many applications. "The general rule is that conduct or beliefs spread among people, as fashion clearly does, with the probability of any individual adopting it increasing with the proportion, which have already done so. As more people come to believe in something, others also "hop on the bandwagon" regardless of the underlying evidence. The tendency to follow the actions or beliefs of others can occur because individuals directly prefer to conform or because individuals derive information from others." *(Bandwagon effect, Wikipedia)*

"*Herd behavior* describes how individuals in a group can act together without planned direction. The term pertains to the behavior of animals in herds, flocks, and schools, and to human conduct during activities such as stock market bubbles and crashes, street demonstrations, sporting events, episodes of mob violence and even everyday decision making, judgment and opinion forming" *(Bandwagon effect, Wikipedia)*. Historically, because large groups of people have been able to bring about dramatic and sudden social change in a manner that bypasses established due process, they have also provoked controversy. "The main idea of *Sigmund Freud's crowd behavior theory* is that people who are in a crowd act differently towards people than those who are thinking individually. The minds of the group would merge together to form a way of thinking. Each member's enthusiasm would be increased as a result, and one becomes less aware of the true nature of one's actions *(Bandwagon effect, Wikipedia)*.

German Hyperinflation 1923: A German woman feeding a fireplace with German Marks, which burned longer than the amount of firewood people could buy with them
Source: Wikipedia, "Inflation in the Weimar Republic"

In 1922 a loaf of bread cost 163 Mark, by September 1923 this figure had reached 1,500,000 Mark and at the peak of hyperinflation in November 1923 a loaf of bread cost 200,000,000,000 Mark. The impact of the *German hyperinflation* was enormous:

- People were paid by the hour and rushed to pass money to loved ones so that it could be spent before its value meant it was worthless.
- People had to shop with wheel barrows full of money.
- Bartering became common - exchanging something for something else but not accepting money for it.
- Pensioners on fixed incomes suffered as pensions became worthless.
- Restaurants did not print menus as by the time food arrived the price had gone up.

- The poor people became even poorer and the winter of 1923 meant that many people lived in freezing conditions and burning furniture to get some heat.
- The very asset rich people suffered least because they had sufficient contacts to get food etcetera. Most of the very rich were land owners and could produce food on their own estates.
- The group that suffered a great deal - proportional to their income - was the middle class. Their hard earned savings disappeared overnight. They did not have the wealth or land to fall back on as the asset rich had. Many middle class families had to sell family heirlooms to survive. It is not surprising that many of those middle class, who suffered in 1923, were to turn to the *Nazi Party*.

Perhaps the most important implications of the *German hyperinflation* were:

- The disappearance of goods – particularly essentials such as food and heating – from the shelves.
- The disillusionment and the dissatisfaction with the German Government at that time.
- Social tensions with violence at "street battles".
- With the acceptance of the inflationary currency depreciation the economic and social weights of the lost war on the masses of the dependent employees and the pure financial resources owners could be diminished.
- An essential part of the middle class found itself in poverty. Their financial reserves melted away in the inflation up to destitute rests.
- Parts of the social middle class, the small and middle bourgeoisies, felt cheated by the republic. Growing parts of the work force were able to see nothing in defending the values of this government anymore.
- Vice versa there was also the inflation winner. So the real-estate owners became in the inflation actually entirely free of debts, while the real estate maintained its value *(Holtfrerich, Wikipedia, Deutsche Inflation 1914-1923).*

Salemi regards as very important effects of the *German hyperinflation:*

- One effect with serious consequences is the reallocation of wealth. Hyperinflations transfer wealth from the general public, which holds money, to the government, which issues money.
- Hyperinflations also cause borrowers to gain at the expense of lenders when loan contracts are signed prior to the worst inflation.
- Businesses that hold stores of raw materials and commodities gain at the expense of the general public.
- Renters gained at the expense of property owners because rent ceilings did not keep pace with the general level of prices *(Salemi 2007).*

Sennholz reached the conclusion: "Finally, the rapid depreciation of currency greatly reduced all tax liabilities during the time interval between the taxable transaction and the date of tax payments. The taxpayer usually paid a sum whose real value was greatly reduced by inflation...The growing deficits then were met with even larger quantities of printing press money, which in turn generated ever larger deficits *(Sennholz 1979, 79-83).*

Although the inflation ended with the introduction of the *Rentenmark* and the *Weimar Republic* continued for a decade afterwards, the *German hyperinflation* is widely believed to have contributed to the Nazi takeover of Germany. "*Adolf Hitler* himself in his book, *Mein Kampf*, makes many references to the German debt and the negative consequences that brought about the 'necessity' of *National Socialism*. The inflation also raised doubts about the competence of liberal institutions, especially amongst a middle class who had held cash savings and bonds. It also produced resentment of Germany's bankers and speculators, many of them Jewish, whom the government and press blamed for the inflation" *(German Hyperinflation, Wikipedia).*

The hyperinflation caused and left an unthinkable *chaos* in the German economic, social and legal area. Nearly the whole economic life came more or less to a stagnation and standstill, because the overwhelming transactions between the agents of the system depended on a sufficiently stable currency. Against all moral and constitutional obligations to prevent German citizens from misery and foster the well-being of their people, the relevant German authorities were incompetent or deliberately did not disclose that the hyperinflation happened with traumatic experiences to come for the majority of the people. The hyperinflation should have been terminated earlier than in 1923, at least sometime in the years 1920 to 1922, and such a development to an unthinkable excess should not have been tolerated. One might pardon the *German Government* and the *German Parliament* that such a hyperinflation was known sufficiently neither in its size nor in its genesis – apart from those politicians, who saw a new currency coming and they tried to achieve for their political clientele the most advantages. The *conventional economics* and socio-political concepts did not seem to have coped with this phenomenon of the hyperinflation. The *economic chaos* and collapse was followed therefore not by a given equilibrium, for which the economists in the 19th and 20th century always aimed and in theory as possible deemed. Instead the system developed itself far away from equilibrium and the entropy expanded with subsequently the degree of disorder of the system increased much faster until finally the system collapsed and a new plateau was in sight.

Today it can be explored neither empirically nor social-psychologically why in August 1923 the already existing *hyperinflation collapsed.* The causes are due likely in the area of irrational behaviour (or one might define it as non-rational behaviour), anxiety and fear of losing everything such as material possessions, money, properties, shares, and social status overall, distrust, survival strategies etcetera and not reducible to a few economic factors and correlations.[74] The modern *Complexity Economics* – still being in the development – could be asked as a challenge to find out a more satisfactory answer than the current traditional Economics has delivered so far. One has to keep in mind that the reduction to deterministic explanation might be very limited. *Niall Ferguson* arguably called into question the causality of historical events "Meanwhile, causal relationships are often nonlinear, which means that traditional methods of generalizing through observation (such as trend analysis and sampling) are of little use. Some theorists of complexity would go so far as to say that complex systems are wholly nondeterministic, meaning that it is impossible to make predictions about their future behavior based on existing data" *(Ferguson 2010, 8).*

---

74 See Chapter 4 and Chapter 6.3.

5.3 Introduction of the Rentenmark 1923 & the Reichsmark 1924

The hyperinflation reached its peak by November 1923, but ended when a new currency the *Rentenmark* was introduced. The government stated that this new currency had a fixed value, secured by real estate, and this was widely accepted by the public. Why the German hyperinflation came to an end? *Salemi* points out two major conditions for the successful termination (*Salemi 2007*):

- "The standard answer is that governments have to make a credible commitment to halting the rapid growth in the stock of money."
- "Proponents of the standard answer argue that the guarantee of convertibility is properly viewed as a promise to cease the rapid issue of money."
- "An alternative view held by some economists is that not just monetary reform, but also fiscal reform, is needed to end a hyperinflation."
- "*Thomas Sargent*, a proponent of this second view, argues that the German reform of 1923 was successful because it created an independent central bank that could refuse to monetize the government deficit and because it included provisions for higher taxes and lower government expenditures."

However, as a very important factor in this complex matter of bringing a hyperinflation to a halt should be identified the psychological issue of trust, in particular people's trust in the new economic, social and legal situation and respectively in the new currency. This new currency has not to be backed by gold or other commodities necessarily, but it should have a value – whatever specific value that might be – in the people's mind at least. Once a currency has entered the state of affairs as a sole *"paper-currency"*, the flight from the worthless currency into real values is a largely historically guaranteed reaction of these money owners who can carry out such a transaction according to their assets.

The German hyperinflation reached tremendous price levels and for example on the 1st of November 1923 one pound of bread cost 3 milliard Mark[75], one pound of meat cost 36 milliard Mark and one glass of beer was charged at 4 milliard Mark.

Under the *Enabling Law of October 13, 1923 (RGB1 I 943)* the German Government issued the *Rentenbank Decree of October 15 (RGB1 I 963)*. The scheme for stabilisation was the immediate responsibility of the monetary policy spearheaded by *Dr. Hjalmar Schacht,* the President of the German Reserve Bank *(Reichsbank)*, together with the fiscal policy of the German *Chancellor Gustav Stresemann* and *Finance Minister Hans Luther*, which brought the inflation in Germany to an end. The victorious powers demanded this stabilization also as a presupposition of negotiations about the *war reparation payments* which led to the *Dawes plan.*

The greatest source of inflation was blocked on the 15th of November 1923, when the *Reichsbank* ceased to discount treasury bills. On the same day the *Rentenbank* opened, which issued the new currency *Rentenmark* to replace the worthless 'paper' *Mark*. The *Rentenmark*

[75] 'Billion' and 'trillion' are used in their American sense. A billion is one thousand million (10^8, corresponds to English and German 'milliard'). A trillion is a million million (10^9, corresponds to English and German 'billion').

was only introduced to discontinue the hyperinflation and to provide the *German Government* and the *German Reserve Bank (Reichsbank)* a pause to consider their new fiscal and monetary policies. The *Rentenmark* (literally, 'Security Mark') was not backed by gold, which was hardly available after WWI in Germany. Therefore the *Rentenbank* mortgaged land and industrial goods worth 3.2 billion *Rentenmark* to back the new currency. The *Rentenmark* was secured by a hypothetical mortgage on industrial and agricultural property and the size of the issued amount on money was restricted to 3.2 billion *Rentenmark (Wikipedia, German Rentenmark)*. The *Rentenmark* was only an intermediate currency and was not legal tender.

Five Rentenmark (Fünf Rentenmark)

The *Rentenmark* was introduced at a rate *1 Rentenmark* = *1:*10^{12} *Mark (1:1trillion)*, by an established exchange rate of *1 US dollar = 4.2 Rentenmark*. The German people widely accepted this new intermediate currency in this *unofficial dual currency system* and the German hyperinflation effectively had been brought to an end.

The *Reichsmark (RM)* as the new legal tender was finally introduced by the *coin law (Münzgesetz) of the 30*th *of August 1924 (RGBl. II p. 254)* as a substitute for the completely devaluated 'paper' *Mark* from the previous hyperinflation in the years 1922 and 1923. The exchange rate of *Mark* to *Reichsmark* amounted to 1.000.000.000.000:1 (a trillion to one). Thus a trillion Mark was worth 0.24 US dollar, the value of one *Mark before the war*. Furthermore the exchange rate was then 1 *Rentenmark* = 1 *Reichsmark*. The *Reichsmark (RM)*[76] was the official currency in *Germany* from 1924 to 1948. This includes a part of the time of the *Weimar Republic*, the time of the *National Socialism* as well as after the WWII in the occupied zones of Germany up to the introduction of the new currency *Deutsche Mark (DM)* in June 1948.

A fictitious *gold reserve* was legally assigned to one *Reichsmark* by 1/2.790 kg of fine gold. This corresponded to the formal prewar gold reserve. However, the *Reichsmark*, in contrast to the pre-wartime Mark, was not redeemable by the citizens, even partly in currency gold coins at the Reichsbank, and the Reichsmark was not a pure *gold standard currency*.

Five Reichsmark 1942 (Fünf Reichsmark)

76 1 Reichsmark (1924-1936) = 3.32 Euro (2000).

Legally the responsibility for *redemption* of the *Reichsmark* bills had been fixed in gold according to §31 of the *Reichsbank law (Reichsbankgesetz)* – however, practically it was never legally enforced *(Southern 1979, p.D1030)*. The *Reichsmark* was a so-called *gold core currency* without visible gold coin circulation and with it practically a paper currency like today. The so-called 'gold core' had in essence only a symbolic importance in connection with payment balance occurrences with foreign countries.

The salvation of the German currency marked the doom of holders of any form of asset expressed in 'paper' Mark. Financial assets of all kinds were swallowed up in the maw of inflation *(Southern 1979, p.D1030)*. "Currency depreciation is 'a terrible instrument for the redistribution of wealth'. 'Inflation constitutes the euthanasis of the rentier'[77] *(J. M. Keynes, General Theory of Employment, Interest and Money, London, 1936, 375)* and 3.6 million people of independent means lost both income and capital" *(Southern 1979, p.D1030)*.

Nevertheless, in spite of all success in the fight against the German hyperinflation, the *trust* of large circles of the German population in the first German Republic *(Deutsches Reich – 'Weimarer Republik')* was traumatized. Extreme political drafts won increasingly the interest of the German population and veiled the real complex circumstances of the birth, the course and the consequences of the German hyperinflation.

One may regard the causes of the hyperinflation as a result of the financing of WWI with war bonds, the lack of a sufficient tax base and in addition the financial burden of war reparations. *Holtfrerich* concluded that "In the long term the growth of the money supply was at least a permissive factor in the process of currency depreciation, though not perhaps its direct determinant. In the short term changes in the value of the mark, external and domestic, were determined rather by variations in the demand for money (or the velocity of circulation) and in the rate of productive activity" *(Holtfrerich 1986, 331)*. Furthermore he summarized that "The hyperinflation began, however, when foreigners lost confidence in the future external value of the mark, because of the diplomatic crisis over Reparations. Capital imports ceased and the 'cake' for distribution among Germans grew smaller" *(Holtfrerich 1986, 333)*.

But the conclusions mentioned above seem too uncomplicated. The entire process of the German hyperinflation is much more complex, in particular taking into account the limited period during August 1923 until November 1923 as part of the inflationary process. *The pathology of money*[78] might perhaps make a relevant contribution to analyzing the *process of the tremendous acceleration* of the German hyperinflation in 1923.

One can imagine the events of a hyperinflation a little bit more if one considers the multiplicity of the emotional determinants of human action. *Susan Schmierer* has stated this very impressively in an interview with *Hedwig Sabert*, who at the time of the inflation was a young girl living on the *Island of Rügen*:

> "My father came upstairs one evening, from the store below, to tell us that he had sold the store and all of its contents to an American for $500 and five steamship tickets to New York. At the time we really did not

[77] A rentier is an individual who depends on income derived from rents.
[78] See Chapter 4.

> understand why he did it, but later we realized how serious things must have been to uproot a man of my father's age – he was over seventy – and force him to move with his family to a new world. Later, on the ship to New York, there was to be a costume party but I had nothing to wear. Then, I remembered the trunk of money we had brought, (just in case,) from Germany. With my mother's help and father's permission I made a dress with millions of marks – I was the belle of the ball." *(Schmierer 1979, 29)*

Susan Schmierer has appropriately summarized the *moral decay* of the German society during the period of the German hyperinflation: "Time became short, tensions rose, the pace of life quickened, and the need to spend the worthless money grew increasingly intense. Alcohol, drugs and prostitution spread through the society as people tried to grab hold of something tangible, or tried to wash it all away" *(Schmierer 1979, 30)*. *Joseph Szebenyei*, a contemporary author, described similar the moral decay in Germany and Eastern Europe as well: "The constant depreciation of currency seems to have a deteriorating influence upon morality. Newspapers are full of political scandals, public corruption, and the misdoings of bank swindlers, defalcators, and petty thieves. The respect for property is diminishing in proportion to its higher money value; and the amounts in which dishonesty deals are counted in millions. It is not worth while to steal less" *(Szebenyei 1922, 417)*.[79]

[79] Joseph Szebenyei describes as a contemporary author very illustrative the various events associate with high inflation and hyperinflation in his article "The Dollar in Wonderland".

Chapter 6 "A Mark is worth a Mark"

Wolfgang Chr. Fischer

> *La Loi, conçue dans sa signification large, comme un rapport nécessaire dérivant de la nature des choses. La Loi devient, chez l'homme, une règle voulue, instituée pour assurer la sécurité et la liberté. L'idée de séparation des pouvoirs: le législatif, l'exécutif et le judiciaire. (Montesquieu, De l'esprit des lois, Genève 1748)*

Charles de Secondat, Baron de La Brède et de Montesquieu (1689-1755)

6.1 Constitution of Weimar Republic 1919 [Deutsches Reich] & Social Responsibility

The *Weimar Republic* was the republican-democratic form of government of *Germany* (officially *Deutsches Reich*) in the years 1918-1933, designated after the place of *Weimar* in which the constitution-giving *National Assembly* sat from the 6th February to the 30th September, 1919. Although the constitution came into effect only on the 11th August, 1919 and formally, even if in the substance emaciated, it remained valid until 1945, one counts the duration of the *Weimar Republic* from the proclamation of the republic on the 9th November, 1918 up to the formation of the *Government Hitler* on the 30th January, 1933.

The *Weimar Republic* was not built on the formation of a long term peaceful evolution rather it was established after numerous violent, controversial and eruptive processes. Nevertheless the *Constitution of the Weimar Republic* implemented some elements of the *Constitution of the German Empire from 28th of March 1849*, based on the *German National Assembly in the Frankfurt Paulskirche 1848.*

19. März 1848: Nach den Barrikadenkämpfen in Berlin

March 1848 at the barricades in Berlin

Die Nationalversammlung in der Paulskirche

German National Assembly Frankfurter Paulskirche 1848

Constitution of the German Empire 28th of March 1849 [Verfassung des Deutschen Reiches]
Some selected articles:

- §. 39 The imperial authority is entitled to remit imperial laws about the commerce nature and to supervise the execution of the same.
- §. 137 [1] Before the law no difference of the states applies. The aristocracy as a state is abolished. [3] The Germans are equal before the law.
- §. 164 [1] The property is inviolable. [2] An expropriation can be carried out only from consideration of the common welfare, only on the basis of a law and for fair compensation.

However this *Constitution of 1849* never came into effect due to the military actions of the Prussian King *Friedrich-Wilhelm IV*, who dissolved the *German National Assembly sitting in the Frankfurt Paulskirche 1848–1849* and crushed the revolutionary troops in *Berlin* by military force.

After the formation of the *German Empire [Deutsches Kaiserreich]* in 1871 the *Chancellor of the German Empire Otto von Bismarck* tried in the first place to stop the new state, the workers to join the *Social Democratic Party of Germany (SPD)* and the *Unions* through banning the SPD by law, which utterly failed.

Graf Otto von Bismarck, Herzog von Lauenburg (1815-1898)
Chancellor of the German Empire [Deutsches Kaiserreich] (1871-1890)

Nevertheless he predicted the downfall of the nobility by not setting "noble" standards in their relation to the working class. Finally Bismarck agreed to *social reforms*, initiated in the *German Parliament (Deutscher Reichstag)*: in 1883 a law about compulsory health insurance, in 1883 a law about compulsory accident insurance, in 1889 a law about compulsory invalidity insurance, in 1889 a law about old-age pension insurance, and in 1891 laws about workplace protection, such as child employment, women's work, unhealthy work and Sunday's rest, and in 1891 an amendment to the industrial code establishing worker's councils.

Crucial for the establishment of a *German republic* with a great deal of social responsibility was then the downfall of the *German Empire*, headed by *Emperor Wilhelm II (Deutscher Kaiser 1881-1918,* in the *World War I (The Great War). World War One* had a devastating impact on Germany. Throughout World War One, the people of Germany had been led to believe by their government that they were winning the war. The Government propaganda had been used to great effect. Only the military leaders such as *von Ludendorff* and *von Hindenburg* knew the true state of Germany's military plight which had become even more apparent when America had joined in the war in 1917. Germany itself was being starved of food and all goods as a result of the British Navy's blockade of her ports in the north. With such a small coastline, the British Navy found it a relatively easy task to blockade her. German troops were poorly equipped and what food there was went to the war effort leaving the people of Germany very short of food in particular during the winter of 1917 (turnip winter). Despite the great military attacks in spring 1918, which nearly won the war for Germany, in autumn 1918 the Allies launched a massive attack on the German lines. The German Army could not stand up to such an attack and in just a few weeks the German Army had collapsed. Many Germans could not accept that they had lost the war. The blame was put on weak politicians rather than on military exhaustion. The two months of October and November 1918 are crucial in setting the scene for the Weimar Republic. In October 1918, Germany's naval command at Kiel decided to take on the might of the British Navy which was blockading Germany's northern ports. British submarines patrolled off the north German coast and such a mission would have been all but suicidal. The *Sailors of Kiel* mutinied rather than go on such a mission. This one incident seemed to have been the catalyst that sparked off total anger in Germany. The army was not sent to crush this mutiny as the Emperor and his government could not trust that they would not join the sailors. In fact, demonstrations took place all over Germany and those who worked went on strike. Soldiers did join the protests. By early November 1918, many cities had been taken over by workers' and soldiers' councils. This was very similar to what had happened in *Russia* during the communist takeover of 1917 and politicians were fearful of another communist takeover in Germany itself. In the space of two months, Germany had gone from being a fighting nation to a defeated one; from a nation with its leader *Kaiser William II* to one with politicians leading the country.

Kaiser Wilhelm II (1859-1941)

With revolution spreading to *Berlin, Wilhelm II* was forced to abdicate on the 9th of November 1918. *Chancellor Max von Baden* pre-empted Wilhelm's decision by announcing his abdication to the public. *Wilhelm II* sought exile in Holland, which refused to extradite him as a war criminal to the Allies following the Armistice.

Wilhelm II's Abdication

I herewith renounce for all time claims to the throne of Prussia and to the German Imperial throne connected therewith. At the same time I release all officials of the German Empire and of Prussia, as well as all officers, non-commissioned officers and men of the navy and of the Prussian army, as well as the troops of the federated states of Germany, from the oath of fidelity which they tendered to me as their Emperor, King and Commander-in-Chief. I expect of them that until the re-establishment of order in the German Empire they shall render assistance to those in actual power in Germany, in protecting the German people from the threatening dangers of anarchy, famine, and foreign rule.
Proclaimed under our own hand and with the imperial seal attached.
Signed Wilhelm *Amerongen, 28 November, 1918*

The removal of the *Emperor* left an apparent power vacuum, with no Head of State the political structure of the *Deutsches Reich* was obsolete, and an alternative form of government would have to be established. In October of 1918 a significant change was instigated: The *Chancellor* and his ministers were no longer accountable directly to the Kaiser. From this point onwards the *Chancellor* was accountable to the *Reichstag*. Thus the first moves towards a democratic state were made prior to the abdication of *Wilhelm II*. Upon the Emperor's abdication, there was still a form of government in which authority, no matter how much weakened, was held. This meant that to an extent the power vacuum left by the abdication was filled, even left in an extremely precarious political and economic situation.

On the 9th of November *1918 Philip Scheidemann* proclaimed the German Republic at the balcony of the German Parliament and two hours later *Karl Liebknecht* proclaimed the *Free Socialist Republic of Germany* at Berlin. Philip Scheidemann, concerned in the face of a possible workers' revolution in Berlin, proclaimed the Republic without consulting any of his colleagues. The decision proved irrevocable. The civil unrest had its cause and drastically increased to the fringe of a civil war in Germany.

Philipp Scheidemann (1865-1939)

Also on November 9th 1918 *Prince Max von Baden,* the *Imperial Chancellor*, transferred his own position of Chancellor to *Friedrich Ebert*, leader of the *SPD*. Ebert immediately set about forming a coalition government, the *Council of the People's Representatives (Rat der Volksbeauftragten),* that could administer Germany in the interim. He made an agreement with the *USPD*, a Socialist party later known as *KPD (Communist Party of Germany)*, which placated many of the disillusioned workers, soldiers and sailors. *Workers and Soldiers Councils* confirmed this on the 10th November 1918. Also on 10th November 1918 the armed forces agreed to support the new German Government, on the understanding that the government would support the *High Command* in its attempts to preserve high levels of discipline within the forces. The interim government was faced almost immediately with problems. Finally on the 11th of November 1918 an *armistice* was declared. In December 1918 the left wing *Spartacist* group held a demonstration that had to be suppressed by use of armed force. In January this group again threatened the fledgling government, as the *Spartacist Uprising* occurred. Again the interim government made use of force to quell the rebellion. Following the successful defeat of the *Spartacists* elections were held across Germany for the *National Assembly*.

The Spartacists defending Berlin

Free Corps men on the march

The *Free Corps* were lead by *Wolfgang Kapp* - a right wing nationalist who hated the government for signing the Versailles Treaty. This incident is called the *Kapp Putsch*. The Free Corps was joined by the Berlin police. The putsch failed because the workers of Berlin, who were not sympathetic to the Free Corps, went on a general strike and paralysed the city. There were no buses, trams, trains and fuel supplies were ended. Kapp held Berlin for just 100 hours before he fled to Sweden. The putsch failed miserably. But once again, it was not the government that restored order. The government's power was being maintained by others.

In the November revolution a government authority was formed with equal representatives from the *SPD* and *USPD* as *Council of the People's Representatives* under the presidency from *Friedrich Ebert* and *H. Haase*, and it had to carry the weight of the war ending. However, the differences in opinion existing among its members from the beginning could be bridged only with difficultly. While the *SPD* representatives aimed at a continuation of the parliamentary concept already introduced in the war and pursued, therefore, the quick summoning of a *National Assembly*, the *USPD* representatives saw their priority aimed at a fundamental transformation of social and economic relations. They retired on 29.12.1918 from the council. Nevertheless, the concept of the *German Constitution* was controversial right from the beginning of the republic and *Friedrich Ebert* had to make compromises to various political groups to win support for the establishment of a German Constitution as soon as possible. The new *German Constitution* had to seek a balance between economic prosperity and social exigencies.

Karl Liebknecht achieved fame immediately after the war by leading with *Rosa Luxemburg* the *Spartacists* in the *so-called German Revolution* against the government of *Friedrich Ebert*. *Liebknecht* was a member of the *Social Democratic Party* and was elected to the *Reichstag (German Parliament)* in 1912. Liebknecht was very opposed to Germany fighting in World War I though he was essentially a lone voice in Germany as few shared his belief. One who did was *Rosa Luxemburg* and they formed an underground organisation called the *'Spartacus League'* which printed an illegal newspaper called the *"Spartacus Letters"*. They got the name *Spartacus* after the slave who led a failed revolt against the mighty Roman Army. Liebknecht was arrested and conscripted into the German Army. After refusing to fight, he was made to bury the dead on the Eastern Front. In October 1915, he was allowed back to Germany as his health had become so poor. The military success of the German Army in Russia had fuelled the support for the war in Germany so support for Liebknecht and the Spartacists was relatively limited. In May 1916, the *Spartacists* went public and called for an end to the war. Liebknecht was arrested and spent the rest of the war in prison only being released in October 1918 when *Prince Max von Baden* granted an amnesty to all political prisoners *(Wikipedia, "Karl Liebknecht")*.

Karl Liebknecht (1871-1919) *Rosa Luxemburg (1870-1919)*

Liebknecht led the 'German Revolution' which started in January 1919. The Spartacists were defeated by the Freikorps and the *German Army (Reichswehr)*. Liebknecht was killed on January 15th, 1919. He and *Rosa Luxemburg* were being held at a hotel in Berlin. From here they were to be moved to a prison but at sometime during that journey, or possibly before it began, both were murdered.

Proclamation of the Free Socialist Republic of Germany

> "The day of the revolution has come. We have enforced peace. Peace has been concluded in this moment. The old has gone. The rule of the Hohenzollern, who has resided in this palace for centuries, is over. In this very hour we proclaim the Free Socialist Republic of Germany. We greet our Russian brethren, which has been ignominiously chased out four days ago.......The day of liberty has begun. Never again a Hohenzollern will enter this place. 70 years ago at this place, Friedrich Wilhelm IV was standing, and he had to take off his cap to honour the 50 corpses, covered in blood, of those who had died fighting at the barricades in the defence of the cause of liberty. Another defile passes here today. It is the spirits of the millions who have given their lives for the sacred cause of the proletariat. With a split skull, soaked in blood, these victims of the rule of force totter along, followed by the spirits of the millions of women and children who were depraved in the cause of the proletariat. And further millions of blood victims of this very world war follow them. Today an incalculable mass of inspired proletarians stands in this very place, to pay homage to the liberty newly gained. Party comrades, I proclaim the Free Socialist Republic of Germany, which we shall include all tribes, where there are no servants, where every honest worker will receive his honest pay. The rule of capitalism, which has turned Europe into a cemetery, is broken. We have to collect all our force to establish a government of workers and soldiers, to create a new stately order of the proletariat, an order of peace, of fortune, of liberty or our German brethren and of our brethren all over the world. We stretch out our hands to them and call on them to complete the world revolution."
>
> *Karl Liebknecht,* November 9th, 1918.
>
> Source: http://www.zum.de/psm/weimar/liebknecht_e.php

The *Dialectic of Spontaneity and Organisation* was the central feature of *Rosa Luxemburg's* political philosophy, wherein "spontaneity" is a grass roots, even anarchistic, approach to organising a party-oriented class struggle. Spontaneity and organisation are not separable or separate activities, but different moments of one political process; one does not exist without the other. These beliefs arose from her view that there is an elementary, spontaneous class struggle from which class struggle evolves to a higher level. Her sharp criticism of the *October Revolution* and the Bolsheviks was lessened insofar as she explained the errors of the revolution and of the *Bolsheviks* with the complete failure of the international proletariat *(Wikipedia, Rosa Luxemburg).*

> "Freedom only for the members of the government, only for the members of the Party — though they are quite numerous — is no freedom at all. Freedom is always the freedom of dissenters. The essence of political freedom depends not on the fanatics of 'justice', but rather on all the invigorating, beneficial, and deterrent effects of dissenters. If 'freedom' becomes 'privilege', the workings of political freedom are broken."
> *(From the Junius Pamphlet – most likely a reference to Lucius Junius Brutus, a legendary republican hero of ancient Rome) Rosa Luxemburg.* Source: Wikipedia, Rosa Luxemburg

The leading party in the *German Parliament (Reichstag)* was the *Social Democrat Party.* It was lead by *Friedrich Ebert.* He was born in Heidelberg in February 1871 and died in February 1925 in office. *Friedrich Ebert* was Germany's first President and he was instrumental in introducing the *German Constitution 1919.* In January 1919, general elections were held in Germany. The coalition which *Ebert* led got 85% support. On the 11th of February 1919 *Friedrich Ebert* was elected *President of the German Republic* - a position he held until his death in 1925.

Friedrich Ebert (1871-1925) Reichspräsident 1919-1925
First President of the German Republic (Deutsches Reich)

In this time he had to contend with the shame many Germans felt at losing the war, the humiliation of the *Treaty of Versailles,* the economic plight Germany was in, the *invasion of the Ruhr* by Belgian and French troops to secure the payments for reparations and the devastating impact of *hyperinflation.*

Friedrich Ebert had inherited a far worse problem. The war had brought:

- Economic disaster to Germany;
- Serious loss of man power (2 million men in the war);
- Near total disrespect for the government;
- Many thousands of armed and disillusioned former soldiers roaming the streets;

- A civilian population traumatised by the impact of the war.

These were the core of Germany's work force and Germany's industrial base could not recover without them. Therefore, it seemed that in December 1918, Germany was condemned to economic weakness. Such was the fear of communism and what had occurred in Russia that most Germans were content to turn a blind eye to what was done in the name of the government. These events also showed that Ebert was willing to use a strong hand against anybody who threatened the stability of Germany. The loss of face *Friedrich Ebert* experienced by having to leave the capital *Berlin* and move to the safer city of *Weimar* during the 'revolution', may explain why he treated those who fought against his government with such harshness.

The defeat of *Imperial Germany* in 1918 offered the opportunity for the complete recasting of German government through the election of a parliament constituted on the basis of democracy and elected under universal suffrage by the German people. Thus a new *German National Assembly* met in the town of *Weimar* in February 1919 and the post-war German state acquired its first democratic constitution *The Constitution of the German Federation of the 11th of August 1919 (see Appendix 5, Selected Articles of the German Constitution of the 11th of August 1919).* It was a federal constitution for the German confederacy of seventeen states large and small comprising some 62 million Germans. The early meetings of the newly elected *National Assembly* were held in the quiet town of *Weimar.* Between February and August much of the work of the *representatives* was focused upon forming a construction and establishing the mechanisms within which democratic government would work within the *German Republic.* The process was lengthy as many aspects of the constitution had to be redrafted as they moved power from state governments to the central authorities. The constitution also had a section that guaranteed the basic rights of German citizens. In this section the constitution outlined the right to localised self-government, a 'dignified existence for all people' economic freedoms, religious freedom and freedom of the Trade Unions. These rights were not only guaranteed but also supported by the development of additional welfare measures such as unemployment benefits, sick pay and the establishment of labour exchanges.

On the 31st July, 1919 the *National Assembly* accepted with overwhelming majority the new *German Constitution* which came into effect after her signing by the *German President Friedrich Ebert* on the 14th August 1919. Central constitutional principles were the people's sovereignty *(Article 1),* the division of power and the fundamental rights, among it for the first time the civil and family-legal equalization of the women *(Article 109, 119).* In addition, the Constitution brought together different structure elements from German and international democratic traditions: the representative democracy with a government responsible to the parliament, the plebiscite democracy with referenda (Switzerland) and the presidential democracy with a strong, directly chosen president (the USA, France). The German federalism survived in weakened form: the competence of the *German Government* (Reichsregierung) was extended. Bismarck's social legislation was further developed considerably *(Mosler 1964, p. 18).*

1919	Philipp Scheidemann
- 1919 to 1920	Gustav Bauer
- 1920	Hermann Müller
- 1920 to 1921	Constantin Fehrenbach
- 1921 to 1922	Joseph Wirth
- 1922 to 1923	Wilhelm Cuno
- 1923	Gustav Stresemann
- 1923 to 1925	Wilhelm Marx
- 1925 to 1926	Hans Luther
- 1926 to 1928	Wilhelm Marx
- 1928 to 1930	Hermann Müller
- 1930 to 1932	Heinrich Brüning
- 1932	Franz von Papen
- 1932 to 1933	Kurt von Schleicher

Reichskanzler (German Chancellors) 1919-1933

The *welfare state* made considerable progress compared to the *German Empire (Deutsches Kaiserreich). Article 159* guaranteed the freedom of coalition (that is the social and economic union freedom) and a constitutional existence and activities right awarded to *labour unions* like entrepreneur's groups. *Article 161* anchored the social insurance by *Bismarck* reasonably in the constitution. In addition, *article 163* from the 'moral' working obligation of the individual derived the obligation of the state to care for the 'necessary maintenance' of those to which an 'appropriate working opportunity cannot be provided'. This meant a constitutional order to the arrangement of a state employment-finding and unemployment insurance. *Article 146* laid down not least for the first time and still today existing 'for all common elementary school' as a basis of the divided school system constructed on it - an educational construction which implied a standardization tendency which went too far for conservative critics, on the contrary for the left went not far enough *(Bundeszentrale fuer Politische Bildung 1998)*.

The *council movement* of the revolution found a certain precipitation in the constitution. Members of the *workers committee,* after economic areas were divided into district workers councils and then a *German Workers Council* should be formed and come together with appropriate entrepreneur's representations to district economic councils and a *German Economic Council (Article 165)*. With the exception of the *German Economic Council* no political, but purely economic tasks were intended for them. The external operational councils should help, first of all, in the completing of socialization: *Article 153 paragraph 2* allowed expropriations 'to the well-being of the common good' on a legal basis, namely 'aligned with appropriate compensation, until a German law determines something else'. Because there were, however, no political majorities for socialization, these councils have - so far they were formed actually - never had an effect.

The *German Economic Council* according to *Article 165* was established on the 4th of May 1920.

Article 165

(1) The workers and office workers are called to help equally in community with the entrepreneurs in the regulation of the wage conditions and working

conditions as well as in the whole economic development of the productive forces. The mutual organizations and their agreements are recognized.
(3) ...The District Economic Councils and the German Economic Council are to be formed so that all important occupational groups are represented according to their economic and social importance in it.
(4) Socio-political and economic bills of fundamental importance should be submitted by the German Government before their incorporation to the German Economic Council for investigation. The German Economic Council has the right to apply even for such bills. If the German Government does not agree to them, so it has to take nevertheless the bill under the statement of her point of view to a vote in the German Parliament.

Demands for an economic parliament with legislative power arose during the constitutional discussions from different sides. A curtailment of the parliamentary competence by the creation of an economic parliament with legislative power found no majority in the *German National Assembly*. The finally enacted *Article 165* of the *German Constitution* did not intend legislative rights any more. But the *German Economic Council* got the right to present laws and to examine bills, however, the *German Economic Council* had no right to insert a veto against the laws passed by the *German Parliament*.

In evaluation of the thought of the councils movement of the 'November revolution' the constitution intended the construction of an economic councils organization. Regional and local worker's councils and economic councils with the *German Economic Council* as a central institution were intended. The *German Economic Council* consisted of 326 members who were partitioned first into 10 occupational groups and representatives' groups. The members were sent by professional interests and trade associations. In addition, appointed members came from the *German Government* and the *German Council (Reichsrat)*, the second chamber of the *German Parliament*. Sixty-eight representatives from agriculture and forestry belonged to the council, among these 25 employee's representatives, 6 representatives of market gardening and fishing, 68 representatives of the industry, 44 from trade, banks and insurance companies, 34 representatives from the traffic area and the public enterprises, 36 representatives of the trades, among these also 22 employees, 30 representatives of the consumers, as well as a representative of the liberal professions and employees. In addition, 12 members were appointed by the German Council *(Reichsrat)* from the regional economic life as well as 12 personalities appointed by the *German Government* came possibly from the science *(see Excursus: Political Activities of Contemporary German Social Democrats, Heinrich August Trinowitz)*. In spite of the extensive activity of the *German Economic Council* the real influence on the decisions of the parliament remained closely limited. From a certain importance one was the completion of the substantial *Economic and Social Enquête* between 1928 till 1932.

Whether the *German Constitution* laid the foundation for *Adolf Hitler*'s terrible misuse of the constitution to establish his terror regime, as so many historians argue, this is here not the issue. In the context of the German hyperinflation the *German Constitution* has to be seen as an important legal framework that had been taken by the *German Supreme Court (Reichsgericht)* as the basis to confirm the *Law about the Revaluation of Mortgages and other Claims [Revaluation Act 1925]* as valid and being consistent with the constitution.

6.2 Nominalism versus Valorism

The notion of *nominalism*, also nominal value principle or nominal principle, named *"Mark-gleich-Mark-Grundsatz" (Mark is worth a Mark)*, says that a pecuniary claim running on a certain sum can be fulfilled by the achievement exactly of the originally arranged number of nominal monetary units. Changes of the purchasing power between the start of the demand and their redemption *(inflation, currency depreciation)* are not considered in the nominal principle. It is insignificant whether with the delivery of the arranged number of nominal monetary units of transferred purchasing power is the same compared to the purchasing power of the appropriate number of monetary units at the time of the agreement of the money debt. With short terms and smaller nominal amounts the nominal principle corresponds to usual day-to-day business.

However, with big demand amounts and or long terms of the demands interests are arranged as a rule. Then the pecuniary claim gets the character of a credit. The described definition today is called *'money debt-legal nominalism'.* Under *technical nominalism* one understands that the money marks which represent an equally high value after the overprint on the separate money marks are also treated as equivalent. The respective material state is without meaning what is common with the current monetary system and currency nature, but not in earlier times *(metallism)*. Metallism lost its importance when the function of money ceased to be a commodity and became instead a currency as a nominal measure of value, a legal tender in private law and an instrument of governmental policy *(Grzybowski 1971)*.

The opposite standpoint is *valorismus. Valorism* is a theory which regards the extent of the monetary obligations as determined not by the nominal sum of units of currency but by their intrinsic value. "In contrast with metallism, which made currency a commodity, *valorism* stresses the *purchasing power of money*. Consequently, the *nominalistic principle* may be seen playing into the hands of authoritarian or totalitarian regimes, favoring policies of change and incompatible with a liberal, democratic and stable society. At the same time, nominalism, although politically dangerous, strengthens continuity and stability, which are threatened by excessive valorism and which may be seen as a means to maintain an economic balance between parties to contracts and the economic value of mutual debts and obligations" *(Grzybowski 1971)*.

The lesson should be drawn from the past experience when the only answer to the ills produced by the excessive *nominalism* was the recourse to limited or general *revaluation*. In conclusion, while our author recognizes that in modern conditions, the nominalistic principle is the only practical solution, it cannot be permitted to operate without control and correctives *(Hirschberg 1971, p.138)*. "Control must reflect the fact that currency serves both the state and social needs. While nominalism is a principle of public law, it is also the principle of economics and private law relations. It straddles these three levels of human existence and must preserve justice and good faith in contracts and obligations; it must assure stability and certainty in order to assure economic growth and public confidence; and it must also serve the state" *(Grzybowski 1971)*. This theory played in the time of the hyperinflation 1922/1923 a certain, but legally not generally recognized role. Today this theory is not generally accepted, but in the case of a hyperinflation, even in an economic situation with high inflation it could be revitalised.

6.3 Law about the Revaluation of Mortgages and other Claims [Revaluation Act 1925]

Revaluation (*Aufwertung*) has two meanings. In its customary sense it refers to the raising of the exchange rate of one national currency against other currencies. It also means *"revalorization"* – the restoration of the value of a currency depreciated by inflation. The German inflation of 1923 led to the inauguration of a wide-ranging programme designed to give people back in part the money which they had lost as a result of the currency devaluation (*(Southern 1979, p.D1030).*

The German government had the choice either by means of a *revaluation law* to finish the hyperinflation quickly or to allow sprawling and the political and violent disturbances on the streets. The campaign for revaluation centred round the middle class, those declining sections of the middle class who felt that history was leaving them behind and demanded that the state should rescue them and restore them to their true place in the social order. The aim of the revaluation movement was to make good the financial losses of the inflation. *Gustav Stresemann* declared as Reich Chancellor on August 22, 1923 *(Southern 1979, p.D1030):*

> "The loss of this cultural group is for us insupportable. I recognize completely the duty of the state to help these groups first of all, for if they have suffered misfortune then it is on account of their loyalty to the state (Staatsgesinnung). They were the repository of patriotism, they subscribed to the war-loans and so they were also the owners of all the wealth which has been swallowed up in the war-loans". *(Stresemann's Nobel Peace Prize speech of June 29, 1927).*

Therefore the German Government presented on the 25th of April 1925 to the German Parliament *(Reichstag)* the *Draft of a law about the revaluation of mortgages and other claims (Reichstag III. Wahlperiode 1924/25, Nr. 804)* [Entwurf eines Gesetzes ueber die Aufwertung von Hypotheken und anderen Anspruechen] *(see appendix 1). In the Explanation of the German Government to article 1* it is said: Claims from legal relationships before the 14th February 1924 are revalued in accordance with the sections 2 to 11a if they have the payment in specific in mark or in another no more valid domestic currency expressed sum of money to the subject and it is about investments [mortgages, mortgage bonds, debenture bonds, credit at public savings banks, claims of the insured persons from life insurance contracts, health insurance, accident insurance and liability insurance] which are devaluated by the currency decay.

In the attachment *"Economic reason for the conversion relation to the gold mark calculation"* to the explanations of the German Government to the Draft of a law about the revaluation of mortgages and other claims *(see appendix 1)* the German Government argues in detail that the interests of creditors and debtors had to be fair and balanced. Neither the *living standard price index* nor the *share price index* or the *property price index* (for this time, however, not existing) were judged as relevant, because the investments not with priority in consumption, shares or properties were granted to supposed-priority taken place, but credits were given also to the continued existence of enterprises and other money investments. The calculation of the *conversion relation* was considerably judged to the dollar index as well as to the wholesale price index. The *wholesale price index* is the price of a representative basket of wholesale goods. Some countries use the changes in this index to measure inflation in their economies. The wholesale price index focuses on the price of goods traded between corporations, rather than goods bought by consumers, which is measured by the consumer price index. The purpose of the *wholesale price index* is to monitor price movements that reflect supply and demand in industry, manufacturing and construction. This helps in analyzing both macroeconomic and microeconomic conditions. The wholesale price index tends to be a leading indicator, moving earlier in trade cycles than the retail price index. The indicator tracks the price movement of each commodity individually. Based on this individual movement, the wholesale price index is determined through the averaging principle. The inside *mark depreciation* arrived temporally to a certain extent always only with a delay on the state reached by the dollar rate. The wholesale price index, with which the big bulk goods, particularly as far as they came from abroad, showed less staying behind the dollar rate and caused a rapid adjustment to the dollar, although the prices of the agricultural products carry out a restraining effect. In principle the German government followed the line of market orientated reasoning that the *dollar index* and *the wholesale price index* would roughly indicate the "true" price level in general over the period of high inflation and hyperinflation. In addition the revaluation was bound on the exchange rate Mark and North American Dollar, based on the *Berlin Bourse* to obtain the value of the *"Goldmark" (Gribel 1925, 55).*

The German government furthermore revealed its method of reason for the conversion relation to the gold mark calculation in technical *"Explanations of the computation method for the revaluation numbers in appendix 1 to the law" (see appendix 1).* The revaluation measured data is the relevant central index, that the conversion relation of the inflated mark to the gold mark is the main resultant. The revaluation measured data arises in general from the arithmetic average between dollar index (the respective dollar rate divided by the pre-war parity) and *wholesale price index* (1913 = set 1); only in the cases in which the wholesale price index exceeds the dollar index does the dollar index represent only the revaluation measured data *(Draft of a law about the revaluation of mortgages and other claims (Reichstag III. Wahlperiode 1924/25, Nr. 804, Section II of Attachment).* The wholesale trade measuring figures required to the calculations had to be taken to interpolation where the quotation did not correspond to the entirely shorter periods chosen for the revaluation measured data. These took place in the following way: for the moments from which wholesale trade figures were present (setting time for measurement) the relation of these index figures to the appropriate dollar index was determined by division. Then for the other calculation it was assumed by the acceptance that the relation has changed one by the next setting time for measurement in even development between dollar and wholesale price index. (*Draft of a law about the revaluation of mortgages and other claims (Reichstag III. Wahlperiode 1924/25, Nr. 804, Section III of Attachment)).*

To form simply the application of the revaluation measured data, the *paper mark* values of the given (indicated) periods (from the 1st January, 1918 to the 30th November, 1923 and the following days) are converted into gold mark. If, for example, in the time from the 21st to the 31st October, 1920 the revaluation measured data (central index) 16.0 ~ amounted, 1 Papiermark = 1/16.08=0.06219 GM, or 100 Papiermark = 6.22 GM are to be placed *(Draft of a law about the revaluation of mortgages and other claims (Reichstag III. Wahlperiode 1924/25, Nr. 804, Section IV of Attachment)).*

The *Law about the Revaluation of Mortgages and other Claims, Appendix (Revaluation Act 1925),* issued the 16th of July, 1925, *(Aufwertungsgesetz vom 16. Juli 1925, Anhang),* finally included only the relation of *paper mark* to *gold mark (GM)* for the period from the 1st of January, 1918 to the 30th of November, 1923 and the following days *(see appendix 2).*

Earlier than the *Law about the Revaluation of Mortgages and other Claims,* issued the 16th of July, 1925, the *Reichsmark* became by the *Coin Law* (Münzgesetz) from the 30th of August, 1924 (RGBl. II S. 254) a substitute for the completely devaluated paper mark (Mark), introduced after the currency had been stabilized by the introduction of the Rentenmark (RM) *[see chapter 5.3 Introduction of the Rentenmark 1923 & the Reichsmark 1924].* The exchange rate of paper mark to Reichsmark amounted to 1.000.000.000.000:1 (a trillion to one). 1 Reichsmark or Rentenmark (RM) = 100 Reichspfennig or 100 Rentenpfennig (Rpf.).

"The key to stabilisation was contraction of the amount of currency in circulation. The dollar exchange rate rose from 630 billion paper marks to a dollar on November 12, 1923, to 4.2 trillions on November 20. At this point the value of the mark was held. Thus a trillion paper marks was worth 0.24 American dollars, the value of one gold mark before the war. By a voluntary rate of conversion the *Rentenmark* was taken as equal in value to the gold mark. Hence the ratio of exchange was fixed at a trillion paper marks to one *Rentenmark*. The *Rentenmark* was intended to serve as a bridge to a gold-based currency. In 1924 it was replaced by the Reichsmark and the exchange rate of a trillion paper marks to one Reichsmark was given legal force" (§5 Law of August 30, 1924 RGB1 II 255)" *(Southern 1979, p.D1031).* Germany went through its worst inflation in 1923. In 1922, the highest denomination was 50,000 Mark. By 1923, the highest denomination was 100,000,000,000,000 Mark. In December 1923 the exchange rate was 4,200,000,000,000 Marks to 1 US dollar. In 1923, the rate of inflation hit 3.25×10^6 percent per month (prices double every two days). Beginning on November 20, 1923, 1,000,000,000,000 old Mark were exchanged for 1 *Rentenmark* so that 4.2 Rentenmarks were worth 1 US dollar, exactly the same rate the *Mark* had in 1914 *((Southern 1979, p.D1031).* Finally, the German Government regulated the revaluation of the substantial national debts by law. The *Public Loan Discharge Law [Gesetz über die Ablösung öffentlicher Anleihen] July 16, 1925, RGBL I, 137* broke entirely new ground, that is war-loans and other paper mark debts of the Reich, Länder and Local Authorities were converted into a new Reich loan stock at a ratio of 40:1, i.e. 1,000 paper marks of old stock became exchangeable under the law for 25 Reichsmark of new stock. ("old" meant the possession of continuous ownership by the 1925 holder or his legal successors since June 1, 1920, or earlier.) *(Southern 1979, p.D1045)*

Revaluation Act 1925 - Conversion Table

Datum	"Reichs"Mark	"Gold"Mark	1 "Gold"Mark = "Reichs"Mark
January-June 1918	10	8,00	1,25
December 1918	10	5,00	2,00
June 1919	10	3,11	3,21
December 1919	10	1,04	9,61
March 1920	100	4,87	20,53
December 1920	100	6,88	14,53
August 1921	100	5,82	17,18
December 1921	100	2,87	34,84
July 1922	1000	9,50	105,26
November 1922	10000	7,80	1.282,05
23. July 1923	1 Million	9,89	101.112,23
17. August 1923	10 Million	9,81	1.019.367,99
7. September 1923	100 Million	7,82	12.787.723,78
3. October 1923	1 Milliarde	9,21	108.577.633,00
16. October 1923	10 Milliarde	8,06	1.240.694.789,00
22. October 1923	100 Milliarde	8,18	12.224.938.875,00
5. November 1923	1 Billion	8,65	115.607.000.000,00
30. November 1923	1 Billion	1,00	1.000.000.000.000,00

Note: 1 Milliarde in German Terms (1,000 Million) = 1 Billion in US Terms;
1 Billion in German Terms (1,000,000 Million) = 1 Trillion in US Terms;
1 "Gold"Mark value in grammes of fine gold (1913) = 0.35842g;
"Reichs"Mark = Currency not tied to the goldstandard in 1918 to 1924.

Source: Law about the Revaluation of Mortgages and other Claims (Revaluation Act 1925), issued the 16th of July, 1925 (Aufwertungsgesetz, Reichsgesetzblatt, Teil I, 1925, p.133-135) and Author's calculations.

1 "Gold"Mark = "Reichs"Mark 1918-1923

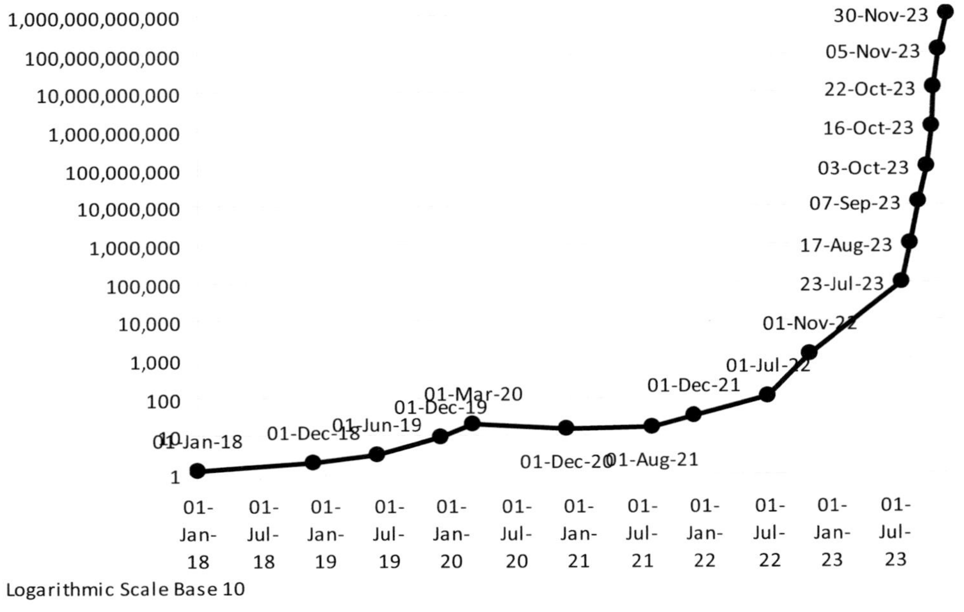

Note: 1 "Gold"Mark value in grammes of fine gold (1913) = 0.35842g;
"Reichs"Mark = Currency not tied to the goldstandard in 1918 to 1924.

Source: Law about the Revaluation of Mortgages and other Claims (Revaluation Act 1925), issued the 16th of July, 1925 (Aufwertungsgesetz, Reichsgesetzblatt, Teil I, 1925, p.133-135) and Author's calculations.

6.4 Revaluation Law and German Supreme Court [Reichsgericht]

Bundesverwaltungsgericht Leipzig
[Formerly Reichsgericht, German Supreme Court]

"The most remarkable expression of the revived quasi-natural law occurred in the field of civil law, as a result of the hyperinflation of 1923. Germany had before the First World War made paper marks compulsory legal tender for the settlement of liquidated obligations. Nominalist principle was enshrined in the rule *Mark gleich Mark* (a mark is worth a mark). Legal tender was made inconvertible at the outbreak of the First World War." *(Southern 1988, 63)* Only hesitantly and under cover of various legal constructions did the courts authorize departures from the rule *"A Mark is worth a mark"*. Finally the courts felt emboldened to reject the rule and declare it to be superseded by a higher law. In overriding the positive law the courts laid claim to what the *Reichsgericht* called *"the plenitude of power of the judge"* in circumstances where both legislation and the contract made by parties had failed to protect vital social interests (*Entscheidung des Reichsgerichts in Zivilsachen, RGZ 104,394*). In the judicial rejection of nominalism in favour of revaluation a pioneering role was played by the President of the Court of Appeal *(Oberlandesgericht)* in Darmstadt - March 29 & May 18, 1923 *(Southern 1979, p. D1052).*

The *stabilisation of the mark* in November 1923 seemed to mark the doom of the victims of the inflation. However, on November 28, 1923, the Reichsgericht proclaimed that the legal tender legislation was invalid and mortgages must be revalued to compensate for the depreciation of the currency. The legal rule that payment in paper marks was a good legal discharge of money obligations was no obstacle to revaluation, because changed circumstances had invalidated the law, which must yield to the paramount rule of equity and good faith contained in §242 of the Civil Code (§242 "Treu und Glauben", BGB). This was judicial rebellion against the law. The judges proclaimed that the *law was subordinate to the judge, not the judge to the law.* For a century judges had been inculcated with the doctrine of the subordination of the judge to positive law. Now the judges purported to declare positive laws invalid by invoking a higher law of their own making. The 5th Civil Senate of the Reichsgericht had been responsible for this judgement *(Southern 1979, p.D1052).*

Almost revolutionary under the impression of the worldwide economic crisis was the developed revaluation jurisdiction with which the *Supreme Court of the German Reich [Reichsgericht]* awarded itself for the first time the competence to check laws on their validity (*RGZIII, 320, Urt. from the 4th November, 1925*). This led to the fact which was given up the *"A Mark is worth a mark"* principle [*Mark-gleich-Mark-Grundsatz*] recognized till then (nominal value principle, nominalism) because of the galloping inflation.

The judgement of the *Supreme Court of the German Reich Leipzig [Reichsgericht, 4th of November, 1925, 5th Civil Senate (see Appendix 3)*, was based on the following legal matters:

1. Are the courts authorized to test the constitutional moderateness of German laws [Reichsgesetze]?
2. Is the regulation happened in the *Law about the Revaluation of Mortgages and other Claims (Revaluation Act 1925), issued the 16th of July, 1925 (Aufwertungsgesetz, Reichsgesetzblatt, Teil I, 1925, p.133-135)* under the Section 62,63 falling claims inconsistent with rules of the *German Constitution [Reichsverfassung]?*
3. According to which rules is a credit claim to be revalued whose security on mortgage has diminished before the beginning of the currency decay?
4. Is an acceptance of the credit present for the purposes of Section 14 of the *Law about the Revaluation of Mortgages and other Claims (Revaluation Act 1925), issued the 16th of July, 1925 (Aufwertungsgesetz, Reichsgesetzblatt, Teil I, 1925, p.133-135* if the creditor has drawn the nominal value of its credit amount in paper mark on the basis of an obtained court seizure decision from the debtor?

The important principle question for the *German Supreme Court (Reichsgericht)* was: if the application of the rules of the *Law about the Revaluation of Mortgages and other Claims (Revaluation Act 1925), issued the 16th of July, 1925 (Aufwertungsgesetz, Reichsgesetzblatt, Teil I, 1925, p.133-135)* with no vigorous reflections is given against the constitutional moderateness of the law which has come about with a simple majority of the *German Parliament [Reichstag]*. Afterwards in public raised attacks against the legal validity of the revaluation law it appeared reasonable for the Supreme Court to submit the constitutional moderateness of the law officially to a test *(RGZ III, 322, 4th of November, 1925)*. The German Constitution has accepted the principle in article 102 that the judges are independent and they are subjected only to the law. This does not expel that a law can be deprived of its validity by the judge. This is the case if a law contradicts a legal principle set up in the German Constitution and with its enactment by article 76 of the German Constitution for constitutional amendment necessary requirements not have been present. Since the rules of the German Constitution can be annulled only by a regularly voted for constitution-changing law.

The 5th Senate of the *German Supreme Court [Reichsgericht]* ruled with the judgement of 4th November 1925 that it has been by the regulation of the revaluation by the *Law about the Revaluation of Mortgages and other Claims (Revaluation Act 1925), issued the 16th of July, 1925* not about an extraction of well-founded rights, but about a fixing and limitation of the content by the currency depreciation and the economic decay in their bases completely devastated facts of the legal regulations for the purposes of the Article 153, Section1, Sentence 2, German Constitution [Reichsverfassung] *(RGZ III,325, Judgement of 4th November 1925)*.

Article 153, German Constitution of 11th August 1919 [Reichsverfassung]
1. The property is guaranteed by the constitution. Its content and its barriers arise from the laws.
2. An expropriation can be carried out only to the well-being of the Society and on legal basis. It takes place against appropriate compensation, until a law determines something else.
3. Property obligations: Its use should at the same time serve in society's best interests.

Even if the regulation of the revaluation would be fulfilled in Article 153, Section 2, which set up requirements for the validity of the expropriation, one could think about the notion of the expropriation falling extraction of creditors' rights. The legal basis which requires Section 2, Sentence 1, for a permissible expropriation is where the expropriation happens directly by a German law [Reichsgesetz], given in the law by itself *(RGZ III, 325, Judgement of 4th November 1925).*

With regard to the basic methodology of the revaluation - either an individual method of revaluation or a schematic method of revaluation - the *5th Senate of the German Supreme Court [Reichsgericht* ruled that in particular the divergence of the individual revaluation happened for the reason of recovery of peace, order and security within the republic and in the tax economy was offered an immediate clear and concluding regulation of the revaluation question at all costs, and this did not appear possible without a schematic method. The restoration of peace, order and security serves the well-being of the generality and, therefore, an expropriation carried out for this purpose cannot be respected as inadmissible *(RGZ III, 326, Judgement of 4th November 1925).*

The *German Supreme Court [Reichsgericht]* argued that it is a generally recognized principle that the well-being of the individual citizen must be set back behind the public welfare. This principle is expressed in Article 153, Section 2 that the property can be taken away for the purposes of the well-being of the generality. Property has to be seen not only as real estate but also as rights as well. Certain guarantees are created in Article 153, Section 2, for the fact that no arbitrary property extraction can take place, while it is strictly settled that the expropriation can be carried out only for the well-being of the generality and only on a legal basis *(RGZ III, 327, Judgement of 4th November 1925).*

Article 109, German Constitution of 11th August 1919 [Reichsverfassung]
1. All Germans are equal before the law.
2. Under public law privileges or disadvantages of the birth or the status are to be abolished. Aristocracy titles are considered only as a part of the name and may not be awarded any more.

With regard to the legal matter, whether the *Law about the Revaluation of Mortgages and other Claims (Revaluation Act 1925), issued the 16th of July, 1925* is contradictory *to Article 109, Section 1, German Constitution of 11th August 1919 [Reichsverfassung],* the Supreme Court ruled in favour of dismissal. The principle of the equality before the law can have only the meaning that the facts of the law are to be treated on an equal basis as to treat incomparably would mean arbitrariness. A different treatment which is justified by no reason would appear as arbitrary and offend against the equality principle *(RGZ III, 329, Judgement of 4th November 1925).*

"For a century German jurists had inculcated the doctrine of the absolute subordination of the judge to the positive law. Ever since *Savigny* natural law had been considered as something dead and buried. Now the proponents of revaluation, led by the judges of the Reichsgericht, hoisted natural law as their standard." *(Southern 1988, 63-83) David Southern* argued that "the overriding of legal rules by judicial discretion became a marked feature of many other fields of German law in the Weimar period. The legislature endorsed and accelerated this process by enacting measures which contained a minimum of concrete elements" *(Southern 1988, 63-83).*

The public objection to the *Law about the Revaluation of Mortgages and other Claims (Revaluation Act 1925)* culminated in 1927, in particular due to political activities of the newly formed

Reichsarbeitsgemeinschaft der Aufwertungsgeschaedigten (Association of people disadvantaged by the revaluation). This organisation was campaigning for a *referendum to the recovery of the national wealth (Volksbegehren zur Wiederherstellung des Volksvermoegens)*. The German Constitution of 1919 makes possible a referendum under certain conditions appropriately the articles 73 to 76, particularly in regard to article 73.

Article 73, German Constitution of 11th August 1919 [Reichsverfassung (1) A law passed by the Reichstag shall, before its promulgation, be submitted to the popular vote if the President so decides within one month. (2) A law of which the promulgation has been postponed at the instance of one-third of the members of the Reichstag [as provided by art. 72] is to be submitted to the popular vote upon the demand of one-twentieth of those entitled to vote. (3) A referendum is to be instigated farther if the tenth of the entitled to vote puts the referendum to the popular vote after the rejection of a bill. A bill must underlie the referendum. It is to be submitted from the government under statement of its statement to the Reichstag. (5) The procedure with the referendum regulates a law. *[See Law about the referendum 27th of June in 1921*

Already in 1926 the agitation for a referendum to alter the *Revaluation Act 1925* enhanced momentum. The *German Government (Chancellor Wilhelm Marx)* declared on the 24th of June 1926 to the *German Parliament (Reichstag)* that the material attitude of the current government to the problem of the revaluation is the same as those of the last government. She holds it for economically dangerous to materialize the revaluation problem again *(Aufwertungsgesetz, zweites Gesetz über den Volksentscheid)*.

Reichskanzler Wilhelm Marx

Ultimately the *Minister of Justice* argued in the meeting of the German Government's Cabinet on the 2nd of March 1927 that in his view all by the revaluation party intended radical changes of the existing regulation are to be declined because the main features of the current regulation must be held by all means. This is a pressing order of the whole German national economy, which must develop in the once fixed paths, and farther also an imperious necessity for the maintenance of an ordered administration of justice. These arguments were strongly supported by the *German Chancellor Wilhelm Marx (Kabinett Marx III/IV, Band 1, Dokumente, Nr. 191 Kabinettssitzung vom 2. März 1927, 1630 Uhr, Top 2 Aufwertungsfragen)*. *Wilhelm Marx* was *German Chancellor* (Reichskanzler) in the years 1923/24 as well as in 1926 to 1928. Until 1933 his party, the *German Centre Party* (short designation: *Zentrum*), was the representative of Roman Catholic Germany.

Chapter 7 Hyperinflation in selected Countries

Wolfgang Chr. Fischer

There are different historical episodes of hyperinflations - also prior to the 20th century there were episodes of severe inflation with monthly inflation rates of over 50 per cent. Examples are: 276 - 334 *West Roman Empire*, 1166 *Chinese Empire*, 1719-1720 *France*, and 1789-1796 France.[80]

Highest Monthly Inflation Rates in History

Country	Month with highest inflation rate	Highest monthly inflation rate	Equivalent daily inflation rate	Time required for prices to double
Hungary	July 1946	4.19 x 10^{16} %	207%	15.0 hours
Zimbabwe	Mid-November 2008	79,600,000,000%	98.0%	24.7 hours
Yugoslavia	January 1994	313,000,000%	64.6%	1.4 days
Germany	October 1923	29,500%	20.9%	3.7 days
Greece	October 1944	13,800%	17.9%	4.3 days
China	May 1949	2,178%	11.0%	6.7 days

Notes: The authors calculated "equivalent daily inflation rate" and "time required for prices to double."

Source: Steve H. Hanke and Alex K. F. Kwok, On the Measurement of Zimbabwe's Hyperinflation Cato Journal, Vol. 29, No. 2 (Spring/Summer 2009), p.354

7.1 Peru[81]

Peru went through its worst inflation from 1988 to 1990. In the 1985 currency reform, 1 inti was exchanged for 1,000 soles de oro. In 1986, the highest denomination was 1,000 intis. But in September 1988, monthly inflation went to 132%. In August of 1990, monthly inflation was 397%. The highest denomination was 10,000,000 intis by 1991. In the 1991 currency reform, 1 nuevo sol was exchanged for 1,000,000 intis. The overall impact of hyperinflation: 1 nuevo sol = 1,000,000,000 (old) soles. These are only the financial facts, but what are the social-economic aspects of the Peruvian hyperinflation?

---

80 See Appendix 7.

81 This chapter "Peru" is based on Fischer, Wolfgang Chr., Sozial-ökonomische Folgen der Weltwirtschaftspolitik am Beispiel Peru, Rationelle Hauswirtschaft, XXVI, Heft 8/89, 7-10, Verlag Neuer Merkur, München, 1989.

In spite of the *World Nutritional Conference* in 1974 in *Rome* and the world-wide statement dismissed there about the wiping out of hunger and malnutrition, for the majority of the developing countries there is no growing participation in global prosperity. Large parts of the world population still live in unspeakable poverty; suffer from lack of nutrition, die of hunger or fight daily for the subsistence level. In the 80s *UN* estimates went out from approximately 800 million to a billion undernourished people on the earth in this decade *(Kracht 1984, p. 117).*

There are various causes for the poverty, the faulty nutrition and the relatively low chances of survival for the population of the underdeveloped countries. The rapid growing population has been taken as the major cause, although the available nutritional resources are not adjusted to it. However, rigid family policy, often seen as the only effective means for the containment of the population increase, turns out to be absolutely unrealistic, not only because the fundamental claims to justice are violated, but because it also overlooks the fact that the generative behaviour of the people is persevering, because they see it as essential for their existence in terms of hunger and poverty *(Fischer 1987, p. 4).*

In 1989 approximately 4.8 billion people live on the earth, and according to estimates of the *United Nations* by 2000 the world population will have risen to approximately 6.1 billion people *(Baldeaux 1985, p. 5).* Besides, it is of central importance that the development of the world population which tapers to a point dramatically takes place, first of all, in the developing countries; facts which possess an absolutely explosive importance for considerations to the re-orientation of the world economy, particularly as it is likely that in 2025 approximately 85 per cent of the world population will live in developing countries. In addition, consider the world population is in a rapid growth and will double with the annual growth rate of 1.72 per cent in 41 years *(Baldeaux 1985, p. 59*). In the past it took millennium and centuries.

An optimistic position in regard to the possibility of control of the population process was stated in the *"World Population Action Plan"* of the *United Nations* which was decided at the *First World Population Conference in 1974* in *Bucharest.* Certainly, then it means that every government of a member country should pursue an appropriate population policy for the purposes of the limitation. To limit as an indispensable presupposition, the population explosion, however, a lasting social and economic development was seen undoubtedly and there was belief in its rapid realization. However, at the *Second World Population Conference in 1984* in *Mexico* the bitter realization could not be avoided that the hopes for this progress which should lead to a drastic improvement in the care of the population and with it to a considerable decline in growth of the population was shattered in most developing countries.

The increase in prosperity is still assigned in view of the distribution of the world gross national product as relatively one-sided to the developed industrial nations, particularly for the western governments. The current world trade can be absolutely still considered as colonial. Particularly with the construction of a world-wide trade by European nations since the beginning of mercantilism in the 17th century, and with the establishment of trading companies to enable the economic exploitation of productive overseas regions by the application of colonial instruments of power, the foundation-stone was laid in the bias of international economic relations. Finally by the establishment of enormous plantations and the obligation of the inhabitants to contribute to the raw material production, the native agriculture (*subsistence agriculture*), which had at least provided sufficient nutrition for all society members, became disturbed *(Collins 1980, p. 98)*.

The rapid development of new technologies (microelectronics, biotechnology) subject the international division of labour to a new structure: the expenses calculations of industrial enterprise let a return misalignment of foreign manufacturing from developing countries of the 70s appear advantageous, at least for new investments; that is the wage differential became second-rate in consequence of rationalization stocks. With new technologies provided manufacturing methods let it in future will function likely that aimed locations are chosen by the markets Europe, North America and Japan and neighbouring developing countries as a supplier or as producers with "stored" technology for other partial markets *(Fischer 1987, p. 19)*. Also the strategies dominant till some years ago of the third world aid policy of the industrial nations - exaggeration of the industrialization might be decisive for the purposes of large-scale projects, neglect of conformist technologies and the protection of basic needs as well as the transmission of western consumption patterns- for the living standard of their population. However, on the other hand, it must be also taken into consideration that as the ruling elites were strengthened in several underdeveloped countries and partly still represents increasing unequal country distribution is another cause for the poverty of the population. Certainly, country reforms were propagated frequently; nevertheless considerable success was not registered to meet the migration from the land and the formation of big slum areas in the metropolises. Nevertheless, in *Latin America* only seven per cent of the landowners possess 93 per cent of the agricultural land *(Venzky 1979, p. 13)*.

Der erhoffte Wohlstand blieb aus: Hütten in Ica

The missing Wealth: Huts in Ica, Southern Peru

As an example, *Peru* could guarantee nearly self-sufficient nutrition and an extensive employment of its population from its climatological conditions, the agriculturally usable surface, including the reserves, as well as the ground resources. However it could be shown as an example of the way in which a country of the so-called *"Third World"* got to the stage of not only an undersupply in food and exorbitant unemployment, but, in addition, to a hyperinflation and to national bankruptcy, widening parts of the population even more in poverty.

Menschen in Peru: Leben in Armut und ohne große Hoffnung

People in Peru: Life in Poverty and little Hope

With the conquest of the *Inca Empire* at the beginning of the 16th century by a small Spanish troop under *Francisco Pizarro* and the murder of the last Inca ruler *Atahualpa* in 1533 ended not only the *Inca Empire* which organized itself administratively tightly, was fitted out with considerable streets, bridges, houses and culture sites, as well as having highly developed, agriculturally oriented terraces, but also their culture developed over a about millennium grown cultures. It began the deformation of the natives in cultural, social, economical and political respects. The upper class oriented to *Madrid* established their own economic and political power, supported by superior weapons. It appropriated enormous latifundia on which the Incas were forced in to the production of agricultural products for the European countries; the same one was considered when to the same moment it occurred at gold and silver mines. With it the subsistence economy of the *Incas* disappeared, their capital *Cuzco* in the high *Andes* became unimportant, and in 1535 *Lima* at the South Pacific was created as a metropolis of the Spanish deputy monarchy by *Francisco Pizarro*. Since the independence of Spain in 1821 the handed down dominion relations have hardly changed - the country was controlled by a small group of white, Spanish oriented families economically and politically always in close alliance with the armed forces *(Hermanns 1986, p. 7)*.

In the 20th century, particularly after the *Second World War*, an industrialization process was introduced by the upper class first of all to residents in *Lima* which admittedly was based on foreign companies, who then controlled the mining industry, the oil production, the banking, the foreign trade and parts of the industrially oriented agriculture dependent on foreign capital. In addition, there was a one-sided distribution of land: in 1961 2 200 great land owners held 70 per cent of the farmed ground, while 815 000 plot farmers had to be content with only 10 per cent of the used surface *(Gohla 1986, p. 10)*. Certainly, after the military putsch of 1968 there was land reform, with the enormous latifundia, partly by the size of Belgium, were smashed but only the employed workers got possession title, not, however, the more poor day labourers. Certainly, producers' cooperatives and marketing co-operatives were established themselves, in the bank area and industrial area participation was propagated, improved educational opportunities as an element of a structural reform were aimed for, but from the armed forces ordered mobilization of the population succeeded only to some extent, because for the purposes of a *"revolution from above"* the social and economic position according to education of the majority of the population was overestimated. Rather illusions appeared in the population which cannot be realized economically at the desired pace. After the general strike of 1978 the conservative *President*

Belaunde Terry, formerly thrown out of office by the armed forces, propagating the free market economy, was re-elected with predominant majority *(Gohla 1986, p. 13)*. At the same time, the terrorist organization, the *Sendero Luminoso (shining path)*, a maoistic oriented splinter group of the *Communist Party of Peru*, became active in increasing massive spectacular terrorist attacks. The aim of this guerrilla warfare movement by the descendants of the *Incas* and other native groups was to conduct a civil war against the established power in politics and business *(Hermanns 1986, p. 14)*. These acts of violence caused the death of thousands and represented a considerably destabilizing effect on the potential inflow of foreign investments and might be the cause of an enormous flight of capital *(Bieber 1988, p. 7)*.

Compromising 1.2 million square kilometres *Peru* is more than five times larger than the Federal Republic of Germany, and a land of contrast. Although it is geographically in the tropical belt of the earth it has the narrow coastal plain partly with long sandy deserts and a hot climate, where the cultivation of rice, corn, vegetable, cotton and sugar cane as well as fish-processing industry is pursued on the land. Also it has the always springlike *Andes Highlands* with mountains up to 6,700 metres, where there is agricultural production of for example corn and potatoes as well as plantations for coffee and cotton, and the two thirds of the national territory of the extensive *Amazon Lowlands* consisting of tropical jungle which is undeveloped agriculturally. In 1989 approximately 22 million people lived in Peru and the growth of the population by approximately 2.7 per cent per year might be substantial. Two thirds of the population live in the capital cities; in ethnic groups one finds South American Indian (55 per cent), mestizo (35 per cent), black (8 per cent) and white (12 per cent) *(Unicef 1988)*. Two thirds of the population fit for work are unemployed or at least underworked and the unemployment is spread particularly among the South American Indians in the *Andes (Bieber 1988, p. 7)*. Besides, the processing industry is located 90 per cent in the coastal plain, and only 70 per cent in the area of Lima. 40 per cent of the employed persons of Peru are occupied in agriculture and in the country there is an enormously high hidden unemployment, but apart from the plantations oriented to export most of the agricultural small businesses consist of a subsistence economy with partial market exchange. Because the disposal of the public budget for years was only of low means, because the foreign debt with 14.35 billion US dollars (*state is to be considered in 1986, Sangmeister 1988, p.26)* was extreme in relation to the export proceeds, and because considerable food imports must be effected (only for 384 million US dollars in 1986) which go to weights of necessary investments in the agrarian area, service industries and the processing industry and leave Peru in the typical state of a developing country oriented on a few export products, the flow of countrymen to the bigger cities remains undiminished.

The supposed attraction of the bigger cities, particularly of the metropolis of *Lima,* lies in the expectation of attaining work there somewhere, somehow and sometime. However, the predominant majority of the countrymen and the population from smaller cities land in the *Barriadas*, to the slum areas. The *Barriadas of Lima* in which twice as many people live as in Hamburg/Germany - mostly without water and electricity - grows visibly; more and more Peruvians must survive on the street and live on decaying rubbish; children are exploited and should be protected from working and robbing for their survival; children's traders gain incredible profits through the poverty and misery of mothers *(Stapelfeldt 1984, p. 11)*. Hygiene and potable water supply are faulty in most parts of Peru, not only in the *Barriadas*. The infant mortality rate is 9.4 per cent in 1985, ten times higher than in the Federal Republic of Germany; the average life expectancy is 59 years. The number of illiterate persons amounts to 28 per cent and many children and adults are to be included who have attended school for only one or two years and 40 per cent of the population are undernourished. The misery is hardly conceivable in its intensity and dimension for most inhabitants for instance of the Federal Republic of Germany, never mind comprehension of the conditions.

With the slogan *"To rule means to give to eat"* the *Alianza Popular Revolutionaria Americana (APRA)*, which is the governing party of Peru, won the election in 1985. The current *President Alan Garcia* replaced the conservative *President Terry*. He began with an economic program of stimulation of private demand by state ordered wage increases, by partial price freezes, particularly for basic food, and the promotion of investments on a credit basis *(Bieber 1988, p. 7)*. However, the demand boom which then occurs with it caused raised importations of food, consumer goods and capital goods which would be financeable in consequence of lacking international credits only by growing exports and by the dismantling of the foreign exchange reserves, particularly as the native production could not keep up with such a rapidly grown, private consumption and investment demand. In addition to stimulate the imports the official exchange rate of the native currency, the *Inti* (which means in the language of an Incas "sun"), to the US dollar is held artificially low which worsens on the one hand the export possibilities and favours, on the other hand, the flight of capital anyway initiated by the political change still farther. The confrontation of the Peruvian government with the *World Bank* and, first of all, with the *International Monetary Fund (IMF)* in regard to an one-sided announced payment moratorium with foreign debts - propagated as a model for the developing countries. Because the Peruvian government falsely estimated the world-economic power constellations which led to a largely isolated international position of Peru, and the inflow of capital decreased substantially. Then when the President tried to nationalize the banks, a considerable flight of capital took place again. The demand boom could keep only till 1987 with relative price stability - in South America two-digit inflation rates are considered as "normal" - and then the foreign exchange reserves were used up. Among other things other wage increases, increase of the money circulation, depreciation of the *Inti* and partial restraint of goods for the native market were the consequence of the state economic policy, first to an inflation, a process of constant price increase, and from 1988 to a *hyperinflation* led with monthly price increases of more than 50 per cent *(Hanke 1989, p. 20)*. To limit the hyperinflation which had risen in 1988 to nearly 2,000 per cent, the Government at short notice in September 1988 ordered a package of measures which should limit the private demand. Certainly, the monthly minimum wage was also raised, but this was in no relation to the general price increase position. According to the hyperinflation the native currency lost sequentially its value, and then the purchasing power loss with exorbitant dropped real incomes must be carried by the majority of the population, from those which have no possession in real values and foreign currencies. In this extremely instable economic position of a hyperinflation the US dollar wins the function of a national worth keeping means, and its possession allows a profitable currency speculation. Certainly, the *black market* for foreign exchange was forbidden; however, it had to be admitted in consequence of its considerable extension. Apart from the money speculative transactions, the speculative transactions with basic food, consumer goods and capital goods also substantially increased which cut down once more the temporary market offer and favoured the hyperinflation.

Furthermore it appears that saving is not worthwhile in the native currency for large parts of the population - even with interest rates of 280 per cent for 30-days money in

September 1988, because the old credits are devaluated constantly and an end of the inflationary development is not foreseeable. The very immediate acquisition including an accumulation, at least of vital food, consumer goods and the fuel important for survival, first of all, for heating purposes and cooking purposes is respected as ultima ratio. The hyperinflation is also caused by the fact that western consumption patterns are taken over. Particularly the white upper class and the relatively small middle class follows the way of life of the North Americans which is promoted among other things by extended advertisements on television, radio broadcasting and in newspapers *(Fischer 1983, p. 143).* In addition, the relevant market is controlled for the wider social class by cheap products from the East Asian area.

Index der Lebenshaltungskosten (1979 = 100)	
1976	29
1982	459
1983	970
1984	2038
1985	5328
1986	9551
(Quelle: Bauco Continental 1987)	

Index der Lebenshaltungs-kosten 1976 bis 1986

Cost of Living Index 1976 to 1986

The hyperinflation led to further impoverishment of the more extensive poor social classes. The psychological-social consequences appear in drastically growing violence on the streets, in mass plunders, attacks on tourists and the use of force by the police and the armed forces. An unimaginable brutality occurred everywhere and the author had experienced three times hold ups on the highway by the police on his way from Lima to Arequipa. For a western member of an affluent society it is hardly comprehensible that thousands of people from the poor districts flow into the city to protect their life with plunders at short notice.

Data for the Hyperinflation as of February 1989
Minimum monthly income
41,000 Inti
Exchange rate 1 US Dollar to Inti (black market)
2,000 Inti
Price for 1 pair of jeans
18,000 Inti
Price for 1 pizza (large)
9,000 Inti
Price for 1 can of milk (1/4 litre)
800 Inti
Price for 20 Peruvian cigarettes
1,300 Inti
Price for 1 gallon petrol
1,900 Inti

Source: Author's own investigation in Arequipa, Southern Peru

As a modest valve to the desolate care of the population the extensive smuggling is tolerated in the border places by state authorities and facilitated at least by corruption. Rightly the *European Parliament* in its resolution stated from the 17th to the 18th September, 1980 *The contribution of the European Community to the fight against the hunger in the world*: It would be a hypocrisy and a falsification of the truth to assume that the overcoming of the underdevelopment is to be brought about for the population masses of the Third World by the present production methods and consumer's habits of the industrialised countries in harmony; the solution to the problems of the underdevelopment, and firstly the problem of the hunger, requires – apart from an inside economic and social process of transformation in the underdeveloped countries - also profound social and economic restructuring and a cultural and mental change of substantial consequence in the more advanced countries.

7.2 Zimbabwe

"At Independence in 1980, the *Zimbabwe dollar* was worth about US$ 1.25. Since then, rampant inflation and the collapse of the economy have severely devalued the currency, causing many organisations to favour using the US$ or South African rand instead. Inflation was stable until Robert Mugabe began a program of land reforms…"(*Wikipedia, "Hyperinflation", http://en.wikipedia.org/wiki/Hyperinflation)* in the sense of redistribution of land. One of the consequences was that the food production shrunk substantially and the export revenues decreased. "Inflation reached 624% in early 2004, then fell back to low triple digits before surging to a new high of 1,730% in March 2007. During that time, the Reserve Bank of Zimbabwe revalued their currency on August 1, 2006 at a rate of 1,000 old Zimbabwean dollars to 1 revalued Zimbabwean dollar. In June 2007, inflation in Zimbabwe had risen to 11,000% from an earlier estimate of 9,000%. On August 19, 2008, official figures announced for June estimated the inflation over 11,250,000 percent. Zimbabwe's annual inflation was 231 million percent in July" (*Wikipedia, "Hyperinflation", http://en.wikipedia.org/wiki/Hyperinflation*). The hyperinflation officially ended in January 2009 when official inflation rates in US$ were announced.

"There is a consensus among economists that, over relatively short periods of time and at relatively low inflation rates, the link between exchange rates and price levels is loose. But as inflation rates increase, the link becomes tighter. In a study of the German hyperinflation of 1921–23, *Jacob Frenkel (1976)* found that correlations between various German price indices and the German mark/U.S. dollar exchange rate were all close to one."*(Hanke&Kwok 2009, 357-358)*. On this benchmark of exchange rates and price levels with the depreciated Zimbabwe dollar as the outcome various foreign currencies became the unofficial currencies in circulation, in particular the US$ and the *South African rand.*

"Zimbabwe's hyperinflation came to an abrupt halt. The trigger was an intervention by the Reserve Bank of Zimbabwe. On November 20, 2008, the Reserve Bank's governor, *Dr. Gideon Gono,* stated that the entire economy was 'being priced via the Old Mutual rate whose share price movements had no relationship with economic fundamentals, let alone actual corporate performance of Old Mutual itself'"*(Hanke & Kwok 2009, 361-362). Old Mutual* is a stock, which is listed on both the London Stock Exchange and the Harare Stock Exchange and enabled the exchange rate British pound to Zimbabwe dollar.

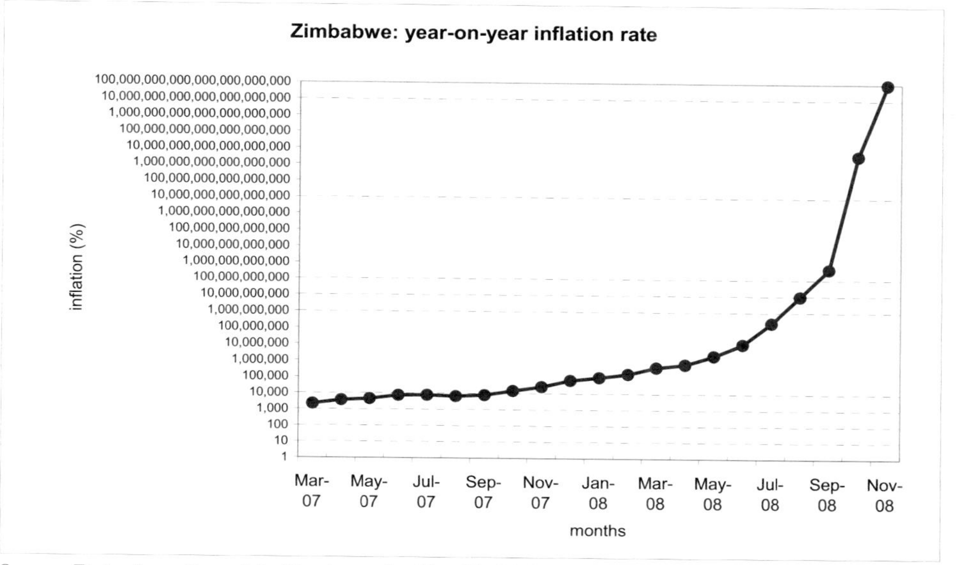

Source: Data from Steve H. Hanke and Alex K. F. Kwok: On the Measurement of Zimbabwe's Hyperinflation, Cato Journal, Vol. 29, No. 2 (Spring/Summer 2009), p.354

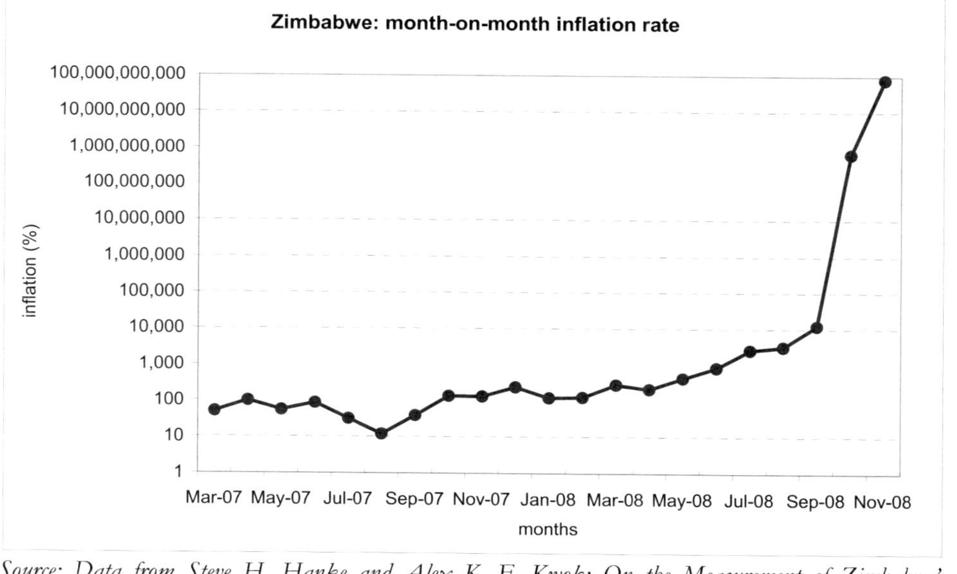

Source: Data from Steve H. Hanke and Alex K. F. Kwok: On the Measurement of Zimbabwe's Hyperinflation, Cato Journal, Vol. 29, No. 2 (Spring/Summer 2009), p.354

Even on the scale of month-on-month inflation rate, like the German hyperinflation, the gigantic acceleration of the *Zimbabwean hyperinflation* occurred within a short period of time from August 2008 to November 2008. Again, there is no sufficient explanation why the hyperinflation in Zimbabwe went out of any reasonable control. Political upheavals or the lack of political will of the Zimbabwe government to bring the hyperinflation to a halt are determinants of the inflationary process but the behaviour of people in such a period of an economic downfall is not resolved yet.

100 trillion Zimbabwe dollar banknote (16th of January 2009)
The highest denomination of a banknote in the history of money

Zimbabwe had unveiled on the 16th of January 2009 the 100 trillion Zimbabwe dollar banknote, which would be worth as of 25th of February 2010 roughly US Cents 31 *(http://www.bloomberg.com/markets/currencies/eurafr_currencies.html).* Astronomical numbers were the result of a "free fall hyperinflation". "Figures from November 2008 estimated Zimbabwe's annual inflation rate at 89.7 sextillion (10^{21}) percent. In April 2009, Zimbabwe abandoned printing of the Zimbabwean dollar, and the South African rand and US dollar became the standard currencies for exchange *(Wikipedia, Hyperinflation in Zimbabwe).* Finally in February 2009 the *Government of Zimbabwe* revalued its currency: "One of these new Zimbabwean dollars is worth one trillion of the previous. This move took the number of decimal places removed during the period of hyperinflation to 25 (10^{25} = 10 septillion; thus, if no revaluations had taken place, Zimbabwe would now be issuing 10 septillion dollar notes)" *(Wikipedia, Hyperinflation in Zimbabwe). Sebastien Berger,* Southern African Correspondent of the UK Telegraph spoke out on the 23rd of November 2008 what at the time of various hyperinflations came true for the ordinary people: "Supermarkets in Harare are accepting only US dollars and South African rands, leaving those Zimbabweans without access to foreign currency in dire straits" *(Berger, 2008).*

Chapter 8 Inflation: detrimentum or condition sine qua non for economic prosperity?

Daniel J. Goulding

"Restore the depreciated state of the currency and you restore the reward of industry, you restore confidence, you restore production, you restore consumption, you restore everything that constitutes the commercial prosperity of the nation."

— *Thomas Attwood (Attwood 1816, 66)*

"A disordered currency is one of the greatest political evils. It undermines the virtues necessary for the support of the social system, and encourages propensities destructive to its happiness. It wars against industry, frugality and economy, and it fosters evil spirits of extravagance and speculation."

— *Daniel Webster (Everett 1851, 394-395)*

8.1 Introduction

Since the dawn of humanity, the omnipresence of scarcity has been a defining feature of civilisation. Some of our greatest intellectuals have wrestled with this topic, with the goal of whittling away at these shackles on economic prosperity. The Greek philosopher *Aristotle* for example, outlined the benefits of private property, including greater 'progress', more than two thousand years ago *(Aristotle 350 B.C.E, 25)*. While the human race continues to wage war on scarcity, both on a theoretical level and in a practical sense, it cannot be denied that we have come a long way from very modest beginnings.

An important catalyst in the pursuit of higher living standards was the evolution of *money* as a medium of exchange. Its roots can be traced to the limitations of a barter system, which impeded the natural inclination towards ever increasing specialisation. As the English economist and philosopher *John Stuart Mill* wrote on this topic, 'The inconveniences of barter are so great, that without some more commodious means of effecting exchanges, the division of employments could hardly have been carried to any considerable extent' *(Mill [1848] 1868, 18)*. Apart from conquering the problems of indivisibility and the double coincidence of wants, the advent of money was also the necessary springboard for the emergence of monetary calculation and in turn the concept of capital. Serving as a common denominator, *profit seeking entrepreneurs* were provided with an indispensable tool to accord scarce capital goods with the most pressing needs of consumers in a manner consistent with the state of economic wealth. Without money and in turn money prices for all goods, the urgency of various ends can not be calculated in a rational manner leading to a subpar outcome *(Mises [1920] 1990)*. While the advent of money as a medium of exchange was an enormous boon for the human race, like most expedient developments throughout the history of humankind, the concept of money has proven to be a double edged sword.

The Swedish economist *Knut Wicksell* once remarked that 'the state of war seems to persist and remain permanent' in economics *(Wicksell [1904] 1958, 51-52)*. A particularly treacherous minefield in economics is that of *monetary theory*. While differences of opinion are a secular feature of many disciplines, the irreconcilable views held in the realm of monetary affairs can be attributed to a heady cocktail of competing ideologies and political intrigue. Commenting on this issue, the Canadian-American economist *John Kenneth Galbraith* argued, "The study of money, above all other fields in economics, is the one in which complexity is used to disguise truth or to evade truth, not to reveal it" *(Galbraith 1975, 5)*. The subterfuge witnessed in monetary matters is not an unexpected outcome since a monopoly of the supply of money affords the issuer an unprecedented level of control over the economy in addition to furnishing the means to circumvent the production-income nexus *(Rothbard 1963, 281)*. Anticipating the American economist *Murray Rothbard* in this regard, the German banker *Mayer Amschel Rothschild*[82] is alleged to have remarked, "Permit me to issue and control the money of a nation, and I care not who makes its laws." The unbridled influence that accompanies this monopoly however can only be wielded if the monetary authority resorts to a systematic inflation of the supply of money.

The *history of economic thought* offers a litany of debates on the nature and role of inflation in promoting or destabilising economic prosperity. The complexity of the subject matter was neatly encapsulated by the American politician *John Adams*[83] in a letter he penned to his fellow American politician *Thomas Jefferson*[84] on 25 August 1787:

> "All the perplexities, confusion and distresses in America arise not from defects in the constitution or confederation, nor from want of honor or virtue, as much from downright ignorance of the nature of coin, credit, and circulation"*(Adams [1787] 1853, 447)*.

The term *inflation*, in an economic sense, was originally conceived in political discourse in the aftermath of the first economic crisis in the *United States*. It was not until the second half of the nineteenth century however that the word begun to appear with any regular frequency in economic and mainstream circles. While the term was employed in its original context as an increase in the money supply above and beyond the reserve of specie, this definition was never crystallised in theory given the demise of the *Jacksonian Movement,* the main purveyors of the word inflation, in the United States during this period. This led the American economist *William Foster* to remark in 1934, "What is 'inflation', any-way? Not one writer out of a hundred who uses the term even attempts to give a definition of it" *(Foster 1934, 16)*. While the term has subsequently managed to carve out its own niche in mainstream economic literature and in popular culture as being synonymous with rising prices, it is far from reaching a unanimous consensus in this regard. The *Austrian school of economic thought* continues to uphold the historical interpretation of the term, viewing

---

[82] Mayer Amschel Rothschild was described by Forbes Magazine as a 'founding father of international finance' *(Noel 2005)*.

[83] John Adams served as the second President of the United States from 1797 to 1801. He is considered one of the Founding Fathers of the United States *(Wikipedia 2010)*.

[84] Thomas Jefferson served as the third President of the United States, from 1801 to 1809. He is considered one of the most influential of the Founding Fathers of the United States *(Wikipedia 2010)*.

inflation as a condition of the money supply, rather than a consequence for prices. While this stance may be viewed as an exercise in academic pedantry in some quarters, this line of reasoning misconstrues the true nature of inflation.

The *Austrian school* opposes *inflation* for both moral and economic considerations. From a moral standpoint, inflation is viewed as a systematic violation of property rights perpetrated by the government on the general populace. According to the American economist *Henry Wallich*,[85] "Like burglary, [price] inflation is an extralegal form of redistribution" *(Hershey Jr. 1988)*. This redistribution of wealth and income is not just confined to absolute changes in the price level however; it also accompanies changes in the structure of relative prices. *Institutionalised inflation* also serves to unravel the moral fabric of a society over time. In the first instant, it serves to obliterate the 'reciprocity between effort and reward' *(Schama [1987] 1988, 362)*. Following on the heels of protracted inflation are other moral vices. Commenting on the connection between paper money, which is inherently inflationary, and corruption, the English poet *Alexander Pope* in *Moral Essays* remarked, "Blest paper credit! Last and best supply! That lends corruption lighter wings to fly"[86] *(Pope 1797, 240)*. On the economic front, a protracted policy of inflation leads to the emergence of the business cycle or hyperinflation.

8.2 The Nature of Inflation

> "No reader of the literature on currency inflation can fail to be impressed with the great variety and vagueness of meanings attached to the words 'inflation' and 'deflation'. There is no universally accepted meaning of the terms, and relatively few serious attempts have been made to provide precise definitions of them. In most instances in which the terms are used, either with or without definition, there is rarely a thorough-going examination of their implications, with the result that the literature on currency inflation is saturated with inconsistencies and superficialities" *(Spahr 1934, 208)*.

The term *inflation* has evolved significantly throughout the course of economic history. The word was widely used in the nineteenth century to refer to an increase in the money supply without a commensurate increase in specie. Nowadays however, the term has come to signify rising prices, an outcome that was originally attributed to inflation. While most *schools of economic thought* have adopted the contemporary interpretation, the *Austrian school* remains steadfast in employing the term in its historical context as a causal definition.

The term *inflation* made its maiden appearance in the wake of the first major financial crisis in the United States. According to the *Oxford English Dictionary*, the first recorded instance

---

[85] Henry Wallich served as a Governor of the Federal Reserve System from 1974 through to 1986 *(Hershey Jr. 1988)*.

[86] The original wording follows: 'Bleft paper-credit! Laft and beft fupply! That lends Corruption lighter wings to fly *(Pope 1797, 240)*.

of the word[87] is attributable to US Congressman *Daniel Barnard* in 1838 *(Bernholz 2003, 1)*. He employed the term to denote an increase in the quantity of paper money relative to specie *(Barnard 1838, 195)*. Arguing against the merits of property as an anchor for the currency, *Daniel Barnard* warned only a specie basis could prevent a repeat of the 'ruinous' inflation that had subsequently brought the country to its knees *(Barnard 1838)*. While hard-money had been advocated a generation earlier by the *Jeffersonians*,[88] the catalyst for the resurgence of this doctrine was the *Panic of 1819*. This crisis demonstrated to observers that convertibility *per se* was insufficient as a check on the issue of money. As long as the general populace retained confidence in the banking system and refrained from converting bank notes into specie on a widespread basis, the overwhelming tendency towards overissue and its attendant consequences would prevail. Apart from the moral ravages brought about by the depreciation of the currency, the inflation and its subsequent exhaustion of the money supply was viewed as the source of the boom-bust cycle. Accordingly, the *Jacksonians*,[89] the intellectual successors to the *Jeffersonians*, advocated the utilisation of *specie* as money, or the *gold specie standard*. They also recommended the abolishment of fractional reserve banking and central banking, on the grounds that both institutions were inherently inflationary. Their position on monetary affairs set the tone for the term inflation for the next few decades.

Up until the 1860s, the word was predominantly employed in political discourse in a distinctly *Jacksonian* manner. The same year that *Daniel Barnard* is credited with coining the term in an economic context, the term appeared in the New York Senate where the merits of repealing the laws restraining private banking were being debated:

> "... the present pecuniary distress can be traced to its true and only cause with as strong and distinct demonstration as the motion of the heavenly bodies can be followed to its impulse, gravitation. ... The whole country is now suffering under the devastating curse of an inflated and exploded paper currency; and the pecuniary losses and human misery which the inflation and explosion has created, and will yet produce, are greater than could be compensated by all the benefits which could result from the full

---

[87] This honour may be attributed to the political economist *Stephen Simpson* in 1831. He decried the inequitable outcomes accompanying 'the inflation and collapse of those paper balloons [paper currency], denominated *banks*, and their air bubbles, paper credits' *(Simpson 1831, 140)*.

[88] The *Jeffersonians* vehemently opposed central banking and fractional reserve banking on the premise both institutions were mechanisms of inflation. For these theorists, inflation was the root of economic injury and the decay of the moral fabric of society. They also opposed paper money since it was not subject to check.

[89] Coinciding with the development of the *Jacksonian Movement* in the United States was the *Currency School* in England. Like their American hard-money counterparts, these theorists attributed the occurrence of the trade cycle and the depreciation of the currency to the overissue of money. In contrast to their American peers however, the *Currency School* advocated the existence of a central bank, on the premise that one cornerstone bank would prove far easier to regulate.

fruition of an eternity of bank paper" *(New York State Legislature 1838, 2-3).*[90]

Another example can be found in former President *James Polk's*[91] annual message to the Congress of the United States in 1848. Referring to the *Independent Treasury Act*[92] of 1846, he argued:

> "It has tended powerfully to secure an exemption from that inflation and fluctuation of the paper currency so injurious to domestic industry and rendering so uncertain the rewards of labor, and, it is believed, has largely contributed to preserve the whole country from a serious commercial revulsion ..."*(Stryker 1849, 534).*

While the term would ultimately transcend the boundaries of politics, it nevertheless would retain links to its *Jacksonian* heritage.

By the second half of the nineteenth century, the term began to appear in the mainstream media and economic literature. The term continued to be utilised in such a manner as to highlight an artificial increase of the *money supply*, that is, an increase in the supply of money without a corresponding increase in the reserve of *specie*. The American business merchant and economic commentator *Charles Holt Carroll* argued for example:

> "The source of inflation, and of the commercial crisis, is in the nature of the system which pretends to lend money, but creates currency by discounting such bills when there is no such money in existence" *(Carroll [1868] 1964, 333).*

The artificial nature of inflation was reiterated by the cartoonist *Thomas Nast* during a series of cartoons in the late 1870s. His Cartoon *Milk-Tickets for Babies, in Place of Milk* sought to highlight the worthless nature of *paper money (Nast 1876).* Having no intrinsic value of its own, it could be inflated at will. Paper money was no more than a confidence trick *writ large.* In a similar vein, his cartoon *Ideal Money*[93] illustrated the derisive nature of paper

---

[90] The same report also laboured to distinguish between the nature of coin and paper: "All men of ordinary understanding are aware that coin possesses intrinsic value, and that paper does not; that gold and silver are payment, whilst bank notes are mere promises to pay; that the one is fruition and the other hope, the one substance, and the other one a shadow..." *(New York State Legislature 1838, 1-2).*

[91] *James Polk* served as the eleventh President of the United States from 1845 to 1849 *(Wikipedia 2010).*

[92] The Independent Treasury was the brainchild of President *Martin Van Buren*, who served as the eight President of the United States from 1837 to 1841 *(Wikipedia 2010).* He believed that by separating banking from government, the banks ability to inflate using federal deposits as a base would be severely curbed *(Philbin 1991, 92).*

[93] While this cartoon might be considered an excellent example of artistic licence, it is incredulous that a real world parallel would emerge approximately thirty years later. The Hungarian-American journalist *Joseph Szebenyei* penned an anecdote about an Austrian clerk, who declared the coupons of an English soap manufacturer as 'Berengarian currency,' at a coffeehouse exchange. When asked for the prevailing exchange rate by the broker, the

money *(Nast 1878)*. Essentially, debts could be repudiated by simply proclaiming worthless property to be money. Following on his heels was the prominent American economist *Francis Walker*[94] who referred to inflation as the "factitious increase of a medium of paper and credit … above the level which the metallic basis of the currency can support" *(Walker [1878] 2008, 433)*.[95] Essentially any artificial increase of the money supply was inflationary, since it carried with it 'the sting of fraud' *(Walker [1899] 2009, 226)*. An increase in specie on the other hand was not inflationary since it emanated from 'natural means', involving "no sting of injustice" *(Walker [1899] 2009, 227-228)*. With the demise of the influence of the *Jacksonian* Movement in the United States, and the *Currency School* in England however, the term inflation would soon lose its sense of heritage.

Not long after the turn of the twentieth century, the *quantity theory of money* began its gradual encroachment into monetary theory. Accompanying this school of thought was its own rendition of inflation. According to the early American quantity theorist *Edwin Kemmerer*:

> "It is the idea of a redundancy of money or circulating credit or both, a redundancy that results in rising prices … inflation occurs when, at a *given price level*, a country circulating media — cash and deposit currency — increase *relatively* to trade needs" *(Kemmerer 1918, 247)*.

---

clerk promptly replied 20 kronen to the *lotu* – the imaginary name he invented for the currency. The broker subsequently paid him 20 kronen for each of the two hundred coupons he had collected. He returned the very next day to confess his guilt and buy back the coupons at the price that he had sold them for. The broker would have nothing of it answering, 'No, no, my dear fellow; I sold them at twenty-eight, and now you could not buy them for less than 40 kronen a *lotu*. If you wait a day or two, they might drop back to 20' *(Szebenyei 1922, 418)*.

[94] *Francis Walker* served as the first president of the *American Economic Association* (AEA). In recognition of his contribution to economics, the Walker Medal was established in his honour by the AEA. From 1947, it was awarded every five years "to the living American economist who in the judgement of the awarding body has during his career made the greatest contribution to economics". It was discontinued in the wake of the creation of the Nobel Memorial Prize *(American Economic Association 2010)*.

[95] This quote belongs to the English economist *Thomas Tooke*: "The factitious increase of a medium of paper and credit, raising the prices of commodities and of the public funds above the level which the metallic basis of the currency can support, must be succeeded, not only by a destruction of all that artificial medium, but by a temporary contraction of the circulation below the level from which that enlargement took place" *(Tooke 1826, 62)*.

Milk-Tickets for Babies, in Place of Milk

Nast, Thomas (1876) Milk-Tickets for Babies, in Place of Milk [Cartoon] Robinson Crusoe's Money; or, the Remarkable Financial Fortunes and Misfortunes of a Remote Island Community, New York: Harper & Brothers.

Ideal Money

Nast, Thomas (1878) Ideal Money [Cartoon] Harper's Weekly Jan 19 1878.

Criticising the proto-monetarist approach to *inflation* was *James Trant*,[96] the Dean of the College of Commerce of Louisiana State University. He argued that a stable dollar was both impractical and undesirable *(Trant 1934, 45)*. In the case of a growing economy, a stable price level could only be achieved through inflation, the very outcome that the quantity theorists sought to eliminate. Moreover he argued, "we would not recognise the inflation because of the stability of the general price level" *(Trant 1934, 45)*.[97] Policymakers could potentially be caught unaware as in the case of the *Great Depression*, which was preceded by eight years of price stability *(Trant 1934, 45)*. Another harsh critic of this approach was the American economist *Henry Willis*. He defined inflation as the deliberate 'policy' or 'philosophy' of enlarging the quantity of money *(Willis 1933, 18-19)*.[98] According to him, the quantity theory of money[99] was inherently inflationary and theoretically 'shallow' *(Willis 1933, 18-19)*. Summing up his stance, he concluded:

> "Inflation is a will-o'-the-wisp — a sort of modern philosophers' stone — which promises to turn base metals into precious, but whose use succeeds only in the payment of large sums for costly experiment and enriches only the charlatans" *(Willis 1933, 45)*.

---

[96] The analogy put forth by *James Trant* against *Irving Fisher's* ideal of price stability is still applicable today. "The proposal for constantly changing the gold content of the dollar to give it stability causes one to wonder why some great railroad company does not constantly shift the road bed of its trunk line to give stability to the track. The 23.22 grain gold content dollar is the monetary road bed over which American commerce has roared for nearly a century. A number of wrecks have occurred on this road, but the question has not been settled as to whether it was faultiness in the foundation of the road bed, or whether it is the result of some artificial barriers having been placed in front of the train of commerce. It is conceivable that the couplings of the train may not have been properly fastened or that a brakeman may have gone to sleep. It is possible, of course, that the trouble lay in the road bed, but in that case one imagines that a greater number of wrecks would have occurred if the road bed had been constantly changed with the hope of giving stability to the track" *(Trant 1934, 45)*.

[97] The Swedish economist *Axel Leijonhufvud* recently presented a similar argument: "The trouble with [price] inflation targeting...is that a constant inflation rate gives you absolutely no information about whether your monetary policy is right" *(Leijonhufvud 2007, 5)*.

[98] According to *Henry Parker Willis*, a policy of inflation could be enacted by one of several different measures including for example, the abandonment of the specie standard in favour of legal tender notes, a moratorium whereby the redemption in specie is suspended, a specie embargo whereby the maintenance of a *gold exchange standard* is no more than a pretence, and the artificial suppression of the interest rate to stimulate borrowing which would have been otherwise considered imprudent *(Willis 1933, 18)*.

[99] Another critic of *Irving Fisher's* goal of price stability was the American economist *James Boyle*. He attached his plan on several different levels including value: "What is value? Value is opinion, mass opinion. Market value is the consensus of opinion. ... Market values change from day to day as confidence, hope, fear, and other feelings influence our opinions. Dr Fisher says he will stabilize values. But can you stabilize opinion" *(Boyle 1934, 45)*?

While the *quantity theory of money* remained on the fringes of monetary policy during the early twentieth century, it nevertheless set the scene for the future excommunication of money from the concept of inflation.

An important land post in the evolution of inflation was *John Maynard Keynes's The General Theory of Employment, Interest and Money*, published in 1936. While the book did not pass without harsh criticism from some quarters,[100] it nevertheless redefined the macroeconomic landscape in the aftermath of the *Great Depression*. By appealing to *mercantilist*[101] notion that the quantity of money and the general level of prices were segregated entities, and that a monetary expansion primarily impacted the real economy, the Keynesian framework offered an air of legitimacy to inflation as a means of achieving *full employment*. Accordingly, the historical interpretation of the term ultimately fell by the wayside, to be replaced by a contemporary rendition which saw inflation as an increase in the general level of prices. Even though the Keynesian paradigm suffered a major setback during the *stagflation* of the 1970s, the battle on the inflation front had already been decided. It is said that history is written by the victors and this is no more evident than in the definition of inflation which proved to be "a casualty in the theoretical battle over the connection between money growth and the general price level" *(Bryan 1997, 1)*. While the symptomatic interpretation of the term has ultimately carved out its own niche in mainstream economic circles and in the general populace, the *Austrian school of economic thought* continues to remain steadfast in employing the term in a context consistent with its historical roots.

Within the *Austrian school*, two interpretations of the term inflation have arisen. While these definitions are similar in the sense that they are causal definitions, pertaining to money and not prices, the underlying frameworks are sufficiently different that they generate contradicting conclusions under certain circumstances. The monetary equilibrium approach follows the Austrian economist *Ludwig von Mises* in viewing inflation as any increase in the quantity of money that is not offset by an accompanying increase in the demand to hold money *(Mises [1912] 1981, 272)*.[102] While this interpretation has found support from free banking theorists within the Austrian school, it is noteworthy that *Ludwig von Mises* himself undermined the employment of the term in an economic context. Since the demand to hold money is constantly fluctuating in response to changes in the economic environment, he argued that the money supply by this measure must be constantly experiencing either *inflation* or *deflation* rendering these concepts superfluous from an economic standpoint *(Mises [1912] 1981, 272)*. The second approach within the Austrian school was expounded

---

[100] In his critique, the American economist *Henry Hazlitt* concluded that he was 'unable to find in it a single doctrine that is both true and original. What is original in the book is not true; and what is true is not original' *(Hazlitt 1959, 6)*.

[101] *Mercantilism* holds sway over economic thought between the 16th and 18th century. Apart from their promotion of protectionism as a means of increasing national wealth, they achieved economic notoriety by advancing the doctrine of the absence of a link between the quantity of money and the general level of prices *(Humphrey [1998] 1999)*.

[102] While *Ludwig von Mises* favoured this definition throughout most of his career, he did advance an alternative which is more consistent with the definition propagated by *Murray Rothbard*. Specifically, "Inflation, as the term was always used everywhere and especially in this country, means increasing the quantity of money and bank notes in circulation and the quantity of bank deposits subject to check" *(Mises 1990)*.

by the American economist *Murray Rothbard* who viewed inflation in a manner consistent with the *Jacksonian Movement.*[103] In essence, any increase in the quantity of money beyond the increase in specie is inflationary[104] since it generates an unequitable outcome as well as leading to the emergence of the *business cycle* under certain circumstances *(Rothbard [2004] 2009, 1022).* According to *Murray Rothbard,* this interpretation is the only expedient definition of inflation since it directly isolates the cause of economic and social injury *(Rothbard [2004] 2009, 1022).*

While many definitions of inflation have been offered throughout the course of economic history, the original interpretation as an increase in the quantity of money without a parallel increase in specie continues to be the only expedient usage of the term.

8.3 Inflation and Morality

> "The moralist is not more strongly bound than is the economist to denounce every measure having any such design of effect [inflation]".
> — *Francis Amasa Walker (Walker [1899] 2009, 226)*

One theme that is usually glossed over when debating the expediency of alternative monetary outcomes is the moral dimension of inflation *per se.* This result is not surprising since economics is widely regarded as a positive discipline, where value judgements are *persona non grata.* What is perplexing however is the corresponding lack of discourse in contemporary political economy, where social justice is a pertinent issue? This oversight is all the more glaring given that the moral stance against inflation is steeped in history.

The thesis that money is not neutral with respect to its impact on the real economy can be traced back to Irish-French economist *Richard Cantillon* in the eighteenth century. He argued that an inflationary influx necessitates a change in the structure of relative prices since this newfound money is injected into the economy at a specific point *(Cantillon [1755] 1959, 167-171).* The nature of this change in the real economy, referred to as *Cantillon effect,* is predicated on the expenditure patterns of the earliest recipients, who enjoy an increase in their purchasing power. This windfall however, comes at the expense of those laggards who only take receipt of the newfound money, subsequent to its impact on relative prices. These latecomers experience a decline in their purchasing power, since they can no longer afford the quantity of goods and services they previously enjoyed. This unequitable outcome was identified by English academic and churchman *Edward Copleston* who argued:

> "The fact undoubtedly is, that the altered value of money does not affect all prices at the same time: but that wide intervals occur, during which one

---

[103] Writing on the mainstream intepretation, *Murray Rothbard* argued it was theoretically deficient since: "Prices are highly complex phenomena, activated by many different causal factors… To lump all of these causes together is misleading, for it glosses over the separate influences, the isolation of which is the goal of science" *(Rothbard [2004] 2009, 1021).*

[104] In a *fiat currency regime,* any increase in the supply of money counts as inflation since it does not emanate from natural means. As such it involves an unequitable outcome as well as being potentially destabilising.

> class is compelled to buy dear while they sell cheap, and others have no prospect whatever of indemnity, or of regaining the relative position they once occupied" *(Copleston 1819, 25)*.

The arbitrary redistribution of real income and wealth following inflation arises due to the time lag between the new monetary equilibrium and the respective adjustment in the real economy. The relative tardiness of the latter virtually ensures that the brunt of inflation is borne by those individuals who are unable to capitalise on the change in prices *ex ante*. This group typically includes the recipients of fixed income, such as the elderly and the disabled, and those individuals who reside at the lower end of the socioeconomic spectrum. The unconscionable impact on the most vulnerable segments of the population was recognised by the French statesman and economist *Frederic Bastiat* who expounded a scathing indictment of inflation:

> "When once false money (under whatever form it may take) is put into circulation, depreciation will ensue, and manifest itself by the universal rise of every thing which is capable of being sold. But this rise in prices is not instantaneous and equal for all things. Sharp men, brokers, and men of business, will not suffer by it; for it is their trade to watch the fluctuations of prices, to observe the cause, and even to speculate upon it. But little tradesmen, countrymen, and workmen will bear the whole weight of it. The rich man is not any the richer for it, but the poor man becomes poorer by it. Therefore, expedients of this kind have the effect of increasing the distance which separates wealth from poverty, of paralyzing the social tendencies which are incessantly bringing men to the same level, and it will require centuries for the suffering classes to regain the ground which they have lost in their advance towards equality of condition" *(Bastiat 1874, 168)*.

Unfortunately, the redistributional effects accompanying relative prices changes are largely neglected by mainstream economists and policymakers. As far as their theories entail, the inflation of the money supply is a necessary prerequisite for achieving price stability, a condition conducive to financial stability and in turn economic growth. Apart from downplaying these issues of redistribution in the short-term, this commitment to price stability also overlooks the grievous effects of inflation in the long-term.

A policy of protracted inflation has major ramifications with respect to provisioning for the future. In an economy with a stable money supply, long-term economic growth manifests itself as a secular downtrend in prices. While many economists view this outcome with trepidation, a decline in the general level of prices[105] is tantamount to an increase in real wages, an expedient outcome that is enjoyed by all and sundry. A backdrop of declining prices is also conducive to the practice of parsimony, since it is rewarded with an increase in the purchasing power of cash balances over time. In an economy committed to *price stability* however, the natural tendency towards declining prices is countered by the

---

[105] The preoccupation with falling prices stems from the erroneous view that *price deflation* and *depressions* are inexorably linked. For an Austrian treatment of this fallacious doctrine, see either *(Selgin 1997)* or *(Salerno 2003)*. For a mainstream refutation of this thesis, see *(Atkeson & Kehoe 2004)*.

continual augmentation of the money supply. As a result of this monetary intervention, the benefits of economic growth on the price level and in turn the *standard of living* are directly impeded.[106] [107] The task of provisioning for the future is complicated further still if the economy experiences a persistent increase in the general level of prices. The erosion of purchasing power that accompanies this outcome is analogous to a relentless attack on thrift *(Paine [1786] 1838)*.[108] The profligate escape a similar levy however, since they do not have to endure the effects of a depreciating currency. In a similar vein, price inflation favours creditors at the expense of debtors, since a depreciating currency dilutes the value of existing debts. The American economist *William Foster* alluded to this when he argued that price inflation makes "a mockery of thrift. Men sow where they do not reap, and reap where they do not sow" *(Foster 1934, 18)*. While most mainstream economists and policymakers are not oblivious to the injustice imposed by price inflation,[109] their overriding concern is the prevention of price deflation.[110] With long-term monetary intervention undermining the incentive to save, it is inevitable that individuals turn towards other means for provisioning for an uncertain future.

For many individuals who are not in a position to capitalise on price inflation *ex ante*, *speculation* becomes their only method of guarding against the constant erosion of *purchasing*

---

[106] The most important criticism of price stability as a goal for monetary policy, "if it should work, is that it would not prevent inflation and deflation (and that is the object of the plan), but would prevent the public from obtaining the benefits of increased efficiency and lowered costs of production" *(Trant 1934, 45)*.

[107] Arguing against price stability as a goal for monetary policy, the English economist *Dennis Robertson* referenced a letter written by a former Archbishop of Wales to *The Times*: "To a simple fellow like myself it seems that the lower prices which increased production makes possible would benefit everybody, but I recognize there must be a flaw in my thinking, for increased productivity has not brought—and does not seem likely to bring—lower prices. Presumably there is some good reason for this. Will someone explain" *(Selgin 1990, 265)*.

[108] The English-American liberal *Thomas Paine* condemned paper money on the premise it was inherently inflationary, and therefore prone to violating the sanctity of money as the embodiment of toil and thrift: "Money, when considered as the fruit of many years' industry, as the reward of labor, sweat and toil, as the widow's dowry and children's portion, and as the means of procuring the necessaries and alleviating the afflictions of life, and making old age a scene of rest, has something in it sacred that is not to be sported with, or trusted to the airy bubble of paper currency" *(Paine [1786] 1838, 45)*.

[109] A rare exception was the American economist and a former Governor of the Federal Reserve *Henry Wallich*, who remarked that price inflation "is a means by which the strong can more effectively exploit the weak" *(Wallich 1978, 13)*.

[110] Central bankers tend to err on the side of caution. As the Austrian economist and *Nobel Memorial Prize in Economics* winner (1974) *Friedrich von Hayek* explains: "Although there are a few people who deliberately advocate a continuous upward movement of prices, the chief source of the existing inflationary bias is the general belief that deflation, the opposite of inflation, is so much more to be feared that, in order to keep on the safe side, a persistent error in the direction of inflation is preferable. But, as we do not know how to keep prices completely stable and can achieve stability only by correcting any small movement in either direction, the determination to avoid deflation at any cost must result in cumulative inflation" *(Hayek [1972] 2009, 101-102)*.

power.[111] Such an outcome was highlighted by the English-American liberal *Thomas Paine*, when he argued that incessant price inflation, "turns the whole country into stock jobbers" *(Paine [1786] 1838, 45)*. Essentially individuals play an elaborate version of the children's game *hot potato*, whereby they seek to offload the losses of a depreciating currency onto the next person as quickly as possible. When looked upon in this context, *speculation* is not the application of avarice as charged by its detractors, but rather a prudent and predictable response to the inroads of monetary intervention. While the act of speculating may emerge with honourable intentions in mind, the investor psyche is easily swayed however. *Institutionalised price inflation,* which underwrites the existence of secular bull markets[112] [113] in asset markets, ultimately serves to corrupt the investor mindset with the allure of easy money. Spellbound by their relentless rise, many individuals lose their proclivity for the toils of labour, seeking instead to ride the wave of optimism higher. In this environment, speculation becomes a means of circumventing the usual nexus between "effort and productivity, on the one hand, and economic reward on the other" *(Hazlitt 1978, 142)*. Ultimately the quest for easy money takes the form of other moral vices including corruption.[114] The degenerative effects of price inflation on the moral fabric of society were highlighted by former United States of America President *Andrew Jackson* in his Farewell Address of 1837:

> "These ebbs and flows in the currency and these indiscreet extensions of credit naturally engender a spirit of speculation injurious to the habits and character of the people... it will foster this eager desire to amass wealth without labor;... the temptation to obtain money at any sacrifice will become stronger and stronger, and inevitably lead to corruption, which will find its way into your public councils and destroy at no distant day the purity of your Government" *(Woolley and Peters 2010)*.

For the *Jacksonian Movement*, price inflation was a contagion that would ultimately inflict all walks of life, including the private sector and the government.

---

[111] In the presence of hyperinflation, even the act of speculation may prove insufficient as a hedge against the loss of purchasing power. Commenting on the *hyperinflation* that had gripped most of Continental Europe after World War One, the Hungarian-American journalist *Joseph Szebenyei* wrote: "The salaried classes and the wage-earners ... are hardest hit by these conditions. No salary can really be high enough to afford them a bare living — indeed, not even mere semi-starvation. Every wage-earner or salaried worker has to speculate, barter, or steal in order to make both ends meet" *(Szebenyei 1922, 419)*.

[112] The American economist *Henry Willis* wrote: "In many instances of inflation, the process operates chiefly upon stocks and securities..." *(Willis 1933 18)*.

[113] The Austrian economist *Friedrich von Hayek* argued that the price of capital goods or durable assets is inversely correlated with interest rates. If a credit expansion maintains interest rates below that level that would have otherwise prevailed, it creates a tailwind for capital goods including equities *(Hayek 1935)*.

[114] With respect to the conduct of commerce against a backdrop of hyperinflation, the Hungarian-American journalist *Joseph Szebenyei* wrote: "The shifting of values and the greatly unsettled conditions in trade and finance have ... totally upset all moral laws. To cheat the sate, to rob the treasury, has become a praiseworthy deed; to transact crooked business is not looked upon as unfair; nor is it at all unusual..." *(Szebenyei 1922, 418)*.

While most governments throughout the world lay claim to the high ground on morality, their role in the inflationary process is inconsistent with such a stance. As the American economist *Henry Hazlitt* elaborates:

> "When modern governments inflate by increasing the paper-money supply, directly or indirectly, they do in principle what kings once did when they clipped coins. Diluting the money supply with paper is the moral equivalent of diluting the milk supply with water. Notwithstanding all the pious pretenses of governments that inflation is some evil visitation from without, inflation is practically always the result of deliberate governmental policy" *(Hazlitt 1978, 142).*

Governments tend to have a vested interest in *institutionalising inflation.*[115] In the first instance, inflation provides a politically palatable alterative to *taxation.* While both means involve a transfer of purchasing power to the government, the general outcry with taxation is far greater since this affects everyone directly. Inflation also opens up a new avenue for revenue in the way of capital gains. The greater the inflation in this regard, the larger its future revenues. In addition to these benefits which tend to be recurring, if the government has wracked up a significant amount of debt, a depreciating currency serves to dilute the value of its existing debt in real terms.

8.4 The Austrian Theory of the Business Cycle

> "The past instability of the market economy is the consequence of the exclusion of the most important regulator of the market mechanism, money, from itself being regulated by the market process."
>
> — *Friedrich von Hayek (Hayek 1976, 79).*

The Austrian theory of the *business cycle* represents hallowed ground within the Austrian school. An early exposition was offered by *Ludwig von Mises* in 1912 in *Theorie des Geldes und der Umlaufsmittel,* which would later be published as *The Theory of Money and Credit* in the English speaking world. Tying together the capital theory of *Eugene von Böhm-Bawerk* with the work of Swedish economist *Knut Wicksell* on interest rates, *Ludwig von Mises* resurrected and refined the monetary theory of the trade cycle that was delineated by the British *Currency School*[116] in the early nineteenth century. Following on the heels of *Ludwig von Mises, Friedrich von Hayek* would leave his distinct mark on the theory, illustrating how a credit expansion would impact the structure of production in a manner inconsistent with

[115] While the responsibility for inflating the money supply has passed from the government to their respective central bank in many instances, the existence of the central bank itself is an outgrowth of government intervention. Moreover, the central bank's mandate stems directly from the government.

[116] The British *Currency School* attributed the emergence of the trade cycle to the augmentation of credit through the issue of bank notes not backed by specie. They committed a grave error however, by failing to acknowledge that demand deposits were a part of the money supply. As a result, the *Bank Charter Act of 1844* proved ineffective in halting the emergence of the boom-bust cycle and the influence of the *Currency School* fell by the wayside.

consumer preferences and the state of economic wealth. The theory continues to be a work in progress to this day, with a number of contributions having been made by economists of the Austrian stripe, most notably *Murray Rothbard* and the American economist *Roger Garrison (Rothbard 1963b, Garrison 2001).*

The *Austrian theory of the business cycle* describes how monetary intervention in the credit market triggers a sequence of events that inevitably culminates in a bust. The business cycle in this context is not a secular feature of a capitalist market economy[117] but rather the outgrowth of the monetary authority appropriating the interest rate from the spontaneous order of the market and the tendency towards disequilibrium that naturally follows.

In an unhampered economy, market rates of interest would naturally gravitate towards the natural rate of interest.[118] In the Austrian framework, the *natural rate of interest* reflects the time preference of society,[119] the premium placed on the value of *present consumption* versus *future consumption.* Since time preference is a subjective concept that varies across individuals, the natural rate of interest can only be ascertained by the totality of exchanges involving present and future goods. If individuals *en masse* become increasingly concerned about the outlook for the future, thereby placing a relatively greater premium on the provision of future goods, they will curtail present consumption as a means of providing the necessary capital goods[120] required to initiate and sustain an extension of the period of production.[121] Falling time preferences will be reflected in declining rates of market interest. Economic growth that follows in this context will be sustainable since it accords with consumer preferences and the availability of capital goods *(Garrison 2001).*

---

117 The business cycle predates the birth of the capitalistic market economy. According to the Italian economic historian *Carlo Cipolla*: "The current conclusions about the nature and the origins of long trends as a rule derive from the unique experience of the upward movement which accompanied and followed the Industrial Revolution. But from the point of view of both economic theory and economic history it is important to study the trends before the middle of the eighteenth century ... From the end of the thirteenth century and the first decades of the fourteenth there occurred a series of crises comparable in their gravity (if the scale of contemporary economy is taken into account) to the crisis that struck modern economy between 1929 and 1939" *(Cipolla 1949, 181).* The Spanish economist *Jesús Huerta de Soto* attributes these crises to the institution of fractional reserve banking *(Huerta de Soto 2006, 70-77).*

118 The Swedish economist *Knut Wicksell* distinguished between market rates of interest and the natural rate of interest, which is the rate "which would be determined by the supply and demand if real capital were lent in kind without the intervention of money" *(Wicksell 1965, xxv).*

119 The concept of time preference was devised by *Eugene von Böhm-Bawerk* who wrote: "Present goods are as a general rule worth more than future goods of equal quality and quantity. That sentence is the nub and kernel of the theory of interest which I have to present" *(Böhm-Bawerk 1891 259).*

120 Capital goods are those resources utilised in the production of future goods.

121 The period of production is represented by time between the initial employment of the factors of production and the realisation of the final product. Roundabout methods are employed because they yield an increase in output without a commensurate increase in the factors of production.

In an economy where the *market rate of interest* is dictated by the monetary authority, the spontaneous order of the market is taken out of play. The interest rate no longer reflects the time preferences of society in aggregate but serves as a means to an end on the part of the monetary authority and the government. By committing to inflation via the expansion of credit, the market rate of interest can be artificially suppressed, leading to an increase in economic activity as entrepreneurs and businesses take advantage of the low rates to finance new projects or extend old ones. However, since the economic expansion was policy driven rather than being induced by a change in preferences on the part of consumers, many of these projects will be cancelled once entrepreneurs realise they have competing claims against an insufficient quantity of capital goods. Essentially credit has masqueraded as capital, serving to derange the economic calculations of entrepreneurs. As *Ludwig von Mises* contends:

> "What is needed for a sound expansion of production is additional capital goods, not money or fiduciary media. The boom is built on the sands of banknotes and deposits. It must collapse" *(Mises [1949] 1998, 559).*

It is possible to stave off the day of reckoning for as long as the credit expansion maintains an exponential rate of growth, providing entrepreneurs the necessary purchasing power to stay one step ahead of the rising prices of the factors of production. However inflation is a policy that can not be carried out *ad infinitum.* As *Ludwig von Mises* elaborates:

> "The boom can last only as long as the credit expansion progresses at an ever-accelerated pace. The boom comes to an end as soon as additional quantities of fiduciary media are no longer thrown upon the loan market. But it could not last forever even if inflation and credit expansion were to go on endlessly. It would then encounter the barriers which prevent the boundless expansion of circulation credit. It would lead to the crack-up boom and the breakdown of the whole monetary system" *(Mises [1949] 1998, 552).*

It is pertinent to realise that the bust is the healthy part of the *business cycle*, where the economy purges itself of unprofitable investments, so that it can return to a growth trajectory that is consistent with consumer preferences and the state of economic wealth. In this light, a downturn should not be fought with further *monetary stimulus*, as a means of saving capital. For as *John Mills* argued:

> "… Panics do not destroy capital; they merely reveal the extent to which it has been previously destroyed by its betrayal into hopelessly unproductive works … The failure of great banks … and mercantile firms … are the symptoms incident to the disease, not the disease itself" *(Manchester Statistical Society 1868, 18-29).*

Conclusions

> "It is also a social menace. It enables some classes to prosper, through no virtue of their own, while other classes suffer, through no fault of their own."
> *Foster, William (1934) 'Can the Dollar be 'Managed?' The Rotarian, Vol.44, No.1, p.18.*
>
> "What is clear, however, is that the behavior of inflation is much more complex than is assumed in our models. And we understand the relationship between activity and inflation quite poorly, especially at low rates of inflation."
> *Prof. Olivier Blanchard, Econometrician, MIT, February 2010*

The traditional approach to judge the effects of the *German Hyperinflation* mostly ended up in the statement, that the road to the supremacy of the *National Socialist German Labour Party* (NSDAP) and the chancellorship of *Adolf Hitler* in 1933 were one of the inevitable consequences. *David Fraser* illustrates this reasoning very impressively: "New housing for the workers was tackled with enthusiasm – and with a good deal of taste. A 'people's car', a *Volkswagen*, intended to bring motoring into lower-income households than hitherto, was designed. New roads, resembling railways in their conception, were devised and named in consequence '*Autobahnen*'. And, at least for a while, all this appeared to be managed without depreciation of the currency, without that unforgettable inflation of the early 1920s which had ravaged Germany and wiped out the savings of millions. Dr Schacht, President of the Reichsbank, seemed to preside over an economy which pundits might whisper was inherently fragile but which to the mass of Germans seemed once again to be built upon stability, labour and national discipline" *(Fraser 1994, 107).*

Simply a hyperinflation is an uncontrollable inflation with extremely high monthly rates. Although the threshold is arbitrary, economists generally reserve the term *hyperinflation* to describe episodes where the monthly inflation rate is greater than 50 percent. At a monthly rate of 50 percent, it corresponds to an annual rate of approximately 13,000 percent. Additionally, hyperinflation is a highly complex system, which has its roots in not merely macroeconomic factors but also in behavioural factors of human beings. Unfortunately the arrow of time is irreversible for the period of the German Hyperinflation 1922/1923, or in other words, one can not revisit the past, that is one can not observe the actual *German Hyperinflation 1922/1923* as a complicated system at its time. Furthermore, the highly complex process of hyperinflation that is for example in the initial state of the process the substantial variety of factors influencing each other, one can not regard as mono-causal and simply deterministic. Why has the high inflation turned into a hyperinflation in a dramatically colossal way? The conventional economic and socio-political concepts did not seem to have coped with this phenomenon of the hyperinflation. The economic chaos and collapse was followed therefore not by a given equilibrium, for which the economists in the 19th and 20th century always aimed and in theory as possible deemed. Instead the system developed itself far away from equilibrium and the entropy expanded while subsequently the degree of disorder of the system increased much faster until finally the system collapsed and a new plateau was in sight. Today it can be explored neither empirically nor socio-psychologically why in August 1923 the already existing hyperinflation collapsed. The causes are due likely in the area of irrational behaviour (or one might define it as non-rational behaviour), anxiety and fear of losing everything such as material possessions, money, properties, shares, and social status overall, distrust, survival strategies etcetera and not reducible to a few economic factors and correlations. The modern *Complexity Economics* – still being in the development – could be asked as a challenge to find out a more satisfactory answer than the current *traditional Economics* has delivered so far.

Rainhart Schweigert has clearly worked out that the finance of the WWI was basically done by the Government and the Parliament through *war bonds* rather than by imposing *taxes* on the economy. One should bear in mind that the assumption of the politically responsible persons prior to the beginning of *WWI* was as such: the war will last fourteen days and can be financed by the war reparation of France from the *Prussian-Franco War 1871*. Regarded as a symbol for this assumption was the *Juliusturm*, a tower at Spandau (Berlin), where French Francs in gold coins were stored.

Advertisement for the 8th German War Bonds (deutsche Kriegsanleihe) in March 1918

Attempts to introduce for example a sales tax *(Umsatzsteuer)* to finance parts of the war costs, for example the submarine fleet, came far too late to avoid shifting the war costs until after the war period and in addition to further generations. One has to bear in mind that the *Imperial Government* was financially dependent on subsidies (*Matrikularbeiträge*) from the provinces (*Länder*). After WWI the *German Government* introduced various taxes to stabilise the revenue base of the post-war government (*Erzberger Tax Reform*) under the leadership of *Matthias Erzberger.*[122] *Hans G. Gnodtke* conjectured "World War One has been called a tragic European fratricide and most disturbingly despite 9 Million human lives lost it was not the war to end all wars and it did not achieve what victors and vanquished had hoped for and that was to create a new balance of power in Western and Central Europe preventing further armed conflict" *(Gnodtke 2009, 20).* This burden of immense war costs had been laid during the revolution and the abdication of *Kaiser Wilhelm II* onto the new democratically elected government of *Friedrich Ebert.* This infant *German Republic* was highly unstable in so many ways - politically, economically and socially.

Harrison Alexander Amankwah in his chapter "Treaty of Versailles (1919) & League of Nations" made an effort to essay the place of the *Treaty of Versailles* in the early stages of the *Weimar Republic.* As the genesis of the treaty was the *First World War*, an overview of

---

[122] Matthias Erzberger was a prominent German politician in the Centre Party who had signed the Armistice for the German Empire. He was assassinated on 26 Aug 1921 by the Organisation Consul, an ultra-nationalist death squad operating in Germany in 1921 and 1922 (Wikipedia, Matthias Erzberger).

that war was undertaken. It was surmised that perhaps Germany alone ought not to be singled out as the sole culprit to shoulder all the blame regarding the causes of the war. The *League of Nations* was an adjunct of the *Treaty of Versailles* and, also necessitated by it due to the desire of the Founding Fathers of the League to eliminate war as an instrument of national policy in international relations. To that end the *League* was mandated to supervise the observance and enforcement of the treaty. Its coverage in the essay is therefore confined to its role in that regard only. It is noted however that the *League* failed in the realization of its principal objective, because only two decades after its inauguration mankind was confronted with yet another war. The *Weimar Constitution* and the *Weimar Republic* which the constitution brought into existence are discussed. The inherent flaws in the constitution are indicated and the factors which inhibited a successful and efficacious management of the infant republic are similarly outlined.

Kenneth Kaoma Mwenda examined the legal aspects of *payment of reparations* by Germany after World War I, providing some important historical perspectives while drawing analogies and comparisons with claims for reparation relating to the *holocaust* and the *slave trade*. He observed that the issue of Germany's payment of war reparations has not yet abated, and that after Germany's defeat in World War II an international conference decided in 1953 that Germany would pay the remaining debt only after the country had reunified. And, in 1995, after reunification, the new German government announced it would resume payments of the reparations. He established that there is increasing evidence to suggest that customary international law does recognize the *principle of reparation payments*. For a claimant to succeed in a claim of reparation payments, he or she need not necessarily show that he or she is relying on a particular treaty in making that claim. Although many cases show that claimants have relied on conventional international law, or rather treaties, so to speak, the International Commission of Jurists, making a legal submission on *Fiji's Promotion of Reconciliation, Tolerance and Unity Bill 2005*, observed, as we have noted already, that Fiji had an obligation under customary international law to provide reparations for victims of gross human violations. Such a pronouncement supports the view that customary international law does, indeed, recognize the principle of reparation payments. And the *Reparations Agreement between Israel and West Germany*, as alluded to earlier, is seen as a practical guide and precedent for the development of treaty obligations on which African States and their sympathizers can additionally base their claims for reparation payments for slave trade.

Erich Krausbeck concludes in his analysis "The Psychopathology of the Money", which could be a contribution to explain why a high inflation up to 1923 suddenly turned into a hyperinflation, that with the discovery of *mirror neurons* in 1995 by *Giacomo Rizzolatti* and his colleague the *group dynamics phenomenon* was elevated from the realm of *behavioural disorders* to the realm of *psychology*. We humans have no choice other than to feel, think and to act within a social unit. We are unable to remove ourselves from it, because if the person opposite me scratches his head, then in my brain the premotor cortex for my hand and arm is activated, whether I want to or not, and at the same time the sensory centres picks up on the itch by the person opposite and an unpleasant sensation is produced in me, whether I want to or not. In retrospect many a phenomenon can be classified now and until recently it was perhaps only possible to define them in an unsatisfactory way. The question of public opinion is evident not only in the collective unconsciousness coined by *Carl Gustav Jung* and in group dynamics. As a society our absolutely conscious thought processes are performed with our social brains. What connects us therefore is not only what is genetically predisposed – for example the collective fear of snakes – but instead the ideas, whether conscious or unconscious that we bring to the society in which we move. During the *Age of Enlightenment* the individual became aware of liberty. With the discovery of the *social brain*, he must be aware that he assumes responsibility for the actions of others because of the things that he says and does. He is at the same time subject to the feelings, behaviour and views of others. There is no restriction on freedom, but instead there is an extension of the notion of freedom on all of social thinking, in which the individual participates as a vital constituent part. The question why a *Voltaire*, a *Robespierre*, a *Frederick The Great* or a *Catherine the Great* would have discussed the concept of individual freedom during the *Age of Enlightenment*, or debated the relationship of the individual with *God* or with authority, could be explained by the fact that these strong historical figures would not have imagined themselves to be bound to a social way of thinking with their social brains. Only now, with the available technology of a functional *magnetic resonance imaging* (MRI) is it possible to get a better insight into the function of our brains. To refer to brains in the plural is increasingly justified, because with a single brain, such as that of a *Robinson Crusoe,* no further cultural development would be possible. It is collective thinking with all its advantages and risks that has been shaped by the human experience and this makes a cultural narrative possible.

Wolfgang Chr. Fischer analysed the *inflationary process* with all the components and introduced the concept of *complexity economics* as a possible better theory to investigate the various factors of a hyperinflation demonstrated on the *German hyperinflation in 1922/1923* as opposed to the traditional, historical and economic current sciences. He illustrated the crucial *acceleration of the inflation rate* and rejected the simple explanation that the lack of taxes to finance the World War I, neither the war bonds, nor the war reparations, nor the political upheaval on the streets at that time alone would answer the essential question of a sudden and *colossal acceleration of the inflation* into a hyperinflation. Most likely the hyperinflation cannot be put into the right perspective without the implementation of psychological and psychiatric elements of mass behaviour. In particular an accelerated fear of losing all savings and other assets, fear of how to make ends meet each day, in particular for wage and salary earners, a fear of a life depending in some way on *black market* and *bartering* are phenomena associated with hyperinflation. At this time the *German Government* and the *German Parliament* were unable to stop the hyperinflation in a much earlier timeframe that is once the inflation turned into a high inflation. Whether the political will or the precise anticipation what could possibly happen was certainly available but it was obviously politically not opportune to declare the bankruptcy of the current currency, the *Mark*. It happened through *Dr. Hjalmar Schacht* as the President of the *Reichsbank* who finally introduced in November 1923 the *Rentenmark* as a dual currency, which was taken as a dual legal tender and widely accepted due to its being bound on the land assets of the German Republic. The new currency *Reichsmark* was finally introduced in August 1924 as a substitute for the completely devaluated 'paper' Mark from the previous hyperinflation in the years 1922 and 1923. The exchange rate of Mark to Reichsmark amounted to 1.000.000.000.000:1 (a trillion to one). Thus a trillion Mark was worth 0.24 US dollar, the value of one Mark before the war.

Wolfgang Chr. Fischer analysed then the legal implication of establishing a new currency after the hyperinflation with the immense problem to find a *conversion rate* which made it possible to value the assets backwards in time to the end of the World War I. This task was taken over by the *Reichsgericht* in 1925, which acted due to a lack of legal activities in the sense of implementing a relevant juridical background through the *Reichstag* and the *Reichsregierung*. The *Reichsgericht* argued that under the constitution (*Verfassung des Deutschen Reiches*) the court has to act with a politically moderate judgment to stop the nominalist principle enshrined in the rule *Mark gleich Mark* (a mark is worth a mark). The *Reichsgericht* decided to accept the *conversion rate* which was composed by a special committee of the *Reichstag* and declared it as valid in the sense of conformity with the German Constitution. This of course brought winners and losers within the new unstable German Republic but overall it was at least a significant contribution to stop endless discussions about which parts of the German society should bear the burden of the past hyperinflation.

Wolfgang Chr. Fischer asserts that hyperinflations are not simply a matter of so-called underdeveloped countries but also a phenomenon of so-called developed industrial countries in nowadays. As examples he had chosen the hyperinflations in *Peru* and *Zimbabwe* and the initial conditions leading to it. Nevertheless these two examples with all the implications could happen in the present also in so-called developed industrial countries. Given that a highly fragile and complex international financial system may collapse for various reasons and as a consequence potentially inflict further collapses of national economies. Hyperinflations not only obliterate social cohesion, economic and legal structures, but also carry the danger of the decay of democracy in the sense of a broader *retrogressive development*. *John Ralston Saul* assessed: "The very fact that anybody could believe that a democratic society could be led by economics, by self-interest, by definition demotes the citizen and their civilisation to little more than decoration. What that means in practical terms is that since 1945 we put in place around the world we put in place in the international arena, dozens and dozens of international treaties, hundreds of international treaties - but the only ones which are really binding are the economic treaties" *(Saul 1999).*

Soup Kitchen Maryborough, Queensland, Australia 2009

The IMF's *(International Monetary Fund)* recommendation of February 2010 to lift the official inflation rate target (unofficially the inflation rates are much higher in almost every country) for governments from currently 2% up to 4%, to ease further government *stimulation packages* etc. and if governments follow this line then national economies and the world economy probably will suffer inflationary processes with all its consequences of economic, legal and social chaos and destruction, which are beyond the imagination of the younger generations.

As a final exploration *Daniel Jason Goulding* weighed up the pros and contras of inflation as a necessity for economic prosperity. He concludes, according to the *Austrian School of Economics*, that inflation in general and over long time is detrimental to the goals of building prosperous economies at all. He argued that the term *inflation* should be exclusively retained to refer to any increase in the quantity of money that does not emanate from natural and peaceful means. Inflation of this nature, regardless of its magnitude, serves to undermine the *moral fabric of a society* as well as *derange economic calculation*, since it supplants the spontaneous order of a capitalistic market economy. As *Friedrich von Hayek* argued, "The peculiar character of the problem of a rational economic order is determined precisely by the fact that the knowledge of the circumstances of which we must make use never exists in concentrated or integrated form but solely as the dispersed bits of incomplete and frequently contradictory knowledge which all the separate individuals possess" *(Hayek 1948, 77)*. By denying this crucial aspect, inflation can only leave untold misery in its wake.

Attempts to explain the economic drama of *hyperinflation* using *complexity economics* rather than trying defining it away for example using philosophy probably constitutes a fascinating avenue of research into the *process of accelerating inflation.*[123] However, the *complexity economics* is in an infant state and very few outsider economists, yet some respectable physicists, mainly from astrophysics, quantum mechanics physicists and mathematicians are in it, but only a few economists or schools of economics. There is still the belief that with the data available the economists are able to come up with predictions and that they have all the tools to explain economic processes. In this avenue of research there should be also the general concept of a historical analysis with a bond to the near future by establishing the collective conscious with respect to inflation.

Given the various *hyperinflations* in numerous countries and the danger of multiple reoccurrences one has to bear in mind that mankind has to undertake drastic changes in organizing the national and international socio-economic order in the near future to survive. *Anders Johansen* and *Didier Sornette* argued in their article '2050: The End of the Growth Era?' that "the evolution from a growth regime to a balanced symbiosis with nature and with the Earth's resources requires the transition to a knowledge based society, in which knowledge, intellectual, artistic and humanistic values replace the quest for material wealth" *(Johansen & Sornette 2001)*. Revisiting the Introduction, in which *Théodicée* has been mentioned, that is the old philosophical question why *God* (for atheists whatever) let it, for example *World War I* and the following tremendous misery of the *German hyperinflation* with all its implications of breaking down the German society, happen to mankind? This colossal and devastating event of *hyperinflation* with law and order vanished, the breakdown of the social and economic order and the establishment of the general behaviour *'everyone for himself'* may be explained through rational reasoning, for example through the social science's *'mass hysteria'* or *'bandwagon effect'*, through the medical discovery of the *'social brain'* or *'mirror neurons'*, through the *'Austrian theory of the business cycle'* or through the *'Complexity Economics'*. However, there is something behind it all, something mankind can not explain like in physics, in which *quantum mechanics* has to concede that "in the subatomic world the behaviour of particles is generally unpredictable. From one moment to the next you cannot be sure what a particle is going to do. The outcome is intrinsically random" *(Davies 1983, 34/35)*. *Albert Einstein* rejected this theory in his famous retort *"God does not play dice"*.[124]

123 See also Paul Davies (2005) About time: Einstein's unfinished revolution, p. 278, in his pledge for further studies of the 'flow of time'.
124 Paul Davies (1983) God and the New Physics, 35.

Excursus:

Political Activities of Contemporary German Social Democrats

In this Excursus three biographies will be presented: The political activities of the contemporary social democratic revolutionaries *Heinrich A. Trinowitz* and *Robert Fischer* (Grandfathers of Wolfgang Chr. Fischer), which may illustrate the individual courageousness of social democrats and labour movement representatives at the time of the *Early Weimar Republic*. In addition some aspects of the political life of the social democratic journalist *Kurt Krausbeck* (Father of Erich Krausbeck) in the succeeding National Socialist German Workers Party (*Nationalsozialistische Deutsche Arbeiterpartei, NSDAP, 1920-1945)* Regime from 1933 to 1945 may demonstrate the very hardship of ordinary Germans during this period.

1. Heinrich August Trinowitz (1879-1929), Member of Parliament (MdL, Landtag Preussen) & Member of the German Council of Economic Affairs (Reichswirtschaftsrat), MdRWR[125]

Wolfgang Chr. Fischer

Heinrich August Trinowitz * 20th of Mai 1879 in Fichthorst; † 18th of April 1929 in *Tilsit* was a notable German unionist and social democratic politician *(Sozialdemokratische Partei Deutschlands).*

Heinrich August Trinowitz

After an elementary education he completed an apprenticeship as cabinetmaker and pursued this trade until 1911. From 1906 to 1911 he was a member on the board of directors of the local sickness-fund for cabinetmakers (Ortskrankenkasse der Tischler). Furthermore he was the chairman of the local branch of the Woodworkers Union as well as a member of the Industrial Court at Elbing from 1909 to 1911. After that *Trinowitz* was the branch manager of East Prussia of the German *Woodworkers Union* from 1911 until he

125 http://en.wikipedia.org/wiki/Heinrich_Trinowitz
Matull, Wilhelm (1973) Ostdeutschlands Arbeiterbewegung – Abriss ihrer Geschichte, Leistung und Opfer, Holzner Verlag, Würburg, Germany, p.366-372.

met his death in 1929. His post was Tilsit. In the years 1912, in 1922 as well as in 1925 Trinowitz was delegate at the German labour union congresses of the wood workers.

In Tilsit Trinowitz was also the chairman of the local Social Democratic Party of Germany's Council of Education as well as a member on the board of directors of the local Consumers' Co-operative from 1914 onwards. He was unfit for military service in WW1 due to a work related accident as cabinetmaker, which caused the loss of his right hand thumb. Prior to WW1 he encountered difficulties with the police by a defamation of Emperor Wilhelm II in a public speech.

Trinowitz was from 1919 to 1921 *Member of the Prussian State Parliament* (*verfassungsgebenden preußischer Landtag*). In addition he was from 1919 to 1925 *Member of the City Council Tilsit* as well as *Member of the Preliminary German Council on Economic Affairs (Reichswirtschaftsrat)* as a representative of the trades' workers from 1921 until 1929 (*http://biosop.zhsf.uni-koeln.de/ GESIS Leibniz-Institut für Sozialwissenschaften, Bonn, Wilhelm Heinz Schröder: BIOSOP Biographien Sozialdemokratischer Parlamentarier in den deutschen Reichs- und Landtagen 1867 – 1933).*

Heinrich August Trinowitz represented the social democratic politicians and activists of the trade-unionism, who abolished the German Imperial Monarchy *(Deutsches Kaiserreich)* and established the first parliamentarian *German Republic*, known as the Weimar Republic or officially as Deutsches Reich. Also he was a journalist for the party and union press.

2. Robert Fischer (1883-1945), Public Office Holder, Unionist[126]

Wolfgang Chr. Fischer

Robert Fischer * 22 August 1883 in *Lüdenscheid*; missing in 1945 in Königsberg was a German unionist and social democratic politician *(Social Democratic Party of Germany)*

Robert Fischer

After an elementary education he completed an apprenticeship as metal processer and pursued this trade until 1906. From 1906 to 1911 he was the chief executive officer of the regional branch of the *Metalworkers Union* (*Deutscher Metallarbeiterverband)* in *Lüdenscheid.* In this time he was also a worker's secretary and agitation leader of the *Social Democratic Party of Germany (SPD)* in Lüdenscheid. From 1911 to 1919 he was chief executive officer of the

126 http://en.wikipedia.org/wiki/Robert_Fischer_(Unionist)

Metalworkers Union in *Bremerhaven* and on the board of directors of the local Consumers' Co-operative from 1914 onwards. In 1919 he was again chief executive officer of the regional branch of the Metalworkers Union in Lüdenscheid and officially to 20th July, 1925 member of the *City Council Lüdenscheid.* An uncompleted strike in November, 1923 was regarded as a failure by Robert Fischer and as an internal union consequence he gave up his post in Lüdenscheid. Then *Robert Fischer* became a managing director of the Metalworkers Union in *Elbing* at the Baltic Sea. He was later director of the *State Employment Agency (Arbeitsamt) in Königsberg,* until he was relieved of his office in 1933 by the *National Socialist German Workers Party (NSDAP).*

Robert Fischer represented the social democratic politicians and activists of the trade-unionism, who abolished the *German Imperial Monarchy (Deutsches Kaiserreich)* and established the first parliamentarian German Republic, known as the Weimar Republic or officially as Deutsches Reich. Robert Fischer was a victim of the *Nazi's terrorism* in his professional life and most likely the Nazi Regime was responsible for his death in 1945 *(http://en.wikipedia.org/wiki/Robert_Fischer_(Unionist).*

Also he was a journalist for the party and union press; he contributed some articles to the newspaper *"Volksstimme"* published in *Mannheim* / Germany *(see Appendix 4).*

3. Kurt Krausbeck (1907-1981) Journalist[127]

Erich Krausbeck

My father *Kurt Krausbeck* was born in 1907 on the 2nd of February. As he liked to suggest all his life, slightly tongue-in-cheek, they were the "good old days". But the times were not as good any longer, because our side of the Krausbeck family was already impoverished. The hotel director Franz Krausbeck from the Empress Elisabeth Hotel in *Baden-Baden* received 10,000 gold marks from his parents for the wedding, and his bride Eugenie contributed the same amount as her dowry. The young couple bought the Café Sorrento in Lichententaler Avenue in *Baden-Baden.*

Kurt Krausbeck

[127] Arendt, Hanna, Eichmann in Jerusalem, 2. Aufl. 2007, München.
Fontaine, André, Le Camp d`Étrangers Des Milles 1939-1943, Aix-en-Provence 1989.
Reimer, Achim, Stadt zwischen zwei Demokratien, Baden-Baden von 1930 bis 1950, München 2005. Röhm, Eberhard und Thierfelder, Jörg, Juden-Christen-Deutsche Bd. 4/II 1941-1945 Stuttgart 2007.Urteil des Sondergerichts Mannheim vom 10.7.1936, Az.: SO Kms 6/36.

The massive bankruptcy by the family led *Kurt Krausbeck* back to the café because of mismanagement. The hotel continued to be managed by Franz Krausbeck's siblings. Franz and his son Emil were killed in action in Belgium on the same day in the First World War. Despite this Kurt was still able to go to secondary school in *Baden-Baden*. In 1922 he began a bookseller's apprenticeship. At the same time he attended senior level classes at a commercial school. In addition, he took acting lessons because he wanted to go on stage. As his ultimate aim was to be a playwright, he trained at the Baden-Baden Theatre in 1928. At the same time he wrote lighthearted feature articles for various newspapers. From the first of January 1930 onwards he wrote political articles for the *SPD* newspaper *'Das Freie Wort'*. In 1932 he was asked to join the editorial staff of the paper in Berlin. On the first of January 1933 he joined "*Vorwaerts*" as a journalist, where he was active until the National Socialist upheaval. He was on the editorial team as an expert on defence matters and the Labour Service (Arbeitsdienst).

His boss was *Ernst Heilman*. Heilman was a Federal Member of Parliament (Reichstagabgeordeter), party leader of the SPD in the Prussian House of Representatives (Preussischer Landtag) and editor-in-chief of "Vorwaerts". A friendly relationship existed with the young trainee Kurt Krausbeck. Kurt named his first daughter Eva after Heilman's daughter. Ernst Heilman was arrested, as was Kurt Krausbeck, by the Berlin police on the night of the Reichstag fire. Heilman was taken to the Esterwegen concentration camp, but he did not survive. The cabaret artist Werner Finck was later taken to the same concentration camp. Incidentally, Carl von Ossietzky was there as well. The inmates sang "We are the Peat Bog Soldiers" which came straight from the socialist song book.

Werner Fink wrote in his autobiography: "Old Fool, What Now?": "One night we were forcibly pulled from our sleep, forced on to the camp road and made to crawl - along the full length of the hut". They were particularly focused on me. Whenever I wanted to lift my head they shouted: "Stay down, you swine!" and pushed my head back into the dirt again. Until I lifted my head during a break to get some air and then I heard one of the guards call out: "Hey, it's not even Heilman" They had confused me with the hated social democratic Federal Member of Parliament *Ernst Heilman*, who occupied the same hut. The most senior inmate of our barracks was the social democrat *Ernst Leber*".

The wife of *Ernst Heilman* was allowed to visit her husband once in the *concentration camp* before he was murdered. Later this traumatised woman was to arrive at Baden-Baden by train to visit Kurt Krausbeck's mother, *Eugenie Krausbeck*, who had suffered from persecution by the *National Socialists* herself. The security police had forbidden her on the life of her children to talk about the visit to the concentration camp. However, she trusted Mother Krausbeck and unburdened her tormented sole. The *SS* had cut off Ernst Heilman's ears.

Kurt Krausbeck was released after a brief detention because of the *Reichstag fire* and returned to Baden-Baden to his mother, where he was active as a writer of fiction. He reported to the judges of the *Special Court* in July 1936 that his novel was close to completion and he hoped that it would be published soon.

Kurt became a member of the SPD in 1924. He founded the *Socialist Working Youth* (Sozialistische Arbeitsjugend) of Baden-Baden in 1925. The organisation was dissolved in 1926 and was set up again by Kurt and a Dr Weissmann in 1929. In 1930 he became the administrator of the SPD library in Baden-Baden. In 1931 he was the second secretary of the SPD's local branch. He appeared 3 times as an opposing speaker in National Socialist meetings in 1930 and this was noted critically by the police.

With the start of the *Third Reich*, he was unemployed once again in *Berlin,* because Social Democratic newspapers were forbidden. He returned to *Baden-Baden.* On the second of July 1934 he refused to greet the conductor Heinrich Pfahl with the *"German greeting"*. He was sentenced to 10 days in jail under public nuisance legislation. During the proceedings it came out that the secret state police were aware that Kurt had said to his "motherly girlfriend" (he liked to express himself like that): "If both your louts (meant were the woman's two sons, who belonged to the *Hitler Youth*) greet me one more time with Heil Hitler, then they'll have to suffer the consequences". In the criminal proceedings in July 1936 the defendant testified that previously the boys had not greeted him at all, but once he'd broken off his intimate relationship with their mother, they had only used the "German greeting" in order to provoke him.

According to police officer Schoener, the Baden-Baden police had secretly been made aware, and from different sources, that Kurt Krausbeck had referred to the German state in a derogatory and mischievous way. Kurt had testified during his first police interrogation that he considered the social democratic ideas to be the only correct ones. During the second interrogation he said that he could not support the Third Reich as long as his leaders (by which he meant *Heilmann, Leber* and others) were still in the concentration camp. The police officer from Baden-Baden told the court, that in his opinion the defendant was still at the time in 1936 an entrenched and incorrigible social democrat.

The *Third Reich* period is difficult to comprehend for those born afterwards. The best way to reconstruct it is through documents, which stem from that period. The judgement (file number: SO Kms 6/36) of the Special Court on behalf of the *Higher Court of the District of Karlsruhe* in Mannheim at the sitting on the 10th of May, 1936 states that County Court Director *Mickel* sentenced the defendant *Kurt Krausbeck* to six months imprisonment. Kurt had claimed in a conversation with a stranger at the terrace café in the old castle in Baden-Baden, that the revenue from disability insurance was proof that the unemployment level had not gone down to the same extent as claimed by the government. The secret state police (*Gestapo*) in Baden discovered that Krausbeck had claimed "Peace in Germany is not as it seems, because one has to consider that exactly one year and one month ago, 73 people (Roehm and SA) were executed. Such an event would not have occurred in a country that was controlled by parliament". Furthermore, Krausbeck maintained that he had got the impression from the editorials in the Frankfurter Allgemeine that the stability of the Reichsmark had not improved in comparison to other currencies. It is remarkable that the police, as was mentioned in the judgement, had previously received various tip-offs. Today it is known that the *Secret State Police (Gestapo)* for their part had no need to carry out extensive investigations, because there was no shortage of people who were prepared to become informers. The private conversation too, at the terrace café in the old castle and which was the reason for the trial in Mannheim, resulted in the denunciation and led to the arrest of the intellectual. A keen citizen was not worried about the expense and effort required to call the *Secret State Police* from the telephone in the café, in order to inform the police down in Baden-Baden about Krausbeck's divergent point of view. The arrest took place on the way home from the old castle to *Baden-Baden,* where Kurt was on his way by foot with his fiancée Grete. A *Gestapo* car drove towards them from town and two criminal police officers got out. "Are you Kurt Krausbeck?" was how they greeted him and Grete would never forget this. The arrest was made by two criminal police officers from the Gestapo, during which Kurt Krausbeck's nose was broken by a policeman whilst collecting his personal details. Grete remained behind on her own.

It is clear from this trial that there was a broad readiness by the police to deal with fellow citizens, who did not join the new National Socialist way of thinking. It is remarkable that a private verbal communication, critisising the government, had resulted in a six months jail sentence. Furthermore, the content of this communication turned out to be accurate after all. It is to be assumed as well, that the informers, and in this court case there were several people, who independent of each other, assuredly knew that the concentration camps existed and that this twenty-four year young man would be severely punished following the denunciation. This of course gives the informers a feeling of power. The denunciation and the willingness by the police officer to break a nose whilst collecting personal details, was not ordered by Adolf Hitler on any level. Such an order would not have been necessary. The informers would not have been disadvantaged had they not telephoned the police or not provided any confidential tip-offs. Confidential apparently meant that the informers had confidence in the discretion of the police. And the police officer from the criminal police would have not been concerned about a disadvantage to himself either, should he not have struck the journalist during his arrest. There were no orders to be followed in this case, nor any need for self-defence. It was simply the need by a contemporary to dispense justice to the incorrigible social democrat, as was stated in the judgement, and the dubious need by the officer to give credibility to his words.

One thing has to be said in retrospect, even if the participants have all passed away since, and that is that the defendant Kurt Krausbeck's statement was correct. The Third Reich was in fact broke by 1939 and this was noted then by Minister *Joseph Goebbels* in his diaries. Full employment was evidently not supported by a growth in the economy or by a stable economic policy. Full employment was an illusion. The President of the Reich's Reserve Bank, Dr. *Hjalmar Schacht*, stepped down from his position as the Reich's Minister of Economics, because he was unable to prevent the "suppressed" inflation by the Third Reich. Kurt Krausbeck could validate the accuracy of his theory when comparing prices of internationally traded goods, following his escape abroad. The price of a typewriter was his favourite quoted example of the National Socialist government's hidden and desolate economic policy. A typewriter was considerably cheaper in Belgium than in Germany. Foreign exchange control, however, prevented the establishment of a true exchange rate for the mark in line with market conditions. The Nazi government tried to conceal the true inflation level by reducing the supply of money, for example compulsory saving for a VW and by other means. The national debt of the German Reich led to the first serious financial crisis in 1939. The bill was finally paid by the Germans with the currency reform in 1948.

Certainly *Hitler* had with the passing of his ordinance, which introduced the concept of maliciousness and outlawed the Social Democratic party, made this sentence possible. But this case obviously demonstrates that *Adolf Hitler* did not operate in a vacuum and instead that his intentions had fallen on fertile ground and were neither ignored nor boycotted. In addition, it is remarkable that the three judges, the presiding Local Court judge *Mickel* and both Local Court judges *de Millas* and *Dr Gerard*, had as educated and qualified lawyers endorsed the correctness of this sentence. Incidentally this sentence has up to this day not been quashed! Kurt Krausbeck was in the end extremely happy to serve his prison sentence at the Baden-Baden jail and not to be sent after a possible acquittal to the so-called protective custody of a concentration camp. Incidentally, in 1955 the defendant was recognised and greeted by the former Gestapo officer, who was beaming with delight, in the Fress Lane in Baden-Baden. Baden-Baden is a small town and one knows each other. One can run, but one can't hide. Kurt Krausbeck was sentenced to six months imprisonment by the Special Court of Mannheim. The three months during which he was on remand in Baden-Baden were taken into account. During his trial he sat in prison and the court was being built behind the northern wing of the castle. It was possible to go by foot through the castle to the ice rink. The remand prison stood right up to the sixties to the right of the footpath. Kurt was moved by prisoner transport, which took the prisoners in batches from prison to prison, back to Baden-Baden after the trial. In prison he had to be taught to play skat by his cell inmates, but he never played it again. He mentioned when talking about his time in prison that the guards were without exception always civil. They were Justice Department employees, who carried out their occupation unchanged. For his marriage to *Grete Braun*, who was highly pregnant with little Eva, he was given one day's prison leave. Prior to this the bride and groom had to provide proof of Aryan ancestry. The visits on the other days took place when Grete walked along the street on the side of the hill, and she could be seen from the cell. This prison proved to be not worth maintaining and it was replaced by a new building halfway through the forties. The new prison was completed by the end of the war, in time for the Nazis to be imprisoned in their own new building.

Evidently the floor of his cell and Germany became too hot for Kurt Krausbeck. He could expect the police to collect him from the prison gates after his prison sentence and deliver him as an "incorrigible social democrat" to a *concentration camp*. Kurt decided to break out of prison and simulated pain on the right lower side of this stomach. The surgeons at the Baden-Baden's city hospital removed his intact appendix. In those days it was usual to spend two weeks in hospital with such a procedure. Kurt Krausbeck managed to sneak out of the hospital and went to his family on the mountain. His sister *Elisabet* had to withdraw her savings from the bank, in order to make his escape possible. Kurt Krausbeck escaped to Switzerland. He then went to Brussels via Spain. The reason for the move to Spain was to support the fight of the International Brigade against the fascists. The communists, however, did not let him join up as a soldier of the International Brigade, because he was a democrat. The *Spanish Stalinists* demanded that he acknowledge their leadership in order to be allowed to fight with them. Kurt went to Brussels. He was given political asylum there. The police did not give up and continued to look for him. Grete was invited to the police station and they questioned her about Kurt Krausbeck's address. Even later in *Brussels*, the secret state police appeared at Grete Krausbeck's apartment. Even little Eva Krausbeck was questioned by the German police about her father's place of abode, as she played with other children in front of their apartment in Brussels. In those days in free Europe a sophisticated relationship existed with refugees. Refugees were given a residence permit and a work permit too. Kurt met up with other émigrés in *Brussels*. For example, a fellow *émigré,* occupied himself by searching for death notices in German newspapers, so that he could provide data on war casualties to the allies. Kurt gave German lessons and Grete did some housekeeping work. The Belgium employers took on the émigrés and their children. They had a small chemist shop on the Rue de la Violette on the Grande Palace of Belgium. With the attack on Belgium by Germany Kurt Krausbeck had to flee once again. He knew that the security policy would not be far behind the German armed forces.

Kurt fled to France and then further on to the South of France. In France the German *émigrés* were interned. He found himself in the *Les Milles camp* near *Aix-en-Provence.* He shared his fate with many in the camp, amongst them prominent German refugees. *Walter Benjamin, Lion Feuchtwanger and Walter Hasen* (committed suicide at Les Milles on the 5th of August, 1940) were at Le Milles in 1940. Kurt Krausbeck joined the protestant émigré congregation. The camp inmates who belonged to the congregation were permitted to attend *Vicar Manon's* church service every Sunday. The journalist Hans Fraenkel organised ecumenical meetings with the Jews. Kurt was once approached by an old rabbi and asked if he could help. He was taken by the rabbi to a grotto. There he was told to light the candle. With this action he became as a Non-Jew a "Schabbesgoi". When he lit the candle he saw many men in the grotto, who had gathered on a Friday evening after sunset for their service. He was given as a Schabbesgoi an egg as his fee.

The Vicar Manon hid and saved 350 Jewish children from deportation. He cared for the helpless adults after the departure of their children. He managed to accommodate émigrés in French homes. The journalist Krausbeck was hidden in the hills of Pinchinats, east of Aix. But he was captured and sent to the *Gurs camp* in 1943, at the foot of the Pyrenees. The Jewish internees, who were selected for deportation to Auschwitz were taken in several trains on the 11th and 13th of August 1942. From Les Milles 1511 prisoners were deported to Auschwitz. Pastor Manon intervened to the *French Vichy government* on behalf of the internees once again and some prisoners were allowed to leave the train during a stop in Lyon. The French police prefect made difficulties for Manon, because of his intervention on behalf of the condemned prisoners and because he had once called out to them: "You will one day be held responsible for your crime before God".

After the war *Kurt Krausbeck* got in touch with *Alfred Doeblin*, who had been in the Gurs camp in 1940. The situation for the internees in the South of France was not without its problems. No one knew if they would survive this period. Many fled across the Pyrenees to the then neutral Spain. Franco was not averse to letting German intellectuals and anti-fascists cross Spain to neutral havens and to the "Night in Lisbon". The situation changed in the Gurs camp once the deportations of Jewish sections of the population in Germany started. In the autumn of 1940 the Badisch police, in this case the safety police ("Schupp"), arrested all Jews in Baden and Saarpfalz, around 7500 men, women and children and transported them as a first-time deportation project to France. However, this was not foreseen in the truce that was signed with France. For this reason, Adolf Eichmann from the SS, as the organiser of the deportation, accompanied the police to the French border, in order to convince the French station supervisor that it was a "German military transport". In France the matter was handled more satisfactorily from the German point of view: as reported by the former inmate *Hannah Arendt,* the *Vichy government* hid the new "refugees" without further ado in the notorious Gurs concentration camp at the foot of the Pyrenees. It was only later that the next deportation trains were to travel to the east, to Poland and to Latvia. In Germany the uniformed police (Ordnungspolizei) guarded the trains and provided the appropriate escort service. In the east the safety police stood by at the destination stations, in order to receive the trains and to hand over its occupants to the extermination camp authorities. Eventually this became the fate of the Badisch Jews from Gurs, when they were deported further by the French police to Auschwitz.

As Kurt Krausbeck could not immigrate to America, he did not want to abandon his family; he remained in the South of France and managed to get a job in the kitchen at *Gurs*. The camp was notorious as a starvation camp. The new cook of the usual soups, which were made from chick-peas and water, noticed when he started his job that large amounts of the inmates' meat ration went missing. He asked the workers about this, but they referred him nervously to the Red Cross nurse, who had in the meantime become somewhat suspicious. Kurt then looked in the eyes of the nurse and it became clear to him that she was unable to stop the embezzlement of the life-saving meat rations. The nurses' face was very serious. She equipped the black market with the stolen supplies. The amount that was taken by the Red Cross employee consisted roughly of 50% of the camp's meat supplies. Finally the camp was dissolved. Kurt Krausbeck needed a new position In the meantime he had taken on a false identity. He found employment with the Organisation Todt, which was building the Atlantic wall. He was working in the office. A good many people had managed to find their way to *Organisation Todt*. *Todt* and later *Albert Speer* needed the workers urgently, so that the Gestapo did not put a lot of effort into thinning out the number of workers. Until the liberation by the allies, Kurt Krausbeck lived with an assumed name in France. He was then interned in England.

In February 1946 the SPD of Baden-Baden was reformed. As was documented, Haebler, Schneider and the journalist *Kurt Krausbeck* were the most prominent foundation members. The SPD party in the new Baden-Baden city council was led by the journalist Kurt Krausbeck.

Appendices

Appendix 1:

Draft of a law about the revaluation of mortgages and other claims 1925
Attachment 1: Economic reason for the conversion relation to the gold mark calculation; Explanations of the method of computation for the revaluation numbers in appendix 1 to the law

Appendix 2:

Law about the Revaluation of Mortgages and other Claims, issued the 16th of July, 1925 (Aufwertungsgesetz vom 16. Juli 1925)
Conversion rates (Umrechnungstabelle)

Appendix 3:

Reichsgericht Leipzig, V. Zivilsenat, Urteil vom 4. November 1925, RGZ III, 320 ff

Appendix 4:

Robert Fischer: Meine ersten Eindrücke in Bremerhaven

Appendix 5:

Selected Articles of the German Constitution of the 11th of August 1919

Appendix 6:

Complexity Economics Comparison with Traditional Economics

Appendix 7:

Examples of Hyperinflation

Appendix 1

Draft of a law about the revaluation of mortgages and other claims 1925
Attachment 1: Economic reason for the conversion relation to the gold mark calculation; Explanations of the method of computation for the revaluation numbers in appendix 1 to the law

Entwurf eines Gesetzes ueber die Aufwertung von Hypotheken und anderen Anspruechen (Aufwertungsgesetz)
Der Reichsminister der Justiz, Dr. Frenken, III a 2536
Reichstag, III. Wahlperiode 1924/25
Drucksachen des Reichstages Nr. 804

Anlage 1: Wirtschaftliche Begruendung fuer das Umrechnungsverhaeltnis zur Goldmarkberechnung; Erlaeuterungen des Berechnungsverfahrens fuer die Aufwertungszahlen in Anlage 1 zum Gesetz

Wirtschaftliche Begründung für das Umrechnungsverhältnis zur Goldmarkberechnung.

Zur Wahl des Index, nach dem aufgewertet werden soll, wird von Gläubigerseite der Gedanke vertreten, daß eine Aufwertung der in den Inflationsjahren entstandenen Ansprüche nach dem Goldwert beziehungsweise nach dem Dollarkurs insofern unbillig sei, als das Geld in dieser Zeit in der inneren deutschen Wirtschaft eine wesentlich *höhere Kaufkraft* gehabt habe, als der Goldwert ergebe. Dies ist im allgemeinen richtig; seit 1919 sind die Preise in Deutschland gegenüber dem Friedensstand in der Regel nicht unerheblich niedriger gewesen, als sie nach dem Dollarkurse hätten sein können. Die innere Markentwertung kam zeitlich gewissermaßen immer erst mit einiger Verspätung auf dem vom Dollarkurs erreichten Stande an. Dies gilt in erster Linie von den Kleinhandelspreisen, wie sie sich im *Lebenshaltungsindex* darstellen, wobei zu beachten ist, daß die zwangsmäßig niedrig gehaltenen Mieten, die zunächst noch beibehaltene Zwangswirtschaft auf manchen Lebensmittelgebieten, ferner die Preistreibereigesetzgebung sowie die Außenhandelskontrolle starke Hemmnisse gegenüber dem an sich vorhandenen Drange nach Angleichung an den Goldwert bildeten. Ein geringeres Zurückbleiben hinter den Dollarkurs wies der *Großhandelsindex* auf, bei dem die großen Massengüter, insbesondere soweit sie aus dem Ausland stammten, eine raschere Angleichung an den Dollar herbeiführten, trotzdem auch hier die Preise der landwirtschaftlichen Erzeugnisse eine hemmende Wirkung ausübten.

Es ergibt sich zunächst die Frage, ob etwa der *Lebenshaltungsindex* zur Berechnung der Aufwertung herangezogen werden kann. Das ist zu verneinen. Von der Seite des Kapital ausleihenden Gläubigers aus betrachtet, müßte man unterstellen, daß der *Gläubiger*, wenn er sein Kapital nicht ausgeliehen hätte, es zu Käufen von Kleinhandelswaren verwandt hätte. Er hätte dies entweder zu Zwecken der *Konsumtion* oder zu Zwecken der *Kapitalanlage* tun können. Ersteres kommt praktisch nicht in Betracht, da der Konsumtion natürliche Grenzen gezogen sind, und jemand, der Kapital anlegt, damit gerade kundgibt, daß er seine Konsumtion nicht zu steigern wünscht. Ein Ankauf von Konsumgütern zur Kapitalanlage aber kann erst recht hier nicht in Betracht gezogen werden; das wäre unwirtschaftliche Spekulation gewesen, die dem Konsum notwendige Güter entzogen, preistreibend gewirkt und gegebenenfalls auch gegen die Preistreibereigesetzgebung verstoßen hätte. Auch die objektive Möglichkeit zur Anhäufung von Kleinhandelswaren als Kapital war begrenzt; wäre sie stärker erfolgt, so wären die Preise und damit der Lebenshaltungsindex in nicht abzuschätzendem Maße gestiegen.

Noch augenfälliger wird, von der *Schuldnerseite* aus gesehen, die Unmöglichkeit, den Lebenshaltungsindex zugrunde zu legen. Eine Kreditaufnahme kann nur in wenigen Ausnahmefällen zum Zwecke der Konsumtion erfolgt sein; bei solchen Zwecken ist der Kredit gefährdet, und der Gläubiger würde ihn bei Kenntnis dieser Anwendungsabsicht nicht bewilligt haben. In der Regel haben die Kreditnehmer Geld zum Zwecke des Betriebs eines Unternehmens aufgenommen. Für solche Anlagen aber kommen regelmäßig nur Erwerbungen auf Grund des Großhandels- oder des Dollarindexes in Betracht. Wenn aber der Schuldner aus dem Kredit Nutzungen nicht ziehen konnte, die auf der Basis des Lebenshaltungsindexes beruhen, und dies auch der Gläubiger nicht von ihm erwarten durfte, so erscheint es nicht vertretbar und unwirtschaftlich, gewissermaßen rückwärts die Möglichkeit des Mehrverzehrs nach dem Lebenshaltungsindex gegen ihn zu verwerten; die Möglichkeit einer Kapitalanlage gemäß dem Lebenshaltungsindex aber schaltet aus gleichen Gründen aus, wie sie oben für den Gläubiger dargelegt sind.

Man kann auch nicht von der für den Gläubiger günstigen Kapitalanlage in *Aktien* oder *Grundstücken* als Normalfall ausgehen; denn abgesehen davon, daß es für Grundstücke keinen Index für jene Zeit gibt, besteht doch eben die Tatsache, daß auch von der Anlagemöglichkeit in Papiermarkwerten in größtem Umfang Gebrauch gemacht worden ist. Diese kann daher bei dem Finden einer billigen mittleren Grundlage keineswegs ausgeschaltet werden; hierdurch würde aber die Berücksichtigung von Aktien und Grundstücken wieder aufgewogen werden. Weiter aber kommt in Betracht, daß man bei Berücksichtigung von Aktien- und Grundstückswerten den Schuldner so behandeln würde, als ob er derartige Werte erworben hätte, während er doch in der Regel den Kredit zum Weiterbetrieb eines Unternehmens verwendet hat. Da die Aufwertung gegenüber dem damals geltenden Rechte, Mark = Mark ein weitergehendes Recht neu schaffen soll, muß dieses neue Recht notwendig seine Grenze da finden, wo es für den Neubelasteten (Schuldner) nicht mehr in Einklang steht mit der damals für ihn praktisch gegebenen Verwertungsmöglichkeit des Geldes. Wie weit man in der Belastung überhaupt gehen will, ist eine Frage des Aufwertungssatzes; es darf jedoch nicht im Interesse der Gläubiger eine wirtschaftlich nicht tragbare Rechnungsgrundlage gewählt werden.

Es bleiben nach allem zur Berechnung nur der *Großhandels- und der Dollarindex* übrig. Es erschien angezeigt, das Mittel daraus zu wählen. Wenngleich dies für diejenigen Schuldner, die lediglich Einfuhrwaren handelten, die sich nach Dollar richteten, eine Gefahr bedeuten könnte, so kann doch davon ausgegangen werden, daß auch diese Schuldner für Löhne und Gehälter Aufwendungen haben machen müssen, die sich nach einem unter dem Dollarwerte liegenden Maßstab berechnen. Wenn gegen jede Berücksichtigung der inneren Kaufkraft der Einwand erhoben wird, daß derjenige, der ein Nominaldarlehen gegeben hat, dann besser führe, wie derjenige, der einen wertbeständigen Betrag in Gold oder Dollar wirklich vereinbart habe, so ist dieser Einwand grundsätzlich jedenfalls berechtigt; er kann aber beiseite gelassen werden im Hinblick darauf, daß bei der hier gewählten Berechnung die Abweichung vom Dollarindex keine besonders starke ist (vgl. Unteranlage 1b) und daß ja überhaupt der Goldwert nur zu einem Bruchteil wiederhergestellt werden soll.

In denjenigen Zeitabschnitten, in denen infolge Rückganges des Dollars im Jahre 1920 oder Übersteigerung der Inlandspreise in der zweiten Hälfte 1923 der Großhandelsindex über dem Dollarindex lag, ist der reine Dollarindex zugrunde gelegt worden, da die Berücksichtigung des Großhandelsindexes nur im Gläubigerinteresse erfolgen soll und man auch dem Schuldner — vorbehaltlich des Prozentsatzes der Aufwertung — grundsätzlich wird zumuten können, den Goldwert des Empfangenen zugrunde zu legen. Wenn der Schuldner damals nach dem Großhandelsindex Güter erworben hat, so hat er eben teuer eingekauft, ebenso wie er in der Gegenwert 40 bis 50 v. H. über dem Friedensgoldwert einkaufen muß. Eine Berücksichtigung dieser Steigerungen würde vom Prinzip der festen Goldwährung abführen zu einer Indexwährung, welche in der Literatur (Irving Fisher, Keynes) zwar vereinzelt befürwortet, aber keineswegs irgendwo bisher zur praktischen Anwendung gekommen ist.

In der Anlage zum Gesetz ist die Meßzahl wiedergegeben, durch die der Nominalbetrag des Anspruchs zu dividieren ist, um den neuen Goldmarkbetrag zu ergeben. Die Unteranlagen 1 und 2 zur Erläuterung erläutern die Art der Berechnung dieser Meßzahl und geben in den letzten Spalten Zahlen, welche die Umrechnung praktisch erleichtern, indem der neue Goldwert für je 1 000 ℳ bzw. 1 Million Mark hingegebenen Kapitals berechnet wird.

Unteranlage 1
zur Erläuterung

Erläuterung des Berechnungsverfahrens für die Aufwertungszahlen in Anlage 1 zum Gesetz

(hierzu heranzuziehen die Zahlen in Unteranlage 2)

I

Die Aufwertungsmeßzahl ergibt sich im allgemeinen aus dem arithmetischen Durchschnitt zwischen Dollarindex (= der jeweilige Dollarkurs dividiert durch die Vorkriegsparität) und Großhandelsindex (1913 = 1 gesetzt); nur in den Fällen, in denen der Großhandelsindex den Dollarindex übersteigt, stellt der Dollarindex allein die Aufwertungsmeßzahl dar. Bei den Zahlenreihen in dieser Anlage ist in letzteren Fällen die Zahl des Mittelindexes eingeklammert und die statt dessen für die Meßzahl zugrunde gelegte Dollarindexzahl unterstrichen.

Die Aufwertungsmeßzahlen wurden für den Zeitraum vom Januar 1918 bis November 1923 berechnet, und zwar:

von Januar 1918 bis einschließlich Dezember 1919 in Zahlen für je einen oder mehrere Monate,

von Januar 1920 bis einschließlich Mai 1923 in Zahlen für je ein Monatsdrittel (Dekade),

von Juni 1923 bis einschließlich November 1923 in täglichen Zahlen.

Bei den täglichen Berechnungen sind die Sonnabende und Sonntage ausgelassen, da hier keine Notierungen stattfanden. Gemäß der Bestimmung im Gesetz ist für diese die Meßzahl des letztvorhergehenden Tages maßgebend.

II

Dem Dollarindex vom Januar 1918 bis Dezember 1919 wurden die in § 2 Abs. 2 der ersten Verordnung zur Durchführung des Artikels I der Dritten Steuernotverordnung vom 1. Mai 1924 (Reichsgesetzbl. I S. 430) festgesetzten Dollarkurse zugrunde gelegt.

Die Berechnung der Dollarmeßziffern vom Februar 1920 bis Mai 1923 erfolgte durch Mittelung aus den in jede der Dekaden fallenden amtlichen Mittelkurse des nordamerikanischen Dollars an der Berliner Börse. Nur für den Januar 1920, in dem der Dollar in Berlin amtlich nicht notiert wurde, mußte auf Umrechnungen, wie sie von der »Frankfurter Zeitung« vorgenommen worden sind, zurückgegriffen werden.

In dem letzten Zeitabschnitte (vom Juni 1923 ab), der tägliche Meßzahlen vorsieht, wurde jeweilig die auf den betreffenden Stichtag fallende Dollartagesnotierung und die beiden nächstfolgenden gemittelt.

III

Für die zu den Berechnungen erforderlichen G r o ß h a n d e l s m e ß z i f f e r n mußte dort, wo die Notierung nicht den für die Aufwertungsmeßzahlen gewählten, durchweg kürzeren Zeitabschnitten entsprach, zu Interpolationen gegriffen werden. Diese erfolgten in nachstehender Weise:

Für die Zeitpunkte, von denen Großhandelsziffern vorlagen (»Feststellungstermin«), wurde das Verhältnis dieser Indexziffern zu dem entsprechenden Dollarindex durch Division ermittelt. Für die weitere Berechnung wurde dann von der Annahme ausgegangen, daß sich das Verhältnis zwischen Dollar und Großhandelsindex von dem einen zu dem nächsten Feststellungstermin in gleichmäßiger Entwicklung verändert habe. Dadurch wurde es ermöglicht, die zwischen den Feststellungsterminen liegenden, noch fehlenden Großhandelsindexziffern zu bestimmen, da für diese Zeitpunkte der Dollarindex einerseits und das (angenommene) Verhältnis zwischen Dollar und Großhandelsindex anderseits bekannt war. Die auf diese Weise gewonnenen Großhandelsindexziffern erfuhren in der Richtung noch eine Veränderung, als sie in ihrem arithmetischen Mittel mit dem für jeden Monat berechneten Monatsdurchschnitt der Großhandelsindexziffer in Übereinstimmung gebracht wurden. Daraus erklärt sich, daß die nach dieser Methode berechneten Großhandelsmeßziffern in ihren Stichtagsergebnissen von den amtlichen Veröffentlichungen abweichen, in ihren Monatsdurchschnitten sich aber mit diesen decken.

IV

Um die Anwendung der Aufwertungszahlen einfach zu gestalten, sind die Papiermarkwerte für die in I angegebenen Zeitabschnitte in Goldmark umgerechnet. Hierbei sind die Papiermarkbeträge in vollen 10. 100, 1000 usf. stets so angesetzt, daß die Goldmarkbeträge zwischen 1 und 10 liegen. Die Goldmarkbeträge selbst sind auf volle Pfennige abgerundet (d. h. Beträge unter $^1/_2$ Pfennig fortgelassen, Beträge von $^1/_2$ Pfennig und darüber vollgerechnet). Wenn beispielsweise in der Zeit vom 21. bis 31. Oktober 1920 die Aufwertungsmeßzahl (Mittelindex) 16,08 betrug, so ist 1 Papiermark = $^1/_{16,08}$ = 0,06219 *Gℳ*, oder es sind 100 Papiermark = 6,22 *Gℳ* zu setzen.

5*

— 20 —

Unteranlage 2

zur Erläuterung

Zeit	Dollarindex	Großhandelsindex	Mittelindex	Wert von 1000 Mark nach Dollarindex	Wert von 1000 Mark nach Mittelindex	Unterschied in Prozent
1918						
Januar—Juni	**1,25**	2,03	(1,64)	**800**	(610)	—
Juli	**1,40**	2,08	(1,74)	**714**	(575)	—
August	**1,45**	2,35	(1,90)	**690**	(526)	—
September und Oktober	**1,55**	2,32	(1,94)	**645**	(515)	—
November	**1,75**	2,34	(2,05)	**571**	(488)	—
Dezember	**2,00**	2,45	(2,23)	**500**	(448)	—
1919						
Januar	**1,95**	2,62	(2,29)	**513**	(437)	—
Februar	**2,15**	2,70	(2,43)	**465**	(412)	—
März	**2,50**	2,74	(2,62)	**400**	(382)	—
April	3,00	2,86	2,93	333	341	+ 2,4
Mai	3,05	2,97	3,01	328	332	+ 1,2
Juni	3,35	3,08	3,22	299	311	+ 4,0
Juli	3,60	3,39	3,50	278	286	+ 2,9
August	4,50	4,22	4,36	222	229	+ 3,2
September	5,70	4,93	5,32	175	188	+ 7,4
Oktober	6,40	5,62	6,01	156	166	+ 6,4
November	9,10	6,78	7,94	110	126	+ 14,5
Dezember	11,15	8,03	9,59	90	104	+ 15,6
1920						
Januar 1.—10.	11,94	9,73	10,34	83,75	96,71	+ 15,5
11.—20.	13,58	12,21	12,90	73,64	77,52	+ 5,3
21.—31.	18,97	15,73	17,35	52,71	57,64	+ 9,4
Februar 1.—10.	23,60	17,20	20,40	42,37	49,02	+ 13,0
11.—20.	23,77	15,72	19,75	42,07	50,63	+ 20,3
21.—29.	23,55	17,63	20,59	42,46	48,57	+ 14,4
März 1.—10.	22,49	18,58	20,54	44,46	48,69	+ 9,5
11.—20.	16,91	15,78	16,35	59,14	61,16	+ 3,4
21.—31.	17,64	16,91	17,28	56,69	57,87	+ 2,1
April 1.—10.	**14,28**	15,11	(14,70)	**70,03**	(68,03)	—
11.—20.	**14,31**	15,53	(14,92)	**69,88**	(67,02)	—
21.—30.	**14,09**	16,37	(15,23)	**70,97**	(65,66)	—
Mai 1.—10.	**12,72**	16,54	(14,63)	**78,62**	(68,35)	—
11.—20.	**11,88**	15,71	(13,55)	**87,87**	(73,80)	—
21.—31.	**9,08**	12,99	(11,04)	**110,18**	(90,58)	—
Juni 1.—10.	**9,69**	13,68	(11,69)	**103,20**	(85,54)	—
11.—20.	**9,40**	14,20	(11,80)	**106,38**	(84,75)	—
21.—30.	**8,94**	13,57	(11,26)	**111,86**	(88,81)	—
Juli 1.—10.	**9,01**	13,32	(11,17)	**110,99**	(89,53)	—
11.—20.	**9,17**	13,62	(11,40)	**109,05**	(87,72)	—
21.—31.	**9,95**	14,08	(12,02)	**100,50**	(83,19)	—
August 1.—10.	**10,83**	14,68	(12,76)	**92,34**	(78,37)	—
11.—20.	**11,33**	14,56	(12,95)	**88,26**	(77,22)	—
21.—31.	**11,90**	14,26	(13,08)	**84,03**	(76,45)	—
September 1.—10.	**12,14**	14,12	(13,13)	**82,37**	(76,16)	—
11.—20.	**14,70**	15,75	(15,23)	**68,03**	(65,66)	—
21.—30.	**14,70**	15,09	(14,90)	**68,03**	(67,11)	—
Oktober 1.—10.	14,96	14,15	14,56	66,84	68,68	+ 2,8
11.—20.	16,46	14,86	15,66	60,75	63,86	+ 5,1
21.—31.	17,19	14,96	16,08	58,17	62,19	+ 6,9

Zeit		Dollarindex	Großhandelsindex	Mittelindex	Wert von 1000 Mark nach		
					Dollarindex	Mittelindex	Unterschied in Prozent
1920							
November	1.—10.	19,53	16,41	17,97	51,20	55,65	+ 8,7
	11.—20.	18,97	15,33	17,15	52,71	58,31	+ 10,6
	21.—30.	16,56	13,33	15,05	60,39	66,45	+ 10,0
Dezember	1.—10.	17,31	14,03	15,67	57,77	63,82	+ 10,5
	11.—20.	17,52	14,36	15,94	57,08	62,74	+ 9,9
	21.—31.	17,41	14,82	16,12	57,44	62,03	+ 8,0
1921							
Januar	1.—10.	17,47	15,57	16,52	57,24	60,53	+ 5,7
	11.—20.	15,70	14,49	15,10	63,69	66,23	+ 4,0
	21.—31.	13,89	13,11	13,50	71,99	74,07	+ 2,9
Februar	1.—10.	14,94	14,03	14,49	66,93	69,01	+ 3,1
	11.—20.	14,05	13,48	13,77	71,17	72,62	+ 2,0
	21.—28.	14,77	13,77	14,27	67,70	70,08	+ 3,5
März	1.—10.	14,87	13,65	14,26	67,25	70,13	+ 4,3
	11.—20.	14,93	13,29	14,11	66,98	70,87	+ 5,8
	21.—31.	14,89	13,21	14,05	67,16	71,17	+ 6,0
April	1.—10.	14,74	12,90	13,82	67,84	72,36	+ 6,7
	11.—20.	14,93	13,03	13,98	66,98	71,53	+ 6,8
	21.—30.	15,69	13,85	14,77	63,73	67,70	+ 6,2
Mai	1.—10.	15,68	13,86	14,77	63,78	67,70	+ 6,1
	11.—20.	14,23	12,72	13,48	70,27	74,18	+ 5,6
	21.—31.	14,67	12,65	13,66	68,17	73,21	+ 7,4
Juni	1.—10.	15,68	13,37	14,53	63,78	68,82	+ 7,9
	11.—20	16,62	13,63	15,13	60,17	66,09	+ 9,8
	21.—30.	17,30	13,98	15,64	57,80	63,94	+ 10,6
Juli	1.—10.	17,79	13,75	15,77	56,21	63,41	+ 12,8
	11.—20.	18,17	13,83	16,00	55,04	62,50	+ 13,6
	21.—31.	18,77	15,26	17,02	53,28	58,75	+ 10,3
August	1.—10	19,44	18,13	18,79	51,44	53,22	+ 3,5
	11.—20.	20,28	20,05	20,17	49,31	49,58	+ 0,5
	21.—31.	20,56	19,34	19,95	48,64	50,13	+ 3,1
September	1.—10.	22,08	19,42	20,75	45,29	48,19	+ 6,4
	11.—20.	25,31	21,06	23,19	39,51	43,12	+ 9,1
	21.—30.	27,62	21,53	24,58	36,21	40,68	+ 12,3
Oktober	1.—10.	29,46	22,04	25,75	33,94	38,83	+ 14,4
	11.—20.	36,54	25,37	30,96	27,37	32,30	+ 18,0
	21.—31.	40,63	26,39	33,51	24,61	29,84	+ 21,3
November	1.—10.	57,69	31,58	44,64	17,33	22,40	+ 29,3
	11.—20.	64,50	32,69	48,60	15,50	20,58	+ 32,8
	21.—30.	66,14	38,21	52,18	15,12	19,16	+ 26,7
Dezember	1.—10.	49,32	35,15	42,24	20,28	23,67	+ 16,7
	11.—20.	43,56	34,44	39,00	22,96	25,64	+ 11,7
	21.—31.	43,57	35,02	39,30	22,95	25,45	+ 10,9

6

Zeit		Dollarindex	Großhandelsindex	Mittelindex	Wert von 1 Million Mark nach: Dollarindex	Wert von 1 Million Mark nach: Mittelindex	Unterschied in Prozent
1922							
Januar	1.—10.	44,30	35,03	39,67	22 573	25 208	+ 11,7
	11.—20.	44,35	35,63	39,99	22 548	25 006	+ 10,9
	21.—31.	48,27	39,30	43,79	20 717	22 836	+ 10,2
Februar	1.—10.	47,85	39,28	43,57	20 899	22 952	+ 9,8
	11.—20.	48,65	40,46	44,56	20 555	22 442	+ 9,2
	21.—28.	52,61	43,35	47,98	19 008	20 842	+ 9,6
März	1.—10.	59,82	47,71	53,77	16 717	18 598	+ 11,3
	11.—20.	65,61	51,80	58,71	15 242	17 033	+ 11,8
	21.—31.	76,46	63,47	69,97	13 079	14 292	+ 9,3
April	1.—10.	73,93	65,58	69,76	13 526	14 335	+ 6,0
	11.—20.	69,18	64,24	66,71	14 455	14 990	+ 3,7
	21.—30.	64,81	60,83	62,82	15 430	15 918	+ 3,2
Mai	1.—10.	69,15	64,57	66,86	14 461	14 957	+ 3,4
	11.—20.	69,17	65,30	67,24	14 457	14 872	+ 2,9
	21.—31.	68,99	63,87	66,43	14 495	15 053	+ 3,8
Juni	1.—10.	67,49	64,07	65,78	14 817	15 202	+ 2,6
	11.—20.	75,60	70,36	72,98	13 228	13 702	+ 3,6
	21.—30.	82,74	76,48	79,61	12 086	12 561	+ 3,9
Juli	1.—10.	111,70	98,84	105,27	8 953	9 499	+ 6,1
	11.—20	110,90	95,21	103,06	9 017	9 703	+ 7,6
	21.—31.	123,58	107,72	118,15	7 777	8 464	+ 8,8
August	1.—10.	184,36	145,44	164,90	5 424	6 064	+ 11,8
	11.—20.	237,69	171,99	204,84	4 207	4 882	+ 16,0
	21.—31.	373,63	258,62	316,13	2 676	3 163	+ 18,2
September	1.—10.	323,96	277,35	300,66	3 087	3 326	+ 7,7
	11.—20.	359,17	288,50	323,84	2 784	3 088	+ 10,9
	21.—30.	361,61	295,10	328,36	2 765	3 045	+ 10,1
Oktober	1.—10.	534,41	402,73	468,57	1 871	2 134	+ 14,1
	11.—20.	686,65	525,29	605,97	1 456	1 650	+ 13,3
	21.—31.	1 028,20	770,01	899,11	973	1 112	+ 14,3
November	1.—10.	1 619,49	1 010,89	1 315,19	617	760	+ 23,2
	11.—20.	1 751,28	1 194,82	1 473,03	571	679	+ 18,9
	21.—30.	1 773,91	1 247,30	1 510,61	564	662	+ 17,4
Dezember	1.—10.	1 946,98	1 502,55	1 724,77	514	580	+ 12,8
	11.—20.	1 761,36	1 475,55	1 618,46	568	618	+ 8,8
	21.—31.	1 708,55	1 446,25	1 577,40	585	634	+ 8,4
1923							
Januar	1.—10.	2 077	1 969	2 023	481	494	+ 2,7
	11.—20.	3 692	2 512	3 102	271	322	+ 18,8
	21.—31.	6 830	3 874	5 352	146	187	+ 28,1
Februar	1.—10.	8 752	6 019	7 386	114	135	+ 18,4
	11.—20.	**5 360**	5 435	(5 398)	**187**	(185)	—
	21.—28.	5 424	5 305	5 364	184	186	+ 1,1
März	1.—10.	5 173	5 109	5 141	193	195	+ 1,0
	11.—20.	4 971	4 740	4 856	201	206	+ 2,5
	21.—31.	4 983	4 816	4 000	201	204	+ 1,5
April	1.—10.	5 030	4 865	4 958	199	202	+ 1,5
	11.—20.	5 475	4 865	5 220	183	192	+ 4,9
	21.—30.	6 917	5 787	6 332	145	157	+ 8,3
Mai	1.—10.	8 659	6 834	7 747	115	129	+ 12,2
	11.—20.	10 648	7 782	9 215	94	109	+ 16,0
	21.—31.	13 999	9 895	11 947	71	84	+ 18,3

Zeit		Dollarindex	Großhandelsindex	Mittelindex	Wert von 1 Million Mark nach		
					Dollarindex	Mittelindex	Unterschied in Prozent
1923							
Juni	1.	18 199	12 692	15 446	54,95	64,74	+ 17,8
	2.	17 226	12 111	14 669	58,05	68,17	+ 17,4
	4.	17 127	12 138	14 633	58,39	68,34	+ 17,0
	5.	17 389	12 422	14 906	57,51	67,09	+ 16,7
	6.	18 660	13 084	15 872	53,59	63,00	+ 17,6
	7.	19 215	13 219	16 217	52,04	61,66	+ 18,5
	8.	19 315	13 034	16 175	51,77	61,82	+ 19,4
	9.	19 771	13 081	16 426	50,58	60,89	+ 20,4
	11.	20 943	13 580	17 262	47,75	57,93	+ 21,3
	12.	23 106	14 679	18 893	43,28	52,93	+ 22,3
	13.	24 968	15 533	20 251	40,05	49,38	+ 23,3
	14.	26 259	15 990	21 125	38,08	47,34	+ 24,3
	15	29 435	17 536	23 486	33,97	42,58	+ 25,3
	16.	31 999	19 842	25 921	31,25	38,58	+ 23,5
	18.	33 190	21 387	27 289	30,13	36,64	+ 21,6
	19.	31 523	21 079	26 301	31,72	38,02	+ 19,9
	20	31 205	21 625	26 415	32,05	37,86	+ 18,1
	21.	30 530	21 399	26 215	32,75	38,15	+ 16,5
	22.	29 518	21 391	25 705	33,88	38,90	+ 14,8
	23.	28 724	22 000	25 362	34,81	39,43	+ 13,3
	25.	31 285	24 675	27 950	32,03	35,78	+ 11,7
	26	34 064	27 343	30 704	29,36	32,57	+ 10,9
	27.	36 327	29 513	32 970	27,53	30,35	+ 10,2
	28.	36 446	30 164	33 305	27,44	30,03	+ 9,4
	29.	37 240	31 286	34 263	26,85	29,19	+ 8,7
	30.	37 677	32 124	34 901	26,54	28,65	+ 8,0
Juli	2.	38 161	35 138	35 550	26,20	27,29	+ 4,2
	3.	38 637	36 089	37 363	25,88	26,76	+ 3,4
	4.	39 908	38 819	39 364	25,06	25,40	+ 1,4
	5.	**41 131**	41 600	(41 366)	**24,31**	(24,17)	—
	6.	**42 242**	44 267	(43 255)	**23,67**	(23,12)	—
	7.	**43 076**	45 898	(44 987)	**23,21**	(22,23)	—
	9.	**43 949**	49 549	(46 749)	**22,75**	(21,39)	—
	10.	**44 505**	51 896	(48 201)	**22,47**	(20,75)	—
	11.	**44 545**	51 110	(47 828)	**22,45**	(20,91)	—
	12.	**45 228**	51 048	(48 138)	**22,11**	(20,77)	—
	13.	**47 689**	52 935	(50 312)	**20,97**	(19,88)	—
	16.	**50 151**	54 729	(52 440)	**19,94**	(19,07)	—
	17.	**57 170**	61 320	(59 245)	**17,49**	(16,88)	—
	19.	67 651	63 759	65 705	14,78	15,22	+ 3,0
	20.	83 214	67 597	75 406	12,02	13,26	+ 10,3
	23.	121 010	82 552	101 781	8,26	9,83	+ 19,0
	24.	153 565	84 774	119 170	6,51	8,39	+ 28,9
	26.	208 036	124 992	168 514	4,81	6,01	+ 24,9
	27.	235 033	152 679	193 856	4,25	5,16	+ 21,4
	30.	262 030	182 997	222 514	3,82	4,49	+ 17,5
	31.	262 030	195 778	228 904	3,82	4,37	+ 14,4
August	1.	305 701	196 321	251 011	3,27	3,98	+ 21,7
	3.	480 387	280 546	380 467	2,08	2,63	+ 26,4
	6.	778 942	409 568	594 255	1,28	1,68	+ 31,3
	7.	1 033 826	483 458	758 642	0,97	1,32	+ 36,1
	8.	1 081 467	619 875	850 671	0,92	1,18	+ 28,3
	9.	989 360	671 498	830 429	1,01	1,20	+ 18,8
	10.	841 671	660 097	750 884	1,19	1,33	+ 11,8
	13.	746 387	664 143	705 265	1,34	1,42	+ 5,0
	14.	666 984	663 880	665 432	1,50	1,50	0,0
	15.	682 865	678 775	680 820	1,46	1,47	+ 0,7

Zeit		Dollarindex	Großhandelsindex	Mittelindex	Wert von 1 Million Mark nach		
					Dollarindex	Mittelindex	Unterschied in Prozent
1923							
August	16.	801 969	796 083	799 026	1,25	1,25	0,0
	17.	1 024 297	1 015 406	1 019 852	0,98	0,98	0,0
	20.	1 191 043	1 179 109	1 185 076	0,84	0,84	0,0
	21.	1 260 918	1 246 598	1 253 758	0,79	0,80	+ 1,3
	22.	1 197 396	1 152 362	1 174 879	0,84	0,85	+ 1,2
	23.	1 221 216	1 143 217	1 182 217	0,82	0,85	+ 3,7
	24	1 326 028	1 206 513	1 266 271	0,75	0,79	+ 5,3
	27.	1 548 353	1 368 140	1 458 247	0,65	0,69	+ 6,2
	28.	1 977 132	1 695 109	1 836 121	0,51	0,54	+ 5,9
	29.	2 286 803	1 827 910	2 057 357	0,44	0,49	+ 11,4
	30.	2 461 490	1 824 703	2 143 097	0,41	0,47	+ 14,6
	31.	2 620 295	1 790 369	2 205 332	0,38	0,45	+ 18,4

Zeit		Dollarindex	Großhandelsindex	Mittelindex	Wert von 1 Milliarde Mark nach		
					Dollarindex	Mittelindex	Unterschied in Prozent
1923							
September	3.	3 390 503	2 135 807	2 763 155	294,94	361,91	+ 22,7
	4.	5 256 471	3 003 923	4 130 197	190,24	242,12	+ 27,3
	5.	8 432 587	4 822 894	6 627 741	118,59	150,88	+ 27,2
	6.	10 870 256	6 222 120	8 546 188	91,99	117,01	+ 27,2
	7.	13 490 551	7 728 225	10 609 388	74,13	94,26	+ 27,2
	10.	16 904 875	9 691 997	13 298 436	59,15	75,20	+ 27,1
	11.	20 215 976	11 599 695	15 907 836	49,47	62,86	+ 27,1
	12	22 137 526	14 097 549	18 117 538	45,17	55,20	+ 22,2
	13.	25 011 910	17 504 250	21 258 080	39,98	47,04	+ 17,7
	14.	29 585 517	22 569 798	26 077 658	33,80	38,35	+ 13,5
	17.	36 858 822	30 441 563	33 650 193	27,13	29,72	+ 9,5
	18.	40 813 086	36 279 612	38 546 349	24,50	25,94	+ 5,9
	19.	37 636 970	35 650 134	36 643 552	26,57	27,29	+ 2,7
	20.	**34 857 869**	35 049 412	(34 953 641)	**28,69**	(28,61)	—
	21.	**30 014 293**	31 928 587	(30 971 440)	**33,32**	(32,29)	—
	24.	**31 284 789**	35 103 532	(33 194 161)	**31,96**	(30,13)	—
	25.	**30 919 486**	36 495 812	(33 707 649)	**32,34**	(29,67)	—
	26.	**34 016 198**	37 6[illegible]8 887	(35 852 543)	**29,40**	(27,89)	—
	27.	**43 226 933**	44 765 785	(43 996 359)	**23,13**	(22,73)	—
	28.	57 328 887	55 220 322	56 274 605	17,44	17,77	+ 1,9

Zeit		Dollarindex	Großhandelsindex	Mittelindex	Wert von 1 Billion Mark nach		
					Dollarindex	Mittelindex	Unterschied in Prozent
1923		in 1 000	in 1 000	in 1 000			
Oktober	1.	79 562	69 036	74 299	12 569	13 459	+ 7,1
	2.	104 018	82 923	93 471	9 614	10 699	+ 11,3
	3.	126 251	90 905	108 578	7 921	9 210	+ 16,3
	4.	157 853	101 480	129 667	6 335	7 712	+ 21,7
	5.	209 465	118 496	163 981	4 774	6 098	+ 27,7
	8.	398 047	194 466	296 257	2 512	3 375	+ 31,4
	9.	733 286	301 663	517 475	1 364	1 932	+ 41,6
	10.	955 614	459 840	707 727	1 046	1 413	+ 35,1
	11.	1 017 945	560 908	789 427	982,37	1 266,74	+ 28,9
	12.	941 718	584 649	763 684	1 061,89	1 309,44	+ 23,3

Zeit	Dollarindex	Großhandelsindex	Mittelindex	Wert von 1 Billion Mark nach Dollarindex	Wert von 1 Billion Mark nach Mittelindex	Unterschied in Prozent
	in 1 000	in 1 000	in 1 000			
1923						
Oktober 15.	1 060 823	732 652	896 738	942,66	1 115,15	+ 18,3
16.	1 410 195	1 072 404	1 241 300	709,12	805,61	+ 13,6
17.	2 037 478	1 639 150	1 838 314	490,80	543,98	+ 10,8
18.	4 776 878	4 053 382	4 415 130	209,34	226,49	+ 8,2
19.	8 575 512	7 622 390	8 098 951	116,61	123,47	+ 5,9
22.	12 625 060	11 824 845	12 224 953	79,21	81,80	+ 3,3
23.	14 610 132	13 881 986	14 246 059	68,45	70,19	+ 2,5
24.	15 324 758	14 730 750	15 027 754	65,25	66,54	+ 2,0
25.	15 483 564	14 582 852	15 033 208	64,58	66,52	+ 3,0
26.	15 483 564	14 282 303	14 882 934	64,58	67,19	+ 4,0
27.	15 483 564	13 981 602	14 732 583	64,58	67,88	+ 5,1
29.	16 079 085	14 207 247	15 143 166	62,19	66,04	+ 6,2
30.	21 235 364	18 350 992	19 793 178	47,09	50,52	+ 7,3
31.	41 471 010	36 427 490	38 949 250	24,11	25,67	+ 6,5
	in Millionen	in Millionen	in Millionen			
November 1.	69 048	61 772	65 410	14,48	15,29	+ 5,6
2.	92 064	83 674	87 869	10,86	11,38	+ 4,8
3.	100 000	92 312	96 156	10,00	10,40	+ 4,0
5	116 667	109 359	113 013	8,57	8,85	+ 3,3
6.	133 333	126 880	130 076	7,50	7,69	+ 2,5
7.	150 000	136 762	143 381	6,67	6,97	+ 4,5
8.	150 000	130 784	140 392	6,67	7,12	+ 6,7
9.	150 000	124 805	137 403	6,67	7,28	+ 9,1
10.	166 667	132 029	149 348	6,00	6,70	+ 11,7
12.	216 667	163 002	189 835	4,62	5,27	+ 14,1
13.	366 667	261 235	313 951	2,73	3,19	+ 16,8
14.	500 000	412 704	456 352	2,00	2,19	+ 9,5
15.	600 000	563 017	581 509	1,67	1,72	+ 3,0
16.	**600 000**	630 788	(615 394)	**1,67**	(1,62)	—
17.	**733 333**	853 795	(793 564)	**1,36**	(1,26)	—
19.	**866 667**	1 106 924	(986 796)	**1,15**	(1,01)	—
20.	**1 000 000**	1 390 172	(1 195 086)	**1,00**	(0,84)	—
21.	**1 000 000**	1 391 729	(1 195 865)	**1,00**	(0,84)	—
22.	**1 000 000**	1 393 287	(1 196 644)	**1,00**	(0,84)	—
23.	**1 000 000**	1 394 844	(1 197 422)	**1,00**	(0,84)	—
24.	**1 000 000**	1 396 401	(1 198 201)	**1,00**	(0,83)	—
26.	**1 000 000**	1 397 959	(1 198 980)	**1,00**	(0,83)	—
27.	**1 000 000**	1 399 516	(1 199 758)	**1,00**	(0,83)	—
28.	**1 000 000**	1 385 500	(1 192 750)	**1,00**	(0,84)	—
29.	**1 000 000**	1 371 484	(1 185 742)	**1,00**	(0,84)	—
30.	**1 000 000**	1 357 468	(1 178 734)	**1,00**	(0,85)	—

Appendix 2

Law about the Revaluation of Mortgages and other Claims, issued the 16th of July, 1925 (Aufwertungsgesetz vom 16. Juli 1925) Conversion rates (Umrechnungstabelle)

Nr. 31 — Tag der Ausgabe: Berlin, den 17. Juli 1925 188

Anlage

Zeit	Wert von ... Papiermark	Wert in G.M
1918		
Januar—Juni	10	8,00
Juli	10	7,14
August	10	6,90
September—Oktober	10	6,45
November	10	5,71
Dezember	10	5,00
1919		
Januar	10	5,15
Februar	10	4,65
März	10	4,00
April	10	3,41
Mai	10	3,62
Juni	10	3,11
Juli	10	2,66
August	10	2,29
September	10	1,88
Oktober	10	1,86
November	10	1,26
Dezember	10	1,04
1920		
Januar 1.—10.	100	9,67
11.—20.	100	7,75
21.—31.	100	5,76
Februar 1.—10.	100	4,90
11.—20.	100	5,06
21.—29.	100	4,66
März 1.—10.	100	4,87
11.—20.	100	6,12
21.—31.	100	5,79
April 1.—10.	100	7,00
11.—20.	100	6,99
21.—30.	100	7,10
Mai 1.—10.	100	7,86
11.—20.	100	8,79
21.—31.	100	11,01
Juni 1.—10.	100	10,32
11.—20.	100	10,64
21.—30.	100	11,19
Juli 1.—10.	100	11,10
11.—20.	100	10,91
21.—31.	100	10,05
August 1.—10.	100	9,25
11.—20.	100	8,33
21.—31.	100	8,40
September 1.—10.	100	8,24
11.—20.	100	6,80
21.—30.	100	6,80
Oktober 1.—10.	100	6,87
11.—20.	100	6,89
21.—31.	100	6,22
November 1.—10.	100	5,67
11.—20.	100	5,69
21.—30.	100	6,65
Dezember 1.—10.	100	6,88
11.—20.	100	6,27
21.—31.	100	6,20
1921		
Januar 1.—10.	100	6,05
11.—20.	100	6,63
21.—31.	100	7,41
Februar 1.—10.	100	6,90
11.—20.	100	7,26
21.—28.	100	7,01
März 1.—10.	100	7,01
11.—20.	100	7,09
21.—31.	100	7,12
April 1.—10.	100	7,24
11.—20.	100	7,16
21.—30.	100	6,77
Mai 1.—10.	100	6,77
11.—20.	100	7,42
21.—31.	100	7,32
Juni 1.—10.	100	6,88
11.—20.	100	6,61
21.—30.	100	6,39
Juli 1.—10.	100	6,34
11.—20.	100	6,25
21.—31.	100	5,88
August 1.—10.	100	5,82
11.—20.	100	4,96
21.—31.	100	5,01
September 1.—10.	100	4,82
11.—20.	100	4,81
21.—30.	100	4,07
Oktober 1.—10.	100	3,68
11.—20.	100	3,22
21.—31.	100	2,98
November 1.—10.	100	2,24
11.—20.	100	2,08
21.—30.	100	1,92
Dezember 1.—10.	100	2,67
11.—20.	100	2,66
21.—31.	100	2,58
1922		
Januar 1.—10.	100	2,62
11.—20.	100	2,50
21.—31.	100	2,28
Februar 1.—10.	100	2,30
11.—20.	100	2,24
21.—28.	100	2,08

Reichsgesetzbl. 1925 I

43

184 Reichsgesetzblatt, Jahrgang 1925, Teil I

Zeit		Wert von ... Papiermark	Wert in G.M
März	1.—10. ..	100	1,86
	11.—20. ..	100	1,70
	21.—31. ..	100	1,43
April	1.—10. ..	100	1,48
	11.—20. ..	100	1,50
	21.—30. ..	100	1,50
Mai	1.—10. ..	100	1,50
	11.—20. ..	100	1,49
	21.—31. ..	100	1,51
Juni	1.—10. ..	100	1,52
	11.—20. ..	100	1,37
	21.—30. ..	100	1,26
Juli	1.—10. ..	1 000	9,50
	11.—20. ..	1 000	9,70
	21.—31. ..	1 000	8,46
August	1.—10. ..	1 000	6,06
	11.—20. ..	1 000	4,58
	21.—31. ..	1 000	3,16
September	1.—10. ..	1 000	3,33
	11.—20. ..	1 000	3,09
	21.—30. ..	1 000	3,05
Oktober	1.—10. ..	1 000	2,13
	11.—20. ..	1 000	1,66
	21.—31. ..	1 000	1,11
November	1.—10. ..	10 000	7,60
	11.—20. ..	10 000	6,79
	21.—30. ..	10 000	6,62
Dezember	1.—10. ..	10 000	5,80
	11.—20. ..	10 000	6,18
	21.—31. ..	10 000	6,34
1923			
Januar	1.—10. ..	10 000	4,94
	11.—20. ..	10 000	3,22
	21.—31. ..	10 000	1,87
Februar	1.—10. ..	10 000	1,55
	11.—20. ..	10 000	1,57
	21.—28. ..	10 000	1,58
März	1.—10. ..	10 000	1,95
	11.—20. ..	10 000	2,08
	21.—31. ..	10 000	2,04
April	1.—10. ..	10 000	2,02
	11.—20. ..	10 000	1,92
	21.—30. ..	10 000	1,57
Mai	1.—10. ..	10 000	1,29
	11.—20. ..	10 000	1,09
	21.—31. ..	100 000	8,40
Juni	1.	100 000	6,47
	2.	100 000	6,52
	4.	100 000	6,60
	5.	100 000	6,71
	6.	100 000	6,30
	7.	100 000	6,17
	8.	100 000	6,18

Zeit		Wert von ... Papiermark	Wert in G.M
Juni	9.	100 000	6,09
	11.	100 000	5,79
	12.	100 000	5,29
	13.	100 000	4,94
	14.	100 000	4,78
	15.	100 000	4,26
	16.	100 000	3,86
	18.	100 000	3,86
	19.	100 000	3,80
	20.	100 000	3,79
	21.	100 000	3,82
	22.	100 000	3,80
	23.	100 000	3,24
	25.	100 000	3,38
	26.	100 000	3,28
	27.	100 000	3,03
	28.	100 000	3,00
	29.	100 000	2,92
	30.	100 000	2,87
Juli	2.	100 000	2,78
	3.	100 000	2,63
	4.	100 000	2,54
	5.	100 000	2,49
	6.	100 000	2,37
	7.	100 000	2,32
	9.	100 000	2,28
	10.	100 000	2,25
	11.	100 000	2,25
	12.	100 000	2,21
	13.	100 000	2,10
	16.	100 000	1,99
	17.	100 000	1,75
	19.	100 000	1,52
	20.	100 000	1,38
	23.	1 Million	9,89
	24.	1 »	8,30
	26.	1 »	6,01
	27.	1 »	5,16
	30.	1 »	4,49
	31.	1 »	4,37
August	1.	1 »	3,98
	3.	1 »	2,63
	6.	1 »	1,68
	7.	1 »	1,32
	8.	1 »	1,18
	9.	1 »	1,30
	10.	1 »	1,38
	13.	1 »	1,42
	14.	1 »	1,50
	15.	1 »	1,47
	16.	1 »	1,25
	17.	10 Millionen	9,81
	20.	10 »	8,44
	21.	10 »	7,08
	22.	10 »	8,51
	23.	10 »	8,46
	24.	10 »	7,90
	27.	10 »	6,86
	28.	10 »	5,45

Zeit		Wert von ... Papiermark		in G.-M
gust	20.	10	Millionen	4,86
	30.	10	"	4,67
	31.	10	"	4,53
ptember	3.	10	"	3,62
	4.	10	"	2,42
	5.	10	"	1,51
	6.	10	"	1,17
	7.	100	"	0,48
	10.	100	"	7,82
	11.	100	"	6,29
	12.	100	"	5,52
	13.	100	"	4,70
	14.	100	"	3,84
	17.	100	"	2,07
	18.	100	"	2,38
	19.	100	"	2,73
	20.	100	"	2,87
	21.	100	"	3,33
	24.	100	"	3,20
	25.	100	"	3,23
	26.	100	"	2,94
	27.	100	"	2,31
	28.	100	"	1,78
ber	1.	100	"	1,35
	2.	100	"	1,07
	3.	1	Milliarde	0,21
	4.	1	"	7,71
	5.	1	"	6,10
	8.	1	"	3,88
	9.	1	"	1,98
	10.	1	"	1,41
	11.	1	"	1,27
	12.	1	"	1,31
	15.	1	"	1,12
	16.	10	Milliarden	8,06
	17.	10	"	5,44
	18.	10	"	2,28
	19.	10	"	1,29
Oktober	22.	100	Milliarden	8,18
	23.	100	"	7,02
	24.	100	"	6,86
	25.	100	"	6,65
	26.	100	"	6,72
	27.	100	"	6,70
	29.	100	"	6,60
	30.	100	"	5,06
	31.	100	"	2,67
November	1.	100	"	1,63
	2.	100	"	1,14
	3.	100	"	1,04
	5.	1	Billion	8,85
	6.	1	"	7,69
	7.	1	"	6,87
	8.	1	"	7,12
	9.	1	"	7,28
	10.	1	"	6,70
	12.	1	"	5,27
	13.	1	"	3,19
	14.	1	"	2,16
	15.	1	"	1,72
	16.	1	"	1,67
	17.	1	"	1,36
	19.	1	"	1,16
	20.	1	"	1,00
	21.	1	"	1,00
	22.	1	"	1,00
	23.	1	"	1,00
	24.	1	"	1,00
	26.	1	"	1,00
	27.	1	"	1,00
	28.	1	"	1,00
	29.	1	"	1,00
	30. und folgende Tage .	1	"	1,00

Appendix 3

Reichsgericht Leipzig, V. Zivilsenat, Urteil vom 4. November 1925
RGZ III, 320 ff

68. 1. Sind die Gerichte zur Prüfung der Verfassungsmäßigkeit von Reichsgesetzen befugt?

2. Steht die im Aufwertungsgesetz geschehene Regelung der Aufwertung von Hypotheken und der unter die §§ 62, 63 fallenden Ansprüche mit Vorschriften der Reichsverfassung in Widerspruch?

3. Nach welchen Vorschriften ist eine Darlehensforderung aufzuwerten, deren hypothekarische Sicherheit vor dem Beginn des Währungsverfalls fortgefallen ist?

4. Liegt eine Annahme der Leistung im Sinne des § 14 des Aufwertungsgesetzes vor, wenn der Gläubiger den Nennbetrag seiner Forderung in Papiermark auf Grund eines von ihm erwirkten Pfändungs- und Überweisungsbeschlusses vom Drittschuldner eingezogen hat?

Reichsverfassung Art. 105, 109, 134, 152, 153. 3. Steuernotverordnung § 11. Aufwertungsgesetz §§ 14, 15 bis 24, 62, 63, 67, 68

V. Zivilsenat. Urt. v. 4. November 1925 i. S. K. (Bekl.) w. M. (Kl.). V 621/24.

I. Landgericht II Berlin.
II. Kammergericht daselbst.

Der Kläger hat dem Beklagten im März 1909 ein zu 5 v. H. verzinsliches Darlehen von 50000 *M* gegen hypothekarische Sicherstellung gegeben. Das Darlehen war abredegemäß am 1. April 1914 fällig, es wurden aber darauf nur 5000 *M* zurückgezahlt. Das Pfandgrundstück kam im Juni 1914 zur Zwangsversteigerung, wobei die Hypothek des Klägers bis auf 2110,87 *M* ausfiel. Im Jahre 1923 pfändete dieser auf Grund der Schuldurkunde, in der sich der Beklagte der sofortigen Zwangsvollstreckung unterworfen hatte, eine dem Beklagten zustehende Forderung und erhielt durch deren Einziehung von dem Drittschuldner den Nennbetrag des Darlehensrestes ausbezahlt. Demnächst wurde er klagbar, um einen Ausgleich für die Geldentwertung zu erlangen, und zwar forderte er mit der Klage, die er auf die 3. Steuernotverordnung und auf Schuldnerverzug des Beklagten stützte, unter Vorbehalt weitergehender Ansprüche vorläufig Zahlung von 600 Goldmark nebst 5 v. H. Zinsen seit 1. Januar 1914. Der Beklagte wandte unter anderem ein, ein Aufwertungsanspruch des Klägers bestehe nach § 11 der 3. StNVO. nicht mehr, weil der Kläger bei Empfangnahme des Geldes keinen Vorbehalt gemacht habe.

Das Landgericht gab der Klage statt. Berufung und Revision des Beklagten blieben ohne Erfolg.

Aus den Gründen:

1. (Betrifft das Vorhandensein der Revisionssumme.)

2. Was die Sache selbst anbetrifft, so ist die rechtliche Beurteilung des Sachverhalts nicht mehr nach der inzwischen außer Kraft getretenen 3. Steuernotverordnung, sondern auf Grund des Aufwertungsgesetzes vom 16. Juli 1925 vorzunehmen, das mit Wirkung vom 15. Juli 1925 in Kraft getreten ist (§ 88 Abs. 1), daher von diesem Tage an auch auf anhängige Rechtsstreitigkeiten Anwendung finden muß. Daß die Anwendung des Gesetzes auf die bei seinem Inkrafttreten bereits in der Revisionsinstanz anhängigen Sachen zu erfolgen hat, ergeben die Vorschriften des § 68, wonach es bei einer die Aufwertung regelnden rechtskräftigen gerichtlichen Entscheidung sein Bewenden behalten soll mit der Maßgabe, daß der Anwendung der §§ 15 bis 24 über die Aufwertung kraft Rückwirkung auch eine rechtskräftige gerichtliche Entscheidung nicht entgegensteht. Soweit also noch keine rechtskräftige Entscheidung vorliegt, sollen hiernach

die Vorschriften des Aufwertungsgesetzes in vollem Umfang zur Anwendung gebracht werden.

Voraussetzung für die Anwendung der Vorschriften des Aufwertungsgesetzes ist, daß sich keine durchgreifenden Bedenken gegen die Verfassungsmäßigkeit des Gesetzes ergeben, das mit einfacher Mehrheit des Reichstags zustande gekommen ist. Im Hinblick auf die in der Öffentlichkeit gegen die Rechtsgültigkeit des Aufwertungsgesetzes erhobenen Angriffe erscheint es hiernach geboten, die Verfassungsmäßigkeit des Gesetzes von Amts wegen einer Prüfung zu unterziehen.

a) In dieser Hinsicht erhebt sich zunächst die Frage, ob und inwieweit die Gerichte überhaupt berechtigt und verpflichtet sind, die Rechtsgültigkeit eines an sich ordnungsmäßig verkündeten Reichsgesetzes nachzuprüfen. Dabei ist mit dem Urteil des I. Strafsenats vom 15. Dezember 1921 (RGSt. Bd. 56 S. 177) davon auszugehen, daß in erster Reihe etwaige reichsrechtliche Bestimmungen, seien es gesetzliche oder gewohnheitsrechtliche, die unmittelbar oder mittelbar zu der Frage Stellung nehmen, maßgebend sein müssen und daß, soweit solche Bestimmungen fehlen, auf die allgemeinen Grundsätze zurückzugehen ist, die aus dem Wesen der gesetzgebenden oder richterlichen Gewalt und der von diesen Gewalten ausgehenden Betätigungen sowie aus ihrem gegenseitigen Verhältnis abzuleiten sind. Die Reichsverfassung hat im Art. 102 den im § 1 GVG. aufgestellten Grundsatz aufgenommen, daß die Richter unabhängig und nur dem Gesetz unterworfen seien. Diese letztere Bestimmung schließt nicht aus, daß einem Reichsgesetz oder einzelnen seiner Bestimmungen vom Richter die Gültigkeit insoweit aberkannt werden kann, als sie mit anderen, vom Richter zu beachtenden Vorschriften, die ihnen vorgehen, in Widerspruch stehen. Das ist der Fall, wenn ein Gesetz einem in der Reichsverfassung aufgestellten Rechtssatz widerspricht und bei seinem Erlaß die durch Art. 76 RV. für eine Verfassungsänderung vorgeschriebenen Erfordernisse nicht vorgelegen haben. Denn die Vorschriften der Reichsverfassung können nur durch ein ordnungsmäßig zustande gekommenes verfassungsänderndes Gesetz außer Kraft gesetzt werden. Sie bleiben daher auch gegenüber abweichenden Bestimmungen eines späteren, ohne Beobachtung der Erfordernisse des Art. 76 erlassenen Reichsgesetzes für den Richter verbindlich und nötigen ihn, die widersprechenden Bestimmungen des späteren Gesetzes außer Anwendung zu lassen. Da die Reichsverfassung selbst keine Vorschrift enthält, nach der die Entscheidung über die Verfassungsmäßigkeit der Reichsgesetze den Gerichten entzogen und einer bestimmten anderen Stelle übertragen wäre, muß das Recht und die Pflicht des Richters, die Verfassungsmäßigkeit von Reichsgesetzen zu prüfen, anerkannt werden.

b) Die Verfassungsmäßigkeit des Aufwertungsgesetzes wird unter verschiedenen Gesichtspunkten in Zweifel gezogen. Es wird behauptet, daß die im Gesetz vorgenommene Schematisierung der Aufwertung gewisser Rechte durch Festsetzung eines nach bestimmten Regeln zu berechnenden festen Aufwertungsbetrags, die Einführung bestimmter Stichtage für die Zulässigkeit oder die Höhe der Aufwertung, die Abhängigmachung der Aufwertung von einem bei Annahme des gezahlten entwerteten Geldbetrags gemachten Vorbehalt des Gläubigers einen nach Art. 153 RV. unzulässigen Eingriff in das gewährleistete Eigentum enthielten, daß diese Vorschriften sowie einige weitere Bestimmungen, z. B. die Versagung der dem Schuldner gewährten Härteklausel gegenüber dem Gläubiger, den im Art. 109 Abs. 1 RV. aufgestellten Grundsatz der Gleichheit aller Deutschen vor dem Gesetz verletzten, daß die Begründung der ausschließlichen Zuständigkeit der Aufwertungsstelle für die Entscheidung gewisser ihr zugewiesener Streitpunkte mit Art. 105 RV. unvereinbar sei, und daß endlich auch im Hinblick darauf, daß für die Festsetzung des Maßes der Aufwertung Erwägungen steuerpolitischer Natur maßgebend gewesen seien, ein Verstoß gegen Art. 134 RV. vorliege (vgl. Zeiler, Die Rechtsgültigkeit der Aufwertungsgesetzgebung, Halle a. S., Verlag „Der Rechtsstaat"; die Aufsätze: „Der vorläufige Sieg Dr. Luthers und des Großkapitals" und „Verfassungsmäßigkeit der Aufwertungsgesetze" im Rechtsstaat 1925 Nr. 25; Daltrop in JW. 1925 S. 1714; ferner Stampe Aufwertungsurteil, Nachtr. S. 87; Zeiler und Sontag, Brennende Fragen der Aufwertung S. 81 flg.; Oertmann, Die Aufwertungsfrage S. 76). Diese Angriffe gegen die Verfassungsmäßigkeit des Aufwertungsgesetzes decken sich, abgesehen von der Heranziehung des Art. 109, in der Hauptsache mit den Gründen, aus denen schon die Verfassungsmäßigkeit der 3. Steuernotverordnung bekämpft worden ist. Das Reichsgericht hat diese Bedenken bezüglich der letzteren in dem Urteil vom 1. März 1924 (RGZ. Bd. 107 S. 375) zurückgewiesen. An den dort entwickelten Gründen ist auch bei erneuter Prüfung unter Berücksichtigung der dagegen vorgebrachten Bedenken durchweg festzuhalten.

Was zunächst den angeblichen Verstoß gegen Art. 153 RV. anbetrifft, so ist im Urteil vom 1. März 1924 ausgeführt worden: Es könne schon zweifelhaft sein, ob die Regelung der Hypothekenaufwertung überhaupt eine Enteignung, d. h. eine zwangsweise Entziehung von Rechten, darstelle oder nicht vielmehr auf die gesetzliche Normierung des streitig gewordenen zivilrechtlichen Rechtsverhältnisses zwischen Hypothekengläubiger und Hypothekenschuldner sich beschränke. In keinem Falle aber liege eine verfassungsmäßig unzulässige Entziehung von Gläubigerrechten vor, da die im Abs. 2 des Art. 153 aufgestellten Voraussetzungen für die Zulässigkeit einer Enteignung erfüllt seien. Diese Erwägungen treffen auch gegenüber den Vorschriften des Aufwertungsgesetzes zu. Die Geldentwertung und der Wirtschaftsverfall in der Nachkriegszeit hatten zu einer völligen Erschütterung aller wirtschaftlichen Verhältnisse geführt. Wenngleich den Gläubigern in der Rechtsprechung das Recht zugestanden wurde, an Stelle des entwerteten Papiermarkbetrags ihrer Forderungen einen der Billigkeit entsprechend aufgewerteten Betrag zu verlangen, so fehlte es doch an jeder sicheren Grundlage für die Beurteilung, welchen Wert die einzelne Forderung in Wahrheit noch darstellte. Denn dabei waren nicht nur die gesamten in Ansehung des Schuldverhältnisses in Betracht kommenden Verhältnisse, sondern auch die Wirtschaftslage des Gläubigers und des Schuldners und die allgemeine, auf der Verringerung des Volksvermögens beruhende Verarmung zu berücksichtigen. Die Berechnung des Aufwertungsbetrags hing also von einer großen Anzahl an sich unsicherer und schwer feststellbarer Umstände ab, deren Beurteilung in das Ermessen der für die Festsetzung des Aufwertungsbetrags zuständigen Stelle gelegt war. Niemand konnte daher mit annähernder Sicherheit voraussagen, wie hoch die einzelne Forderung ihrem Aufwertungsbetrage nach zu bewerten war. Diese völlige Unsicherheit ließ eine gesetzliche Regelung im Interesse des gesamten Wirtschaftslebens dringend geboten erscheinen und zwar in einer Weise, die möglichst schnell eine sichere feste Grundlage für die Bewertung der durch die Geldentwertung betroffenen Verhältnisse zu schaffen geeignet war. Dieses Ziel schien nur im Wege der Schematisierung der Aufwertung erreichbar. Demgemäß begründete die Mehrheit des Reichstagsausschusses ihren Beschluß, der weiteren Beratung den Regierungsentwurf zugrundezulegen, dahin:

Notwendigkeit einer sofortigen, klaren und abschließenden Regelung im Hinblick auf die öffentlichen und privaten Haushalte zur Wiederherstellung von Ruhe, Ordnung und Sicherheit im Innern und in der Steuerwirtschaft, daher Ablehnung der zwar gerechteren, aber wirtschaftlich unhaltbaren und praktisch undurchführbaren Individualmethode des Best'schen Entwurfs und jeder zeitlichen Hinausschiebung des Aufwertungsergebnisses; vielmehr schematische Lösung unter Anpassung des Normalsatzes, der Zahlungsfristen und Zinshöhe an die Leistungsfähigkeit der Wirtschaft, Ausdehnung der Rückwirkung, Wahrung des öffentlichen Glaubens des Grundbuchs, Zulassung einer Individualregelung, wo sie wirtschaftlich möglich oder aus sozialen Gründen notwendig sei.

Bei dieser Sachlage läßt sich die Annahme vertreten, daß es sich bei der Regelung der Aufwertung durch das Gesetz vom 16. Juli 1925 nicht um eine Entziehung wohlbegründeter Rechte, sondern um eine Festsetzung und Begrenzung des Inhalts der durch die Geldentwertung und den Wirtschaftsverfall in ihren Grundlagen völlig erschütterten Rechtsverhältnisse im Sinne des Art. 153 Abs. 1 Satz 2 RV. gehandelt hat. In dieser Beziehung sei darauf hingewiesen, daß das Aufwertungsgesetz die durch Vereinbarungen oder rechtskräftige Entscheidungen zugunsten der Gläubiger bereits festgestellten weitergehenden Rechte hat bestehen lassen (§§ 67, 68).

Aber auch wenn in der Regelung der Aufwertung eine unter den Begriff der Enteignung fallende Entziehung von Gläubigerrechten zu finden sein sollte, wären die im Abs. 2 des Art. 153 aufgestellten Erfordernisse für die Zulässigkeit der Enteignung erfüllt. Die gesetzliche Grundlage, die Abs. 2 Satz 1 für eine zulässige Enteignung erfordert, ist hier, wo die Enteignung unmittelbar durch ein Reichsgesetz geschieht, in dem Gesetz selbst enthalten. Daß eine Enteignung nicht nur durch einen Verwaltungsakt auf Grund eines ihn rechtfertigenden Gesetzes, sondern unmittelbar durch ein Gesetz selbst erfolgen kann, ist vom Reichsgericht bereits wiederholt ausgesprochen worden (RGZ. Bd. 103 S. 200, Bd. 109 S. 317/18). Der Mangel einer den verkürzten Gläubigern zu gewährenden angemessenen Entschädigung steht der Zulässigkeit der Enteignung nicht entgegen, da Abs. 2 Satz 2 des Art. 153 den Ausschluß einer Entschädigung durch ein Reichsgesetz zuläßt, und demnach für eine durch Reichsgesetz vorgenommene Enteignung das Erfordernis einer Entschädigung überhaupt nicht zwingend vorgeschrieben ist. Im übrigen geht aus den Vorschriften des Aufwertungsgesetzes mit hinreichender Deutlichkeit hervor, daß eine Entschädigung der Gläubiger für ihren etwaigen Rechtsverlust nicht stattfinden soll. Daß endlich auch dem Erfordernis genügt ist, daß die Enteignung „zum Wohle der Allgemeinheit" vorgenommen ist, ergibt sich aus den oben mitgeteilten Erwägungen, die für den Erlaß des Aufwertungsgesetzes und die darin geschehene Regelung der Aufwertung der Hypotheken und anderen Vermögensanlagen maßgebend gewesen sind. Gerade die Abweichung von der Individualaufwertung, in der eine teilweise Enteignung der Gläubiger zu finden sein könnte, geschah aus dem Grunde, weil zur Wiederherstellung von Ruhe, Ordnung und Sicherheit im Innern und in der Steuerwirtschaft eine sofortige klare und abschließende Regelung der Aufwertungsfrage unbedingt geboten war, und diese ohne eine Schematisierung der Aufwertung zur Erreichung des erstrebten Zieles nicht möglich erschien. Die Herstellung von Ruhe, Ordnung und Sicherheit im Innern dient dem Wohle der Allgemeinheit und eine zu diesem Zwecke vorgenommene Enteignung kann daher nicht als unzulässig angesehen werden. Ob der mit dem Gesetz erstrebte gemeinnützige Zweck in dem erhofften Umfang tatsächlich erreicht wird, ist ohne Belang. Wesentlich für die Zulässigkeit einer Enteignung kann immer nur sein, daß ein dem Wohle der Allgemeinheit dienender Zweck erstrebt wird und wenigstens teilweise erreichbar erscheint, und das trifft unter den gegebenen Verhältnissen zu.

Der Einwand, daß die Zulassung einer Enteignung im Interesse der Wirtschaft in Fällen der vorliegenden Art zu einer Aufhebung jeder verfassungsmäßigen Gewähr für das Eigentum der Staatsbürger führe, trifft nicht zu. Die Gewähr für das Eigentum wird von der Verfassung nicht unbedingt geleistet, sie kann nicht nur im Wege einer Verfassungsänderung gänzlich beseitigt werden, sondern sie gilt überhaupt nur mit den sich aus den Vorschriften des Abs. 1

Satz 2 und des Abs. 2 des Art. 153 ergebenden Beschränkungen. Es ist ein allgemein anerkannter Grundsatz, daß das Wohl der einzelnen Staatsbürger hinter dem Allgemeinwohl zurückstehen muß. Dieser Grundsatz kommt in der Vorschrift des Abs. 2 Art. 153 zum Ausdruck, daß das Eigentum zum Wohle der Allgemeinheit entzogen werden kann. Damit wird die im Abs. 1 Satz 1 ausgesprochene Gewährleistung des Eigentums in gewissem Umfang eingeschränkt, aber keineswegs gegenstandslos. Es sind im Abs. 2 bestimmte Garantien dafür geschaffen, daß keine willkürliche Eigentumsentziehung stattfinden kann, indem ausdrücklich festgesetzt wird, daß die Enteignung nur zum Wohle der Allgemeinheit und nur auf gesetzlicher Grundlage vorgenommen werden und mangels abweichender Bestimmung eines Reichsgesetzes nur gegen eine im Rechtswege verfolgbare angemessene Entschädigung erfolgen darf. Gerade in der Festlegung dieser Voraussetzungen für die Vornahme einer Enteignung besteht der Schutz, den die Verfassung mit der im Abs. 1 ausgesprochenen Gewährleistung dem Privateigentum gewähren will. Dieser Schutz versagt, wenn die Voraussetzungen des Abs. 2 für eine Enteignung vorliegen. Soweit dabei das Wohl der Allgemeinheit in Betracht kommt, sind von der Verfassung keine Unterscheidungen gemacht, auf welchem Gebiet die Förderung des Wohles der Allgemeinheit geschehen soll. Sie kann daher auch auf dem Gebiet der allgemeinen Wirtschaft liegen.

Im Gegensatz zu den gegen die 3. Steuernotverordnung gerichteten Angriffen, die deren Verfassungsmäßigkeit in Zweifel zu ziehen suchten, weil sie eine unzulässige Enteignung enthielte, wird jetzt die Ansicht vertreten (Zeiler a. a. O. S. 15), daß das Aufwertungsgesetz gegen Art. 153 RV. verstoße, weil es eine Rechtsentziehung vornehme, die nicht unter den Begriff einer Enteignung falle und daher durch Art. 153 Abs. 2 nicht gedeckt werde. Diese Ansicht beruft sich darauf, daß mit dem Worte Enteignung ein bestimmter, rechtswissenschaftlich feststehender Begriff, wie er sich auf Grund des preußischen Enteignungsgesetzes gebildet habe, verbunden werde und daher auch im Abs. 2 Art. 153 RV. nur in diesem Sinne gebraucht sein könne. Allein mit Recht weist Wolff (Festgabe für Kahl, IV S. 20) darauf hin, daß die Frage, was Enteignung sei, nicht mit der Frage, unter welchen Voraussetzungen eine Enteignung zulässig sei, verwechselt werden dürfe, und daß Abs. 2 des Art. 153 RV. — wie auch das preußische Enteignungsgesetz — nur die Erfordernisse für eine zulässige Enteignung aufstellt, den Begriff der Enteignung jedoch nicht näher bestimmt. Ist aber das Wort „Eigentum" im Abs. 1 Satz 1, wie die heute allgemein herrschende Meinung annimmt, nicht in dem dem Bürgerlichen Gesetzbuch entsprechenden Sprachgebrauch im Sinne von Sacheigentum zu verstehen, sondern im weitesten Sinne auszulegen, so daß darunter auch Rechte aller Art, insbesondere auch Forderungsrechte fallen, so würde auch der Abs. 2, der die Zulässigkeit einer Enteignung regelt, in dem Sinne auszulegen sein, daß darunter eine Entziehung oder Beschränkung des im Abs. 1 Satz 1 gewährleisteten Eigentums zu verstehen ist, also jeder Eingriff der Staatsgewalt in ein durch Abs. 1 Satz 1 geschütztes Recht. Daß darunter nicht nur Eingriffe durch Verwaltungsakt, sondern auch durch den Gesetzgeber selbst fallen, ist, wie oben erwähnt, vom Reichsgericht bereits wiederholt angenommen worden. Ob zum Begriff der Enteignung im Sinne des Art. 153 eine „Überführung" des entzogenen Rechtes in das Vermögen eines anderen Rechtssubjekts erforderlich ist (vgl. Wolff a. a. O. S. 24flg. und die dort S. 25 in Anm. 1 angeführten Schriftsteller), kann dahingestellt bleiben, weil diesem Erfordernis hier dadurch genügt wäre, daß die Schuldner zu dem Betrag, um den die Aufwertungsbeträge der Forderungen durch das Aufwertungsgesetz gegenüber den allgemeinen Vorschriften herabgesetzt worden sind, von ihrer Leistungspflicht befreit worden sind (RGZ. Bd. 103 S. 200, Bd. 109 S. 317/18). Das von Zeiler angeregte Bedenken kann hiernach nicht als durchschlagend anerkannt werden (vgl. auch Triepel, Goldbilanzen-Verordnung S. 25).

Bezüglich der Bedeutung und der Tragweite des Ausspruchs im Art. 109 Abs. 1 RV. besteht Streit, ob sie sich in der Bedeutung erschöpfe, die dem gleichlautenden Ausspruche der preußischen Verfassungsurkunde vom 31. Januar 1850 (Art. 4) beigelegt worden ist, nämlich dahin, daß die Gesetze ohne Unterschied des Standes gegen jeden in vollem Umfang angewendet werden sollen (Entsch. des preuß. OVG. Bd. 56 S. 235; Anschütz, Preuß. VU., Bd. I S. 108flg.) und mithin nur als eine Norm für Justiz und Verwaltung, nicht für die Gesetzgebung selbst aufzufassen sei (Anschütz, Reichsverf.

S. 189; Giese, RV. 6. Aufl. S. 300), oder ob dadurch auch eine Schranke für die Gesetzgebung gezogen worden ist (Triepel, Goldbilanzen-Verordnung, S. 26 flg.; Leibholz, Die Gleichheit vor dem Gesetz, bes. S. 34, 87, 95, 99; Aldag, Die Gleichheit vor dem Gesetz in der RV., bes. S. 38, 41, 51 flg.). Es kann ferner zweifelhaft sein, ob sich Abs. 1 des Art. 109, wie aus dem weiteren Inhalt des Art. 109 gefolgert werden könnte, nur auf reine Persönlichkeits-, nicht auch auf Vermögensrechte bezieht (Daltrop, JW. 1924 S. 1714) oder ob er eine allgemeine, auch das Gebiet des Vermögensrechts umfassende Vorschrift aufstellt. Einer Stellungnahme zu diesen Fragen bedarf es nicht, weil auch eine Prüfung unter dem Gesichtspunkt des Art. 109 Abs. 1 RV. nicht zur Verneinung der Verfassungsmäßigkeit des Aufwertungsgesetzes führt. Der Grundsatz der Gleichheit vor dem Gesetz kann nur die Bedeutung haben, daß Tatbestände vom Gesetz als gleich zu behandeln sind, die ungleich zu behandeln Willkür bedeuten würde. Eine verschiedene Behandlung, die durch keinen auf vernünftigen Erwägungen beruhenden Grund zu rechtfertigen ist, würde als willkürlich erscheinen und gegen den Gleichheitsgrundsatz verstoßen (Triepel, S. 30; Leibholz, S. 87, 95; Aldag, S. 41, 51). Die Regelung der Aufwertung, wie sie im Gesetz vom 16. Juli 1925 geschehen ist, insbesondere ihre Schematisierung, beruht aber, wie die oben wiedergegebene Begründung für die Ablehnung der als gerechter ausdrücklich anerkannten Individualmethode ergibt, auf durchaus vernünftigen Erwägungen, nämlich auf der allseitig betonten und durch die Wirtschaftslage tatsächlich begründeten Notwendigkeit einer sofortigen, klaren und abschließenden Regelung des Aufwertungsproblems unter Anpassung der Regelung im einzelnen an die Leistungsfähigkeit der Wirtschaft, und Zulassung der Individualaufwertung, wo sie wirtschaftlich möglich oder aus sozialen Gründen erforderlich war. Die Unterschiede, die sich aus der Regelung des Gesetzes für die Aufwertung nach der Art der betroffenen Ansprüche und nach gewissen im Gesetz hervorgehobenen Umständen ergeben, können hiernach nicht als willkürliche, den Grundsatz des Art. 109 Abs. 1 RV. verletzende Unterscheidungen angesehen werden, wenngleich damit, wie auch die Reichstagsmehrheit nicht verkannt hat, vielfach große Härten und beklagenswerte Unbilligkeiten, namentlich für die Gläubiger, verbunden sind. Man mag über die Zweckmäßigkeit oder Notwendigkeit einzelner Bestimmungen des Gesetzes streiten können; gerade die umstrittenen Vorschriften sind aber bei den Beratungen im Reichstagsausschuß Gegenstand eingehender Prüfung und Erörterung gewesen und schließlich zur Annahme gelangt, weil eine anderweite Regelung mit dem erstrebten Zwecke des Gesetzes nicht verträglich erschien. Von einer willkürlichen, vernünftiger Erwägungen entbehrenden Regelung kann daher auch in diesen Beziehungen nicht gesprochen werden.

Daß das Aufwertungsgesetz keinen Verstoß gegen die Artikel 105 und 134 RV. enthält, ergibt sich aus den Gründen, aus denen in dem Urteil vom 1. März 1924 (RGZ. Bd. 107 S. 376/377) die Vereinbarkeit der 3. Steuernotverordnung mit den genannten Artikeln angenommen worden ist. Auf die dort gemachten Ausführungen, an denen der Senat festhält, wird hiermit verwiesen. Von Daltrop (JW. 1925 S. 1714) wird die im § 68 Abs. 2 AufwG. vorgeschriebene Ausdehnung der in den §§ 15 bis 24 geregelten Rückwirkung der Aufwertung gegenüber rechtskräftigen gerichtlichen Entscheidungen mit Art. 105 Satz 2 RV. für unvereinbar gehalten. Da indessen grundsätzlich kein Bedenken dagegen besteht, daß ein Gesetz sich rückwirkende Kraft beilegen kann, und auch eine Änderung der Vorschriften der Zivilprozeßordnung über die Rechtskraftwirkung gerichtlicher Entscheidungen im Wege eines einfachen Reichsgesetzes zulässig ist, könnte es sich nur fragen, ob der in Rede stehenden Bestimmung des Aufwertungsgesetzes der Art. 153 RV. entgegensteht. Das ist zu verneinen. Es handelt sich bei der Vorschrift des § 68 Abs. 2 wie auch bei der des § 67 Abs. 2 um die Beseitigung eines Rechtsverlusts des Gläubigers aus Billigkeitsrücksichten, nicht um einen Eingriff in ein konkretes, unter den Eigentumsbegriff im Sinne des Art. 153 Abs. 1 fallendes Vermögensrecht des Schuldners. Will man aber einen derartigen Eingriff als vorliegend ansehen, so wäre er aus den oben zu Art. 153 gemachten Ausführungen als zulässig zu erachten. Ebensowenig enthält § 67 Abs. 2 AufwG. einen unzulässigen Eingriff in den im Art. 152 RV. aufgestellten öffentlich-rechtlichen Grundsatz der Vertragsfreiheit. Denn dieser Grundsatz gilt nach Art. 152 nur „nach Maßgabe der Gesetze". Da hiermit der Gesetzgebung das Recht vorbehalten ist, Beschränkungen der Vertragsfreiheit aufzustellen, steht Art. 152 auch einem im Wege des

Gesetzes erfolgenden Eingriff mit rückwirkender Kraft in schon bestehende Vertragsverhältnisse nicht entgegen (RGZ. Bd. 103 S. 310).

Die im Aufwertungsgesetz vorgenommene Regelung der Aufwertung von Hypotheken und der unter die §§ 62, 63 fallenden Ansprüche verstößt hiernach weder im ganzen noch hinsichtlich der vorstehend erörterten Einzelbestimmungen gegen Vorschriften der Reichsverfassung.

3. Bei der Beurteilung des vorliegenden Streitfalles nach den Vorschriften des Aufwertungsgesetzes erhebt sich zunächst die Frage, ob die Darlehensforderung, deren Aufwertung der Kläger geltend macht, als eine durch Hypothek gesicherte Forderung der Aufwertung gemäß den §§ 8flg. unterliegt, oder ob sie als ungesicherte Forderung nach §§ 62, 63 aufzuwerten ist. Die Forderung ist im Jahre 1909 begründet worden und zunächst durch eine Hypothek gesichert gewesen. Bei der im Frühjahr 1914 erfolgten Zwangsversteigerung des belasteten Grundstücks ist die Hypothek mit 2110,87 ℳ zur Hebung gelangt, der Rest ist ausgefallen und die Hypothek gelöscht worden. Der damals ungetilgt gebliebene Rest der Forderung bestand seitdem ohne hypothekarische Sicherung fort. Das Berufungsgericht hat bei der Beurteilung der Rechtslage auf Grund der 3. Steuernotverordnung angenommen, daß die Forderung, da sie bei Beginn des Währungsverfalls bereits nicht mehr durch Hypothek gesichert war, im Sinne der 3. Steuernotverordnung als eine ungesicherte Vermögensanlage zu behandeln und demnach als ein Anspruch aus einer Vermögensanlage anderer Art gemäß § 12 der 3. Steuernotverordnung aufzuwerten sei. Die Behandlung als einer ungesicherten Forderung erweist sich auch nach den Vorschriften des Aufwertungsgesetzes als zutreffend. Es kann dahingestellt bleiben, ob im Sinne dieses Gesetzes nur die Forderungen, für die bei seinem Inkrafttreten noch eine Hypothek bestand, als durch Hypothek gesichert anzusehen sind, oder ob für diese Frage ein früherer Zeitpunkt, etwa der im § 2 für die Berechnung des Goldmarkbetrags als Stichtag angegebene 1. Januar 1918, als maßgebend anzunehmen wäre. Das Gesetz bezeichnet im § 1 als Gegenstand der Aufwertung Ansprüche, die auf einem vor dem 14. Februar 1924 begründeten Rechtsverhältnis beruhen, wenn sie durch den Währungsverfall betroffen sind. Soweit also das Gesetz eine verschiedene Art der Aufwertung für die durch den Währungsverfall

betroffenen Ansprüche festsetzt, je nachdem sie dinglich gesichert sind oder nicht, können Ansprüche, deren dingliche Sicherheit bereits vor dem Beginn des Währungsverfalls fortgefallen war und die als ungesicherte von dem Währungsverfall betroffen worden sind, für die Aufwertung nur als ungesicherte Ansprüche in Betracht kommen. Der Währungsverfall hat erst im Laufe des Weltkriegs eingesetzt. Da die für die Forderung des Klägers bestellte Hypothek bereits im Jahre 1914 gelöscht worden ist, stellt sich hiernach seine Forderung jedenfalls als eine ungesicherte im Sinne des Aufwertungsgesetzes dar. Anderseits ist dem Berufungsgericht darin beizustimmen, daß die Forderung des Klägers, die als Darlehensforderung begründet worden ist, ihren Charakter als eine Vermögensanlage durch den Fortfall der hypothekarischen Sicherheit nicht verloren hat. Der Umstand, daß eine Forderung hypothekarisch sichergestellt wird, kann bei der Beurteilung, ob eine Vermögensanlage vorliegt, von Erheblichkeit sein, zum Begriff der Vermögensanlage gehört aber das Bestehen einer hypothekarischen Sicherung nicht. Stellt sich eine Forderung als eine solche aus einer Vermögensanlage dar, so bleibt dieser Charakter durch den Ausfall der dafür bestellten Hypothek unberührt.

4. Die Aufwertung der Darlehensforderung des Klägers bestimmt sich hiernach nach § 62 AufwG. und zwar richtet sie sich nach den allgemeinen Vorschriften mit den sich aus § 63 Abs. 1 und 4 ergebenden Maßgaben für die Aufwertung von Vermögensanlagen. Danach ergibt sich kein Anlaß zu einer Beanstandung der vom Berufungsgericht in Ansehung der Klage getroffenen Entscheidung. Denn das Berufungsgericht hat den Aufwertungsanspruch des Klägers auf Grund der allgemeinen Vorschriften, insbesondere der §§ 157, 242 BGB., geprüft und dabei den bisher eingeklagten Betrag, der kaum 2 v. H. des Goldmarkbetrags der Forderung ausmache, als jedenfalls begründet befunden. Da § 63 Abs. 1 AufwG. eine Aufwertung bis zu 25 v. H. des Goldmarkbetrags zuläßt, so ergibt sich in dieser Hinsicht kein rechtliches Bedenken.

Der vom Beklagten auf § 11 der 3. Steuernotverordnung gestützte Einwand, der Kläger habe den Nennbetrag seiner Restforderung vorbehaltlos angenommen, ist vom Berufungsgericht mit der Begründung verworfen worden, daß § 11 nicht bloß Hinnahme der

Leistung, sondern deren Annahme als Erfüllung voraussetze, ein derartiger Tatbestand aber hier nicht dargetan sei, wo der Kläger den Betrag auf Grund einer Pfändung der Forderung des Beklagten vom Drittschuldner eingezogen habe. An sich würde der Mangel eines Vorbehalts bei der Annahme der Zahlung dem Aufwertungsverlangen des Klägers nach § 15 Satz 1 AufwG., der nach § 63 Abs. 1 Satz 2 auch auf die Aufwertung nicht gesicherter Vermögensanlagen entsprechende Anwendung zu finden hat, nicht entgegenstehen, da der Kläger die Zahlung erst im Jahre 1923 erhalten hat. Der Beklagte hat sich aber in der Revisionsinstanz darauf berufen, daß die Voraussetzungen des § 15 Satz 2 für einen Ausschluß der Aufwertung kraft Rückwirkung vorlägen, und ihm Gelegenheit gegeben werden müsse, nach dieser Richtung neue tatsächliche Anführungen zu machen, da er vor dem erst im Laufe der Revisionsinstanz erfolgten Inkrafttreten des Aufwertungsgesetzes nicht in der Lage gewesen sei, seine Verteidigung auf diesen Gesichtspunkt abzustellen. Dieses Verlangen würde an sich berechtigt sein, es kommt aber gegenwärtig auf die Zulässigkeit einer Aufwertung kraft Rückwirkung nicht an, weil der Annahme des Berufungsgerichts zuzustimmen ist, daß es eines Vorbehalts des Klägers zur Erhaltung seines Aufwertungsanspruchs nicht bedurft hat.

Nach § 14 Aufw.G., der nach § 63 Abs. 1 Satz 2 entsprechende Anwendung findet, ist die Aufwertung ausgeschlossen, wenn der Gläubiger sich „bei der Annahme der Leistung" seine Rechte nicht vorbehalten hat. Der § 14 AufwG. schließt sich, soweit er die Aufwertung von einem Vorbehalt des Gläubigers abhängig macht, an § 11 der 3. Steuernotverordnung an. Zur Begründung des § 11 war angeführt, es müsse verhindert werden, daß der wirtschaftliche Erfolg einer nachträglichen Aufwertung bereits erloschener Ansprüche auf Umwegen (ungerechtfertigte Bereicherung, Irrtumsanfechtung) herbeigeführt werde. Der Vorschrift liegt hiernach die Auffassung zugrunde, daß das Schuldverhältnis erlösche, wenn der Gläubiger eine ihm als Erfüllung angebotene unvollständige Leistung als Erfüllung annehme. Wenngleich diese Auffassung nach feststehender Rechtsprechung unrichtig ist, so ist sie doch für die Auslegung der auf ihr beruhenden Vorschriften zu berücksichtigen. Danach ist davon auszugehen, daß unter der Annahme der Leistung im Sinne der genannten

Vorschriften ein Verhalten des Gläubigers zu verstehen ist, das nach Lage des Falles unter Berücksichtigung der Verkehrssitte und der Grundsätze von Treu und Glauben sich als Ausdruck des Willens darstellt, eine ihm zugehende Leistung als Erfüllung gelten zu lassen (Schlegelberger S. 104; Mügel S. 270). Ein derartiges Verhalten mag an sich auch dann vorliegen können, wenn der Gläubiger im Wege der Zwangsvollstreckung gegen den Schuldner vorgeht und von ihm eine Leistung erzwingt. Es ist aber rechtlich nicht zu beanstanden, wenn das Berufungsgericht unter den Umständen des vorliegenden Falles, wo der Kläger auf Grund einer vollstreckbaren Ausfertigung der Schuldurkunde eine Forderung des Beklagten hat pfänden und sich zur Einziehung überweisen lassen, in der Entgegennahme der vom Drittschuldner geleisteten Zahlung des gepfändeten Betrags keine Erklärung des Willens erblickt hat, sich dadurch wegen seiner Forderung gegen den Beklagten für befriedigt zu erklären. Der dem Kläger zur Verfügung stehende vollstreckbare Titel lautete nur über den Nennbetrag seiner Forderung, einen Titel über den Aufwertungsbetrag hatte er nicht, sondern sucht er sich mit der gegenwärtigen Klage erst zu verschaffen. Wenn er sich des ihm zur Verfügung stehenden Vollstreckungstitels bedient hat, um zwangsweise gegen den Beklagten vorzugehen, so bekundete er damit seinen Willen, den Beklagten im Rahmen des vollstreckbaren Titels zu einer Leistung zu zwingen, er gab jedoch damit nicht zu erkennen, daß er diese Leistung als die volle Erfüllung der dem Beklagten obliegenden Verbindlichkeit annehmen wollte. Der Beklagte konnte den Umständen nach das Vorgehen des Klägers auch nicht anders auffassen; denn dem Kläger stand damals eine weitergehende Vollstreckungsmöglichkeit nicht zu Gebote. Ein Anlaß zu einem Vorbehalt dem zahlenden Drittschuldner gegenüber bestand für den Kläger nicht, da die Zahlung des Drittschuldners nicht als Erfüllung der Schuld des Beklagten geleistet wurde, sondern nur zur Tilgung seiner eigenen Schuld in Höhe des vom Kläger gepfändeten Betrags erfolgte. Eine Annahme der Leistung, wie sie § 14 AufwG. voraussetzt, hat seitens des Klägers hiernach nicht stattgefunden, es bedurfte daher zur Erhaltung des Aufwertungsanspruchs des Klägers auch keines Vorbehalts (Schlegelberger S. 105).

Die Ansicht des Oberlandesgerichts Marienwerder (JW. 1924

S. 1269/70), daß auch bei zwangsweiser Beitreibung des Nennbetrags ein Vorbehalt erforderlich sei, ist unrichtig. Das Oberlandesgericht begründet diese Ansicht damit, daß der Gläubiger, wenn er gegen den Schuldner vorgehe, noch besser in der Lage sei, sich zu überlegen, wieviel er fordern könne, als wenn der Schuldner ihm eine Zahlung aufdränge. Daß diese Erwägung nicht zutreffend ist, zeigt der vorliegende Fall, wo der Kläger nicht in der Lage war, auf Grund des vollstreckbaren Titels mehr als den Nennbetrag beizutreiben, wie er es getan hat. . . .

Appendix 4

Robert Fischer:

Meine ersten Eindrücke in Bremerhaven

Bevor ich nach den Unterweserorten kam, war ich nur im damaligen 7. Bezirk des D.M.V. tätig gewesen und hatte dort all die unangenehmen Erscheinungen der Auseinandersetzungen mit den gegnerischen Organisationen zur Genüge kennengelernt und ausgekostet. Um so erfreuter war ich, als ich am 1. Juli 1912 meine Stellung in Bremerhaven antrat, zu finden, daß die auf den Werften und in den handwerklichen Betrieben beschäftigten Metallarbeiter fast restlos im D.M.V. organisiert waren. Mit dieser Einigkeit der Metallarbeiter hatten die Firmen zu rechnen und haben damit gerechnet. Was an anderen Orten mit schlechten Organisationsverhältnissen unbedenklich den Arbeitern geboten werden konnte, in den Unterweserorten war es Dank der guten Organisation unmöglich.

Die Arbeit auf den Werften zur damaligen Zeit brachte es mit sich, daß gelegentlich Überstunden geleistet werden mußten, wenn die Lieferfristen eingehalten werden sollten. Als 1912 wegen Durchführung der Maifeier die Werften die Arbeiter für 3 Tage aussperrten, wurde dieses nicht ruhig hingenommen und beschlossen, in den nächsten 3 Monaten keine Überstunden zu leisten. Dieser Beschluß wurde mit aller Schärfe durchgeführt. Dank der Einigkeit der Arbeiter und ihrem Rückhalt in der Organisation mußten die Werften sich mit dem Beschluß und der Art seiner Durchführung abfinden. Nachdem ich kurze Zeit in Bremerhaven war, nahmen die Kollegen in Abteilungsversammlungen Stellung zu der Frage, „ob nicht die Verweigerung der Überstunden über 3 Monate hinaus bestehen bleiben soll". Im Bewußtsein der durch eine gute Organisation bedingten Stärke bestand bei den Kollegen die Absicht, wenn nicht besondere Zugeständnisse seitens der Werften gemacht würden, den gefaßten Beschluß weiter in Geltung zu lassen.

Mit Rücksicht auf die damals geplanten und z. T. in Ausführung begriffenen Lohnbewegungen mußte die Organisationsleitung Wert darauf legen, daß eine Störung derselben in jeder Form unterblieb. Leicht war es nicht, die Kollegen davon zu überzeugen, daß aus diesem Grunde nach Ablauf der 3 Monate der Beschluß betr. Überstundenverweigerung erledigt sei.

Die Verdienste der Werftarbeiter waren damals nicht so hoch, daß nicht jeder für den durch Überstunden zu erzielenden Mehrverdienst Verwendung gehabt hätte. Um so unvergeßlicher bleibt mir der Opfermut, mit dem die Kollegen bereit waren, den gewerkschaftlichen Kampf in dieser Form weiter zu führen und auch weiterhin auf die Mehreinnahme aus Überstunden zu verzichten.

147

In den Orten, in denen ich vordem für den Verband tätig war, hatte die Organisationsleitung große Mühe, mitunter war es sogar aussichtslos, in den einzelnen Betriebsabteilungen Kollegen zu finden, welche bereit waren, das Amt eines Vertrauensmannes anzunehmen. Um so angenehmer war mein Empfinden, daß in den Unterweserorten ein guter Vertrauensmännerkörper vorhanden war, und darüber hinaus fast jeder Kollege sich im Interesse des weiteren Auf- und Ausbaues des Verbandes betätigte. Mich hiervon zu überzeugen, hatte ich gleich in den ersten Tagen meiner Anwesenheit auf dem Verbandsbüro Gelegenheit; sei es in der Anmeldung von Werkstattversammlungen, sei es bei der Ablieferung von Aufnahmescheinen der in den Betrieben neueingestellten „Binnenländer".

Damals habe ich oft gewünscht, hätte der D.M.V doch in allen Orten eine solche gute Organisation und solch tätige Mitglieder, wie in den Unterweserorten. Um vieles besser wäre in der Vorkriegszeit die Lage der Metallarbeiter gewesen.

Und daß in den Unterweserorten der gute Organisationsgeist noch heute vorhanden ist, erfüllt mich mit besonderer Freude. In den weiterhin notwendigen Kämpfen wünsche ich den Kollegen vollen Erfolg.

Source: 40 Jahre Deutscher Metallarbeiter Verband, Verwaltungsstelle Bremerhaven, 1.September 1891/1931, S. 147-148

Appendix 5

Selected Articles of the German Constitution of the 11th of August 1919

PART I Structure and Tasks of the Federation

Section I. The Federation and the States

Art. 1. The German Federation is a republic. Supreme power emanates from the people.
Art. 4. The rules of international law, universally recognized, are deemed to form part of German federal law and, as such, have obligatory force.
Art. 9. In so far as there is need for uniform regulation, the Federation may legislate upon all matters concerning
(1) Public welfare,
(2) The maintenance of public order and security.
Art. 10. General principles may be laid down by federal legislation concerning the following subjects, viz.
(1) The rights and duties of religious bodies.
(2) Public education, including the universities and scientific libraries.
(3) The status of officials of all public corporations.
(4) Land laws...
(5) The disposal of the dead.
Art. 12. So long and so far as the Federation has not exercised its legislative powers, the states continue free to legislate. This does not, however, hold good of subjects as to which the federation has sole power to legislate...
Art. 13. Federal law overrides state law...
Art. 14. The federal laws are executed by the authorities of the states, in so far as federal laws do not otherwise provide.
Art. 15. .The state governments are bound at the request of the federal government to remedy defects discovered in the execution of federal laws...
Art. 17. Every state must have a republican constitution. The representatives of the people must be elected by the universal, equal, direct and secret suffrage of all German subjects, men and women. Each state government requires the confidence of the state parliament...

Section II. The Reichstag

Art. 20. The deputies are, each of them, representative of the whole people. They are subject to their conscience alone and are not bound by instructions.
Art. 22. The representatives are elected by the universal, equal, direct, and secret suffrage of all men and women over twenty years of age in accordance with the principle of proportional representation...
Art. 23. The Reichstag is elected for four years...
Art. 25. The President of the Federation may dissolve the Reichstag, but only once for any one cause.
The general election is held not later than on the sixtieth day after dissolution.

Section III. The President of the Federation and the Federal Government

Art. 41. The President of the Federation is elected by the whole German people. Every German who has completed his thirty-fifth year is eligible...
Art. 42. When entering upon his office, the President takes the following oath before the Reichstag,
"I swear to devote my strength to the welfare of the German people, to further its interests, to guard it from harm, to observe the constitution and the laws of the Federation, to fulfil my duties conscientiously, and to do justice to all men."
Art. 43. The President remains in office for seven years. Re-election is permitted.
Art. 47. The President has supreme command over the whole of the defence force of the federation.
Art. 48. If a state fails to perform the duties imposed upon it by the federal constitution or by federal law, the President may enforce performance with the aid of the armed forces. If public order and security are seriously disturbed or endangered within the Federation, the President may take all necessary steps for their restoration, intervening, if need be, with the aid of the armed forces. For the said purpose he may suspend for the time being, either wholly or in part, the fundamental rights described in Articles 114, 115, 117, 118, 123, 124, and 153.
The President has to inform the Reichstag without delay of any steps taken in virtue of the first and second paragraphs of this article. The measures to be taken are to be withdrawn upon the demand of the Reichstag.
Where delay is dangerous a state government may take provisional measures of the kind described in paragraph 2 for its own territory. Such measures are to be withdrawn upon the demand of the President...or of the Reichstag.
Art. 50. All orders and decrees of the President, including those relating to the defence force, in order to be valid, must be countersigned by the Federal Chancellor or by the competent Federal Minister...
Art. 53. The President appoints and dismisses the Federal Chancellor and, on the latter's recommendation, the Federal Ministers.
Art. 54. The Federal Chancellor and the Federal Ministers require the confidence of the Reichstag for the exercise of their offices. Any one of them must resign if the Reichstag withdraws its confidence from him by an express resolution.
Art. 56. The Federal Chancellor settles the political program, for which he is responsible to the Reichstag...

Section IV. The Reichsrat

Art. 60. A Reichsrat [upper house] will be formed for the representation of the German states in federal legislation and administration.
Art. 61. In the Reichsrat each state has at least one vote. In the case of the larger states one vote will be assigned for every 700,000 inhabitants...No single state may be represented by more than two-fifths of the total number of votes.
After joining the German Federation, Austria will be entitled to be represented in the Reichsrat by a number of votes proportional to her population. Meanwhile the Austrian representatives may take part in the deliberations, but may not vote...

Section V. Federal Legislation

Art. 68. Bills may be introduced by the Federal Government or may originate in the midst of the Reichstag itself.
Federal laws are enacted by the Reichstag.
Art. 70. The President must authenticate all laws constitutionally enacted...
Art. 73. A law passed by the Reichstag shall, before its promulgation, be submitted to the popular vote if the President so decides within one month.
A law the promulgation of which has been postponed at the instance of one-third of the members of the Reichstag [as provided by art. 72] is to be submitted to the popular vote upon the demand of one-twentieth of those entitled to vote...
Art. 74. The Reichsrat may protest against laws passed by the Reichstag. In case of such protest the law is referred back to the Reichstag for further consideration. If then the Reichstag and the Reichsrat cannot agree, the President may, within three months cause the matter in dispute to be submitted to the popular vote...
Art. 76. The constitution can be amended by legislation. However, resolutions of the Reichstag in favour of an amendment of the constitution are effective only if two-thirds of those present consent thereto...

Section VII. Administration of Justice

Art. 102. Judges are independent and subject to the law only.
Art. 105. Exceptional courts [i.e., those not established according to legal administrative procedures] are forbidden. No one may be withdrawn from his lawful judge...Military courts of honour are abolished.

PART II Fundamental Rights and Duties of Germans

Section I. The Individual

Art. 109. All Germans are equal before the law...Titles of nobility may no longer be conferred.
Art. 114. Personal freedom is inviolable. No restraint or deprivation of personal liberty by the public power is admissible, unless authorized by law...
Art. 115. The residence of every German is a sanctuary for him and inviolable. Exceptions are admitted in virtue of the law only.
Art. 116. No one may be punished for an act unless such act was legally punishable at the time when it was committed.
Art. 117. The secrecy of correspondence, as well as the secrecy of postal, telegraphic and telephonic communications is inviolable. Exceptions may be admitted by federal law only.
Art. 118. Every German is entitled within the limits of the general law freely to express his opinions by word of mouth, writing, printing, pictorial representation, or otherwise... There is no censorship, but the law may otherwise provide as regards cinematographic performances. Legislative measures are also permitted for the purpose of combating base and pornographic publications...

Section II. Social Life

Art. 121. By legislation illegitimate children are to be offered the same opportunities for their physical, mental and social development as legitimate children.
Art. 124. All Germans have the right to form societies or associations for any object that does not run counter to the criminal law...The same provisions apply to religious societies and bodies...
Art. 125. Freedom of elections and secret voting are guaranteed...

Section III. Religion and Religious Bodies

Art. 135. All inhabitants of the Federation enjoy full liberty of faith and of conscience...
Art. 137. There is no State Church...

Section IV. Education and Schools

Art. 144. The whole of the educational system is under the supervision of the state; the latter can assign a share in this task to the local communities...
Art. 145. School attendance is compulsory...up to the completion of the eighteenth year. Instruction and the accessories thereto are gratuitous in elementary and continuation [i.e., high] schools.
Art. 148. In every school the educational aims must be moral training, public spirit, personal and vocational fitness, and, above all, the cultivation of German national character and of the spirit of international reconciliation.

Section V. Economic Life

Art. 151. The organization of economic life must accord with the principles of justice and aim at securing for all conditions of existence worthy of human beings. Within these limits the individual is to be secured the enjoyment of economic freedom...
Art. 159. Freedom to combine for the protection and betterment of their conditions of labour is guaranteed to all and in all occupations...

Source: H. Oppenheimer, The Constitution of the German Republic

Appendix 6

Complexity Economics Comparison with Traditional Economics

	Complexity Economics	**Traditional Economics**
Dynamic	Open, dynamic, non-linear systems, far from equilibrium	Closed, static, linear systems in equilibrium
Agents	Modelled individually; use inductive rules of thumb to make decisions; have incomplete information; are subject to errors and biases; learn to adapt over time; heterogeneous agents	Modelled collectively; use complex deductive calculations to make decisions; have complete information; make no errors and have no biases; have no need for learning or adaptation (are already perfect), mostly homogeneous agents
Networks	Explicitly model bi-lateral interactions between individual agents; networks of relationships change over time	Assume agents only interact indirectly through market mechanisms (e.g. auctions)
Emergence	No distinction between micro/macro economics; macro patterns are emergent result of micro level behaviours and interactions.	Micro-and macroeconomics remain separate disciplines
Evolution	The evolutionary process of differentiation, selection and amplification provides the system with novelty and is responsible for its growth in order and complexity	No mechanism for endogenously creating novelty, or growth in order and complexity
Technology	Technology fluid, endogenous to the system	Technology as given or selected on economic basis

Preferences	Formulation of preferences becomes central; individuals not necessarily selfish	Preferences given; Individuals selfish
Origins from Physical Sciences	Based on Biology (structure, pattern, self-organized, life cycle)	Based on 19th-century physics (equilibrium, stability, deterministic dynamics)
Elements	Patterns and Possibilities	Price and Quantity

Source: Complexity Economics (2010) http://en.wikipedia.org/wiki/Complexity_economics

Appendix 7

Examples of Hyperinflation[128]

Angola

Angola went through its worst inflation from 1991 to 1995. In early 1991, the highest denomination was 50,000 kwanzas. By 1994, it was 500,000 kwanzas. In the 1995 currency reform, 1 kwanza reajustado was exchanged for 1,000 kwanzas. The highest denomination in 1995 was 5,000,000 kwanzas reajustados. In the 1999 currency reform, 1 new kwanza was exchanged for 1,000,000 kwanzas reajustados. The overall impact of hyperinflation: 1 new kwanza = 1,000,000,000 pre 1991 kwanzas.

Argentina

The recent examples of very high inflation have mostly occurred in Latin America. Argentina, Bolivia, Brazil, Chile, Peru, and Uruguay together experienced an average annual inflation rate of 121 percent between 1970 and 1987. The Latin American countries with high inflation also experienced a phenomenon called "dollarization." Dollarization is the use of U.S. dollars by Latin Americans in place of their domestic currency, the bulk of the debt having been taken out by corrupt and unjust governments. Argentina was ruled by a military dictator between 1976-83, under which its external borrowing ballooned from US$8 billion to US$43 billion. In the 15 years since 1975, which was the beginning of a long period of economic stagnation, inflation averaged 300%. The drying up of foreign investment after 1982, and the Argentine government's recourse to printing more money to meet its spending needs, laid the foundation for Argentina's hyperinflation. During the 80's in Argentina, inflation rose exponentially. The rising inflation caused incredible problems within the Argentinean economy. Black market, tax evasion, and bartering became norm. Large banks crashed. People were forced to literally bury or hide their money so they would not lose it in a bank. Citizens switched from the peso to the dollar as fast as they could. All these reactions and effects to the rising inflation in turn made the inflation rise faster. By 1989, Argentina experienced 1,000% inflation. Argentina went through steady inflation from 1975 to 1991. At the beginning of 1975, the highest denomination was 1,000 pesos. In late 1976, the highest denomination was 5,000 pesos. In early 1979, the highest denomination was 10,000 pesos. By the end of 1981, the highest denomination was 1,000,000 pesos. In the 1983 currency reform, 1 Peso argentino was exchanged for 10,000 pesos. In the 1985 currency reform, 1 austral was exchanged for 1,000 pesos argentino. In the 1992 currency reform, 1 new peso was exchanged for 10,000 australes. The overall impact of hyperinflation: 1 (1992) peso = 100,000,000,000 pre-1983 pesos.

Austria

Between 1921 and 1922, inflation in Austria reached 134%.

Belarus

Belarus went through steady inflation from 1994 to 2002. In 1993, the highest denomination was 5,000 rublei. By 1999, it was 5,000,000 rublei. In the 2000 currency reform, the ruble was replaced by the new ruble at an exchange rate of 1 new ruble = 1,000 old rublei. The highest denomination in 2002 was 50,000 rublei, equal to 50,000,000 pre-2000 rublei.

---

[128] Information mainly provided by Wikipedia, Hyperinflation, http://en.wikipedia.org/wiki/Hyperinflation.

Bolivia

Bolivia went through its worst inflation between 1984 and 1986. Before 1984, the highest denomination was 1,000 pesos bolivianos. By 1985, the highest denomination was 10 Million pesos bolivianos. In 1985, a Bolivian note for 1 million pesos was worth 55 cents in US dollars, one-thousandth of its exchange value of $5,000 less than three years previously. In the 1987 currency reform, the Peso Boliviano was replaced by the Boliviano at a rate of 1,000,000 : 1.

Bosnia-Herzegovina

Bosnia-Herzegovina went through its worst inflation in 1993. In 1992, the highest denomination was 1,000 dinara. By 1993, the highest denomination was 100,000,000 dinara. In the Republika Srpska, the highest denomination was 10,000 dinara in 1992 and 10,000,000,000 dinara in 1993. 50,000,000,000 dinara notes were also printed in 1993 but never issued.

Brazil

From 1986 to 1994, the base currency unit was shifted three times to adjust for inflation in the final years of the Brazilian military dictatorship era. A 1960s cruzeiro was, in 1994, worth less than one trillionth of a US cent, after adjusting for multiple devaluations and note changes. A new currency called real was adopted in 1994, and hyperinflation was eventually brought under control. The *real* was also the currency in use until 1942; 1 (current) real is the equivalent of 2,750,000,000,000,000,000 of those old reals (called *réis* in Portuguese).

Chile

Beginning in 1971, during the presidency of Salvador Allende, Chilean inflation began to rise and reached peaks of 1,200% in 1973. As a result of the hyperinflation, food became scarce and overpriced. A 1973 coup d'état deposed Allende and installed a military government led by Augusto Pinochet. Pinochet's free-market economic policy ended the inflation and except for an economic depression in 1981 the economy has recovered.

China

As the first user of fiat currency, China has had an early history of troubles caused by hyperinflation. The Yuan Dynasty printed huge amounts of fiat paper money to fund their wars, and the resulting hyperinflation, coupled with other factors, led to its demise at the hands of a revolution. The Republic of China went through the worst inflation 1948-49. In 1947, the highest denomination was 50,000 yuan. By mid-1948, the highest denomination was 180,000,000 yuan. The 1948 currency reform replaced the yuan by the gold yuan at an exchange rate of 1 gold yuan = 3,000,000 yuan. In less than 1 year, the highest denomination was 10,000,000 gold yuan. The highest denomination by a regional bank was 6,000,000,000 yuan issued by XinJiang Provincial Bank in 1949. After the renminbi was instituted by the new communist government, hyperinflation ceased with a revaluation of 1:10,000 in 1955.

Free City of Danzig

Danzig went through its worst inflation in 1923. In 1922, the highest denomination was 1,000 Mark. By 1923, the highest denomination was 10,000,000,000 Mark.

Georgia

Georgia went through its worst inflation in 1994. In 1993, the highest denomination was 100,000 coupons [kuponi]. By 1994, the highest denomination was 1,000,000 coupons. In the 1995 currency reform, a new currency lari was introduced with 1 lari exchanged for 1,000,000 coupons.

Germany

See Chapter 5.2

Greece

Greece went through its worst inflation in 1944. In 1943, the highest denomination was 25,000 drachmai. By 1944, the highest denomination was 100,000,000,000,000 drachmai. In the 1944 currency reform, 1 new drachma was exchanged for 50,000,000,000 drachmai. Another currency reform in 1953 replaced the drachma at an exchange rate of 1 new drachma = 1,000 old drachma. The overall impact of hyperinflation: 1 (1953) drachma = 50,000,000,000,000 pre 1944 drachmai. The Greek inflation rate reached 8.5 billion percent per month (prices double every 28 hours).

Hungary

Hungary went through the worst inflation ever between the end of 1945 and July of 1946. In 1944, the highest denomination was 1,000 pengő. By the end of 1945, it was 10,000,000 pengő. The highest denomination in mid-1946 was 100,000,000,000,000,000,000 pengő. The rate of inflation was 4.19 quintillion (4.19×10^{18}) per cent. A special currency the adópengő - or tax pengő - was created for tax and postal payments. The value of the adópengő was adjusted each day, by radio announcement. On January 1, 1946 one adópengő equaled one pengő. By late July, one adópengő equaled 2,000,000,000,000,000,000,000 or 2×10^{21}pengő. When the pengo was replaced in August 1946 by the forint, the total value of all Hungarian banknotes in circulation amounted to one-thousandth of one US dollar. It is the most severe known incident of inflation recorded, peaking at 4.19×10^{16} percent per month (prices double every 15 hours). The overall impact of hyperinflation: On the 1st of August, 1946 400,000,000,000,000,000,000,000,000,000 or 4×10^{29} (four hundred octillion) pengő became 1 forint.

Israel

Inflation accelerated in the 1970s, rising steadily from 13% in 1971 to 111% in 1979. From 133% in 1980, it leaped to 191% in 1983 and then to 445% in 1984, threatening to become a four-digit figure within a year or two. In 1985 Israel froze all prices by law. That same year, inflation more than halved, to 185%. Within a few months, the authorities began to lift the price freeze on some items; in other cases it took almost a year. By 1986, inflation was down to 19%.

Japan

After WWII, Japan went through the highest denomination at that time, which was a 75,000,000,000 Yen bank cheque. The Japanese wholesale price index (relative to 1 as the average of 1934 to 1936) shot up to 16.3 in 1946, 127.9 in 1948 and 342.5 in 1951. In the early 1950s, after achieving independence from USA, Japan controlled its own money. Through its rapidly growing export trade, Japan stabilized the Yen quickly.

Krajina

Krajina went through the worst inflation in 1993. In 1992, the highest denomination was 50,000 dinara. By 1993, the highest denomination was 50,000,000,000 dinara. Note that this unrecognized country was reincorporated into Croatia in 1998.

Madagascar

The Malagasy franc had a turbulent time in 2004, losing nearly half its value and sparking rampant inflation. On 1 January 2005 the Malagasy ariary replaced the previous currency at a rate of one ariary for five Malagasy francs. In May 2005 there were riots over rising inflation, although falling prices have since calmed the situation.

Nicaragua

Nicaragua went through the worst inflation from 1987 to 1990. From 1943 to April 1971, one US dollar equalled 7 córdobas. From April 1971 to early 1978, one US dollar was worth 10 córdobas. In early 1986, the highest denomination was 10,000 córdobas. By 1987, it was 1,000,000 córdobas. In the 1988 currency reform, 1 new córdoba was exchanged for 10,000 old córdobas. The highest denomination in 1990 was 100,000,000 new córdobas. In the 1991 currency reform, 1 new córdoba was exchanged for 5,000,000 old córdobas. The overall impact of hyperinflation: 1 (1991) córdoba = 50,000,000,000 pre-1988 córdobas.

Peru

See Chapter 7.1

Poland

Poland went through its worst inflation between 1990 and 1993. The highest denomination in 1989 was 200,000 zlotych. It was 1,000,000 zlotych in 1991 and 2,000,000 zlotych in 1992. In the 1994 currency reform, 1 new zloty was exchanged for 10,000 old zlotych. Previously, between 1922 and 1924, Polish inflation reached 275%.

Republika Srpska

Republika Srpska was the breakaway region of Bosnia. As with Krajina, it pegged its currency, the Republika Srpska dinar, to that of Yugoslavia. Their bills were almost the same as Krajina's, but they issued fewer and didn't issue currency after 1993.

Romania

Romania is still working through steady inflation. The highest denomination in 1998 was 100,000 lei. By 2000 it was 500,000 lei. In early 2005 it was 1,000,000 lei. In July 2005 the leu was replaced by the new leu at 10,000 old lei = 1 new leu. Inflation in 2005 was 9%. In 2006 the highest denomination is 500 lei (= 5,000,000 old lei).

Russia

Between 1921 and 1922 inflation in Soviet Russia reached 213%. In 1992, the first year of post-Soviet economic reform, inflation was 2,520%, the major cause being the decontrol of most prices in January. In 1993 the annual rate was 840%, and in 1994, 224%. The ruble devalued from about 40 r/$ in 1991 to about 30,000 r/$ in 1999.

Turkey

Throughout the 1990s Turkey dealt with severe inflation rates that finally crippled the economy into a recession in 2001. The highest denomination in 1995 was 1,000,000 lira. By 2005 it was 50,000,000 lira. Recently Turkey has achieved single digit inflation for the first time in decades, and in the 2005 currency reform, introduced the New Turkish Lira; 1 was exchanged for 1,000,000 old lira.

Ukraine

Ukraine went through its worst inflation between 1993 and 1995. In 1992, the Ukrainian karbovanets was introduced, which was exchanged with the defunct Soviet ruble at a rate of 1 UAK = 1 SUR. Before 1993, the highest denomination was 1,000 karbovantsiv. By 1995, it was 1,000,000 karbovantsiv. In 1996, during the transition to the Hryvnya and the subsequent phase out of the karbovanets, the exchange rate was 100,000 UAK = 1 UAH. This translates to a hyperinflation rate of approximately 1,400% per month. And to this day Ukraine holds the world record for most inflation in one calendar year, which was set in 1993.

United States

During the Revolutionary War, the Continental Congress authorized the printing of paper currency called continental currency. The easily counterfeited notes depreciated rapidly, giving rise to the expression "not worth a continental." Between January 1861 and April 1865, the Lerner Commodity Price Index of leading cities in the eastern Confederacy states increased from 100 to over 9000. As the U.S. Civil War dragged on the Confederate States of America dollar had less and less value, until it was almost worthless by the last few months of the war.

Yugoslavia

Yugoslavia went through a period of hyperinflation and subsequent currency reforms from 1989 to 1994. The highest denomination in 1988 was 50,000 dinars. By 1989 it was 2,000,000 dinars. In the 1990 currency reform, 1 new dinar was exchanged for 10,000 old dinars. In the 1992 currency reform, 1 new dinar was exchanged for 10 old dinars. The highest denomination in 1992 was 50,000 dinars. By 1993, it was 10,000,000,000 dinars. In the 1993 currency reform, 1 new dinar was exchanged for 1,000,000 old dinars. But before the year was over, the highest denomination was 500,000,000,000 dinars. In the 1994 currency reform, 1 new dinar was exchanged for 1,000,000,000 old dinars. In another currency reform a month later, 1 novi dinar was exchanged for 13 million dinars (1 novi dinar = 1 Pound sterling at the time of exchange). The overall impact of hyperinflation: 1 novi dinar = $1 \times 10^{27} \sim 1.3 \times 10^{27}$ pre 1990 dinars. Yugoslavia's rate of inflation hit 5×10^{15} percent cumulative inflation over the time period 1 October 1993 and 24 January 1994.

Zaire

Zaire went through a period of inflation between 1989 and 1996. In 1988, the highest denomination was 5,000 zaires. By 1992, it was 5,000,000 zaires. In the 1993 currency reform, 1 nouveau zaire was exchanged for 3,000,000 old zaires. The highest denomination in 1996 was 1,000,000 nouveaux zaires. In 1997, Zaire was renamed the Congo Democratic Republic and changed its currency to francs. 1 franc was exchanged for 100,000 nouveaux zaires. The overall impact of hyperinflation: 1 franc = 3×10^{11} pre 1989 zaires.

Zimbabwe

See Chapter 7.2

References

Adams, Charles F. (ed.) (1853) The Works of John Adams, Second President of the United States, Vol. 8, Little, Brown and Company, Boston.

American Economic Association (2010) Francis A. Walker Medal, viewed 26 April 2010, http://www.vanderbilt.edu/AEA/honors_awards/walker_medal.htm.

Answer.com, "Allied Powers" (2008) available Online at: http://www.answers.com/topic/allied-powers, website visited on May 24, 2008.

Answer.com, "Central Powers" (2008(i)) available Online at: http://www.answers.com/topic/central-powers, website visited on May 20, 2008.

Answer.com, "Dawes Plan" (2008(iii)) available Online at: http://www.answers.com/topic/dawes-plan, website visited on May 20, 2008.

Answer.com, "Reparations" (2008(ii)) available Online at: http://www.answers.com/topic/reparations?cat=biz-fin, website visited on May 26, 2008

Answer.com, "Young Plan" (2008(iv)) available Online at: http://www.answers.com/topic/young-plan, website visited on June 1, 2008.

Arendt, Hanna (2007) Eichmann in Jerusalem, 2. Aufl., München.

Aristotle (350 B.C.E, 25) Politics, Translated by Jowett, Benjamin, Batoche Books, Kitchener, Ontario.

Atkeson, Andrew & Kehoe, Patrick (2004) 'Deflation and Depression: Is There an Empirical Link', American Economic Review, Vol. 94, No. 2, pp. 99-103.

Attwood, Thomas (1816) The Remedy; or, Thoughts on the Present Distress, 2nd ed., Baldwin, Cradock and Joy, London.

Aufwertungsgesetz [zweites Gesetz über den Volksentscheid] http://www.bundesarchiv.de/aktenreichskanzlei/1919-1933/0001/ma3/ma31p/kap1_2/kap2_34/para3_1.html.

Bainbridge, Lister & Jones, Peter (1992) The Politics of Tolerance: The Use of Gendered Self in Social Welfare Education and Practice, Paper presented at the Annual National Conference of the Australian Association for Social Work and Welfare Education, Sydney.

Baldeaux, Dieter (1985) Bevoelkerungspolitik der Entwickluingslaender - Beurteilung der Massnahmen seit der Weltbevoelkerungskonferenz 1974, Forschungsberichte des BMWZ, Bd. 66, Koeln, Germany.

Baranger, Michel (2008) Chaos, Complexity, and Entropy – A physics talk for non-physicists, Massachusetts Institute of Technology, Center for Theoretical Physics, No. 3112.

Barnard, Daniel (1838) Speeches and Reports in the Assembly of New York: at the Annual Session of 1838, Oliver Steele, Albany.

Bastiat, Frederic M. (1874) Essays on Political Economy, 4th ed., Provost, London.

Benvenisti, E. (2004) The International Law of Occupation, Princeton University Press, Princeton, NJ.

Berger, Sebastien (2008) Zimbabwe hyperinflation 'will set world record within six weeks', 13 Nov 2008, http://www.telegraph.co.uk/news/worldnews.

Bernholz, Peter (2003) Monetary Regimes and Inflation: History, Economic and Political Relationships, Edward Elgar, Cheltenham.

Best, Diana & McColl-Kennedy, Janet (1994) Consumer Expertise and Involvement in Selected Services, Management Paper No. 17, University of Queensland, Brisbane.

Beyer, Wolfgang (2007) Schönheit im Chaos, http://www.wolfgangbeyer.de.

Bieber, Horst (1988) Peru – Terror und Chaos. In: Die Zeit vom 23.12.1988, Hamburg, Germany.

Bikhchandani, Sushil, Hirshleifer, David, & Welch, Ivo (1992), "A Theory of Fads, Fashion, Custom, and Cultural Change as Informational Cascades," Journal of Political Economy, Volume 100, Issue 5, pp. 992-1026.

Biographien sozialdemokratischer Parlamentarier in den deutschen Reichs- und Landtagen 1867-1933, http://biosop.zhsf.uni-koeln.de/dbzugriff/mainParl.htm & GESIS: Leibniz-Institut fuer Sozialwissenschaften, Bonn.

Böhm-Bawerk, Eugene von (1891) Positive Theory of Capital, translated by Smart, William A (1891) Macmillan and Co., London.

Boettke, Peter (2001) Calculation and Coordination: Essays on Socialism and the Transitional Political Economy, Routledge, New York.

Bookrags, (reproducing an article by an anonymous 1923 author), "Impact of the Treaty of Versailles on Germany," available Online at: http://www.bookrags.com/essay-2005/10/15/12120/002, website visited on June 2, 2008.

Bottigliero, I. (2004) Redress for Victims of Crimes under International Law, Martinus Nijhoff Publishers, The Hague.

Boyle, James E. (1934) 'By Way of Rebuttal to Dr Fisher', The Rotarian, Vol. 45, No. 6, pp. 30, 45.

Bresciani-Turroni, Constantino, [1931] (2003) The Economics of Inflation : a Study of Currency Depreciation in Post-War Germany, translated by Savers, Millicent E. (1937), George Allen & Unwin, London.

Brockhaus-Enzyklopädie, Bd. 24, Brockhaus-Verl. Mannheim.

Brockhaus-Enzyklopädie „Versailler Vertrag", Bd. 23, Mannheim.

Brownlie, I. (1996) Principles of Public International Law, (4th Edition), Clarendon Press, Oxford.

Bryan, Michael F. (1997) 'On the Origin and Evolution of the Word Inflation', Economic Commentary Federal Reserve Bank of Cleveland, October 15, pp. 1-5.

Bundesministerium der Finanzen (1971) Im Gedenken an Reichsfinanzminister Rudolf Hilferding in Blickpunkt Finanzen, Bd. 6, Bonn.

Bundeszentrale fuer Politische Bildung (1998) Informationen zur politischen Bildung, Heft 261, Bonn, Germany.

Cantillon, Richard [1755] Essai sur la Nature du Commerce en General, translated by Higgs, Henry (1959), Frank Cass, London.

Chang, I. (1997) The Rape of Nanking The Forgotten Holocaust of World War II, Basic Books, New York.

Cipolla, Carlo M. (1949) 'Revisions in Economic History: XII. The Trends in Italian Economic History in the Later Middle Ages', The Economic History Review, New Series, Vol. 2, No. 2, pp. 181-184.

Clodfelter, M. (2002) Warfare and Armed Conflicts: A Statistical Reference to Casualty and Other Figures, 1500-2000, (2nd ed.), McFarland, London.

Collins, Joseph & Lappé, Frances (1980) Vom Mythos des Hungers – Die Entlarvung einer Legende – Niemand muss hunger, Frankfurt, Germany.

Complexity Economics (2010) http://en.wikipedia.org/wiki/Complexity_economics.

Copleston, Edward (1819) A letter to the Right Hon. Robert Peel, M.P. for the University of Oxford, on the Pernicious Effects of a Variable Standard of Value, especially as it regards the Condition of the Lower Orders and the Poor Laws / by one of his Constituents, 2nd ed., J. Murray, Oxford.

Davies, Paul (1983) God and the New Physics, Simon & Schuster, New York.

Davies, Paul (1987) The Cosmic Blueprint, Heinemann, London.

Davies, Paul (2005) About time: Einstein's unfinished revolution, Simon & Schuster, New York.

Dieckmann, H. & Popitz, Johannes (1960) Entwicklungen und Wirksamkeit in der Zeit der Weimarer Republik, Berlin.

dtv-Lexikon München, Bd. 20.

Ekklesia News Brief, "C of E should consider reparations for slave trade says Archbishop of Canterbury," available Online at:
http://www.ekklesia.co.uk/node/4940, website visited on June 5, 2008.

Ellis, J. (1993) The World War II databook: the essential facts and figures for all the combatants, Aurum Press, London.

Epstein, K. (1962) M. Enzberger und das Dilemma der deutschen Demokratie, Berlin.

Everett, Edward (ed.) (1851) The Works of Daniel Webster, Volume 3, Little and Brown, Boston.

Ferguson, Niall (2010) "Complexity and Collapse – Empire on the Edge of Chaos", Foreign Affairs, Vol. 89, No. 2, New York.

Ferguson, Niall, http://en.wikipedia.org/Niall_Ferguson.

Findley, C.V. & Rothney, J.A. (2006) Twentieth Century World, (6th ed.), Houghton Mifflin Company, Boston.

Fischer, Wolfgang Chr. (1983) Sozial-oekonomische Aspekte der Ernaehrung in unterentwickelten Laendern – dargestellt am Beispiel Ecuador/Suedamerika. In: Hauswirtschaft & Wissenschaft, 31. Jg., Heft 3, Muenchen, Germany.

Fischer, Wolfgang Chr. (1984) Eine geteilte Gesellschaft - Implikationen fuer die Verbraucherpolitik in westlichen Industriestaaten, Hauswirtschaftliche Bildung, No. 2, Baltmannsweiler, Germany.

Fischer, Wolfgang Chr. (1989) Sozial-oekonomische Folgen der Weltwirtschaftspolitik am Beispiel Peru, Rationelle Hauswirtschaft, XXVI, Heft 8/89, 7-10, Verlag Neuer Merkur, Muenchen, Germany.

Fischer, Wolfgang Chr. & Froeleke, Hartmut (1987) Welternaehrungskrise – Was koennen wir tun? Beitraege zur Arbeits- und Konsumforschung, Heft 4, Bremen, Germany.

Fontaine, André (1989) Le Camp d`Étrangers Des Milles 1939-1943, Aix-en-Provence, France.

Foorman, J.L. & Jehle, M.E. (1982) "Effects of State and Government Succession on Commercial Bank Loans to Foreign Sovereign Borrowers," University of Illinois Law Review, No. 1.

Foster, William (1934) 'Can the Dollar be 'Managed'?' The Rotarian, Vol. 44, No. 1, pp. 16-18, 49-50.

Frankenberg, G. & Knieper, R. (1984) "Legal Problems of the Over-indebtedness of Developing Countries: The Current Relevance of the Doctrine of Odious Debts," International Journal of the Sociology of Law.

Fraser, David (1994) Knight's Cross, A Life of Field Marshal Erwin Rommel, HarperCollins Publishers, London.

Galbraith, John K. (1975) Money, Whence it Came, Where it Went, Houghton Mifflin, Boston.

Garrison, Roger W. (1989) 'The Austrian Theory of the Business Cycle in the Light of Modern Macroeconomics', Review of Austrian Economics, Vol. 3, No. 1, pp. 3-29.

Garrison, Roger W. (2001), Time and Money: The Macroeconomics of Capital Structure, Routledge, London.

Gilbert, M. (1994) Atlas of World War I, Oxford University Press, Oxford.

Gesetz v. 26.06.1916 (RGBl. 1916, 639).

Gnodtke, Hans G. (2009) Sixty Years of the German Basic Law (Constitution of the Federal Republic of Germany 1949) and Twenty Years of German Reunification – a Synopsis, Guest Lecture, School of Law, James Cook University, 26th of May 2009.

Gohla, H.P. (1986) Peru 1968–1980: Das Experiment linker Militaers. In: Misereor, Peru – Bolivien, Aachen, Germany.

Goulding, Daniel J. (2009) Email to author W. Fischer on 2nd September 2009.

Gribel, Carl (1925) Gesetz ueber die Aufwertung von Hypotheken und anderen Anspruechen (Aufwertungsgesetz) vom 16. Juli 1925 unter besonderer Beruecksichtigung der Rechtsprechung des Kammergerichts in Berlin, Verlag von Julius Springer, Berlin.

Grybowski, Kazimierz (1971) The Nominalistic Principle: A Legal Approach to Inflation, Deflation and Revaluation by Eliyahu Hirschberg, Duke Law Journal, Vol. 1971, No. 5, pp.1030-1031.

Haffner, S. (1989) Von Bismarck zu Hitler, 186 ff., Johannes Popitz, München.

Hagen Preuss in Denkschrift zum Verfassungsentwurf v. 03.01.1919, S. 9, Deutscher Reichsanzeiger Nr. 15 v. 20.01.1919.

Hanf, Henning & von Wersebe, Bernhard (1994) Price, Quality, and Consumers Behaviour, Journal of Consumer Policy, Vol. 17, No. 3, The Hague, Netherlands.

Hanke, Steve H. & Kwok, Alex K. F. (2009) On the Measurement of Zimbabwe's Hyperinflation, Cato Journal, Vol. 29, No. 2 (Spring/Summer 2009), New York.

Hanke, Thomas (1989) Peru – Opfer ohne Sinn. In: Die Zeit, Nr. 1, Hamburg, Germany.

Hayek, Friedrich von (1935) Prices and Production, 2nd ed., Routledge & Kegan Paul, London.

Hayek, Friedrich von (1948) Individualism and Economic Order, University of Chicago, Chicago.

Hayek, Friedrich von [1972] A Tiger by the Tail: A 40-Years' Running Commentary on Keynesianism by Hayek, 3rd ed., edited by Shenoy, Sudha R (2009), The Institute of Economic Affairs & the Ludwig von Mises Institute.

Hazlitt, Henry (1959) The Failure of the "New Economics": an Analysis of the Keynesian Fallacies, Van Nostrand, Princeton.

Hazlitt, Henry (1978) The Inflation Crisis, and How to Resolve It, Arlington House, New York.

Hermanns, Johannes (1986) Das taegliche Sattwerden ist die alles beherrschende Frage. In: Misereor, Peru-Bolivien, Aachen, Germany.

Hershey Jr., Robert D. (1988) 'Henry C. Wallich, 74, Dies; Served on Federal Reserve', New York Times, September 16 1998.

Hettlage, Die Finanzverwaltung in Jeserich, Deutsche Verwaltungsgeschichte, Bd. 4.

Hirschberg, Eliyahu (1971) The Nominalistic Principle: A Legal Approach to Inflation, Deflation and Revaluation, Bar Ilan University Press, Israel.

Holt Carroll, Charles (1964) Organization of Debt into Currency and Other Papers; edited by Simmons, Edward C, D. Van Nostrand Company, Princeton.

Holtfrerich, Carl-Ludwig, Deutsche Inflation 1914-1923, http://de.wikipedia.org/wiki/Deutsche_Inflation_1914_bis_1923.

Holtfrerich, Carl-Ludwig (1986) The German inflation 1914-1923 - Causes and Effects in International Perspective, Berlin-New York.

Honig, F. (1954) "The Reparations Agreement between Israel and the Federal Republic of Germany," The American Journal of International Law, Vol. 48, No. 4 Oct.

Hübschmann, Kommentar zur Abgabenordnung, Einf. A, S. 5.

Huerta de Soto, Jesús [1998] Money, Bank Credit, and Economic Cycles, translated by Stroup, Melinda A (2006) Ludwig von Mises Institute, Auburn, Alabama.

Huerta de Soto, Jesús (2006) Money, Bank Credit, and Economic Cycles, Ludwig von Mises Institute, Auburn, Alabama.

Humphrey, Thomas (1981) Keynes on Inflation, Federal Reserve Bank of Richmond, Economic Review, January/February 1981.

Humphrey, Thomas [1998] (1999) 'Mercantilists and Classicals: Insights from Doctrinal History', Federal Reserve Bank of Richmond Economic Quarterly, Vol. 85, No. 2, pp. 55-82.

International Commission of Jurists, "Fiji: Legal Submission on the Promotion of Reconciliation, Tolerance and Unity Bill 2005," (August 2005), available Online at: http://www.humanrights.org.fj/pdf/ICJ_submission.pdf, website visited on June 2, 2008.

Jefferson, Thomas (1830) Memoir, Correspondence, and Miscellanies, from the Papers of Thomas Jefferson, Vol. 4; edited by Randolph, Thomas Jefferson (1830), Gray and Bowen, Boston.

Johansen, Anders & Sornette, Didier (2001) 2050: The End of the Growth Era?, Institute of Geophysics and Planetary Physics, University of California at Los Angeles, USA.

Kabinett Marx III/IV, Band 1, Dokumente, Nr. 191 Kabinettssitzung vom 2. März 1927, 1630 Uhr, Top 2. Aufwertungsfragen http://www.bundesarchiv.de/aktenreichskanzlei/1919-933/0000/ma3/ma31p/kap1_2/kap2_191/para3_2.html.

Keen, Steve (2009) "The Roving Cavaliers of Credit", DebtWatch No 31 February 2009: http://www.debtdeflation.com/blogs/2009/01/31/therovingcavaliersofcredit, January 31st, 2009.

Kemmerer, Edwin W. (1918) 'Inflation', The American Economic Review, Vol. 8, No. 2, pp. 247-269.

Keylor, W. (1998) "Versailles and International Diplomacy," in Boemeke, M.F., Feldman, G.D. & Glaser, E. (eds.), The Treaty of Versailles: A Reassessment after 75 Years, Cambridge University Press and The German Historical Institute, Cambridge, New York, Melbourne, pp. 469-506.

Kirchhof, P. (2007) Matthias Enzberger, Patriot u. Visionär, Hohenheim.

Kracht, Uwe (1984) "Ausrottung" von Hunger und Unterernaehrung: Perspektiven des Welternaehrungsproblems im Wandel. In: Ernaehrungs-Umschau, 31. Jg., Heft 4, Frankfurt, Germany.

Krugman, Paul (2009) How Did Economists Get It So Wrong? In: New York Times, 2nd of September.

Krugman, Paul & Wells, Robin (2009) Principles of Economics, 2nd edition, Worth Publisher.

Lancaster, Kelvin (1991) Modern Consumer Theory, Brookfield.

Landreth, Harry & Colander, David C. (2002) History of Economic Thought, Houghton Mifflin Company, Boston & Toronto.

Laremont, R.R. (1999) "Political versus Legal Strategies for the African Slavery Reparations Movement," African Studies Quarterly, Vol. 2, No. 4, available Online at: http://web.africa.ufl.edu/asq/v2/v2i4a3.htm, website visited on June 6, 2008.

Lawson, Robert & Tidwell, Paula & Rainbird, Paul & Loudon, David & Della Bitta, Albert (1996) Consumer Behaviour in Australia & New Zealand, McGraw-Hill, Sydney, New York.

Leaphart, J.V. (2002) "The World Conference against Racism: What was really achieved?" The Fletcher Forum of World Affairs, Vol. 26, No. 2, Summer/Fall.

Leidel, H. (1964)Die Begründung der Reichsfinanzverwaltung, Bundesminister der Finanzen, Bonn.

Leijonhufvud, Axel (2007) 'Monetary and Financial Instability', Centre for Economic Policy, Research Policy Insight, No. 14.

Machlup, Fritz [1931] (1940) The Stock Market, Credit and Capital Formation, revised ed., William Hodge, London.

Manchester Statistical Society (1868) Transactions of the Manchester Statistical Society 1867-68, The Society, Manchester.

Marks, S. (1976) The Illusion of Peace, International Relations in Europe, 1918-1933, St. Martin's Press, New York.

Marx, Karl (1867) Das Kapital, http://en.wikipedia.org/wiki/Das_Kapital.

Matull, Wilhelm (1973) Ostdeutschlands Arbeiterbewegung – Abriss ihrer Geschichte, Leistung und Opfer, Holzner Verlag, Würburg, Germany.

Maynes, E. Scott (1976) Decision Making for Consumers: An Introduction to Consumer Economics, New York.

McKercher, B.J.C. (ed.) (1991) Anglo-American Relations in the 1920s: the struggle for supremacy, Macmillans and the University of Alberta Press, London and Edmonton.

Mill, John Stuart [1848] (1868) Principles of Political Economy: with some of their Applications to Social Philosophy, Vol. 2, D. Appleton, London.

Mises, Ludwig von [1912] The Theory of Money and Credit, translated by Baston, Harold (1981), Liberty Fund, Indianapolis.

Mises, Ludwig von [1949] (1998) Human Action: A Treatise on Economics, Scholars' Edition, Ludwig von Mises Institute, Auburn, Alabama.

Mises, Ludwig von (1990) Economic Freedom and Interventionism: An Anthology of Articles and Essays by Ludwig von Mises, edited by Greaves, Bettina, Irvington-on-Hudson, Foundation for Economic Education, New York.

Mosler, Hermann (1964) Die Verfassung des deutschen Reichs vom 11. August 1919, Stuttgart, Germany.

Nast, Thomas (1876) Milk-Tickets for Babies, in Place of Milk [Cartoon] Robinson Crusoe's Money; or, the Remarkable Financial Fortunes and Misfortunes of a Remote Island Community, Harper & Brothers, New York.

Nast, Thomas (1878) Ideal Money [Cartoon] Harper's Weekly Jan 19 1878.

New York State Legislature (1838) Documents of the Senate of the State of New York, Sixty-First Session, Vol. 2, E Croswell, Albany.

Noel, Michael (2005) The Twenty Most Influential Businessman of All Time, Forbes, 29 July 2005, viewed 1 April 2010. http://www.forbes.com/2005/07/29/most-influential-businessmen-cx_mn_0729bizmenintro.html.

Ormerod, Paul (1994) Free-Marketeers Opt for Chaos, in Theory, The Age, Melbourne.

Paine, Thomas 1786 1838 (1786) Dissertations on Government, the Affairs of the Bank, and Paper Money, Charles Cist, Philadelphia.

Philbin, James (1991) 'An Austrian Perspective on Some Leading Jacksonian Monetary Theorists', The Journal of Libertarian Studies, Vol. 10, No. 1, pp. 83-95.

Phillips, Chester A & McManus, Thomas F & Nelson, Richard W (1937) Banking and the Business Cycle, Macmillan, New York.

Plait, Philip C. (2002) Bad Astronomy; Misconceptions and Misuses Revealed, from Astrology to the Moon Landing "Hoax", Wiley, New York.

Pope, Alexander (1797) The Works of Alexander Pope, Esq., Volume 3, edited by Warton, Joseph, Law, Johnson & Dilly, London.

Popitz, J. Die Finanzpolitik seit 1918 in Zehn Jahren deutsche Geschichte 1918 – 1928.

Raguet, Condy (1839) A Treatise on Currency and Banking: Addressed to John W. Cowell, Esq., Agent of the Bank of England in the United States, Ridgway, Piccadilly & Miller, London.

Rau u.a. (2009) Kommentar zum UmsatzsteuerG, Einf. vor § 1 (Rz. 3, 6, 8, 11), Köln.

Rede zur Neuordnung des deutschen Finanzwesens vom Reichsminister der Finanzen, S. 82, Berlin 1919, Verlag Hobbing.

Reichsmark, Wikipedia, http://de.wikipedia.org/wiki/Reichsmark.

Reichswirtschaftsrat, Wikipedia (2009) http://de.wikipedia.org/wiki/Reichswirtschaftsrat.

Reimer, Achim (2005) Stadt zwischen zwei Demokratien, Baden-Baden von 1930 bis 1950, München.

RGBl. 1918, 959; Popitz, StuW 1928.

Richarz, Irmintraut (1992) Household Management: Historical and Future Perspectives, Journal of the Home Economics Association of Australia, Vol. 24, No. 2.

Rizzolatti, G., Fadiga, L., Gallese, V. & Fogassi, L. (1996) Premotor cortex and recognition of motor actions, Cogn Brain Res 3, pp. 131-41.

Robbins, Lionel (1937) in: Chi-Yuen Wu, An Outline of International Price Theories, George Routledge and Sons, p. xi.

Röhm, Eberhard & Thierfelder, Jörg (2007) Juden-Christen-Deutsche Bd. 4/II 1941-1945 Stuttgart, Germany.

Rothbard, Murray N. (1963a) Money, the State and Modern Mercantilism, Modern Age, Summer 1963, pp. 279-289.

Rothbard, Murray N. [1963b] (2000) America's Great Depression, 5th ed., von Mises Institute, Auburn, Alabama.

Rothbard, Murray N. [1995] (2006) Economic Thought before Adam Smith: An Austrian Perspective on the History of Economic Thought, Vol.1, Ludwig von Mises Institute. Auburn, Alabama.

Rothbard, Murray N. [1995] (2006) Classical Economics: An Austrian Perspective on the History of Economic Thought, Vol.2, Ludwig von Mises Institute, Auburn, Alabama.

Rothbard, Murray N. [2004] (2009) Man, Economy, and State: a Treatise on Economic Principles; with Power and Market: Government and the Economy, Ludwig von Mises Institute, Auburn, Alabama.

Salemi, Michael K. (2007) Hyperinflation, The Concise Encyclopedia of Economics, 2nd Edition, Library of Economics and Liberty, Indianapolis, USA.

Salerno, Joseph (1999) 'Money and Gold in the 1920s and 1930s: An Austrian View', The Freeman, Vol. 49, No. 10, pp. 31-33.

Salerno, Joseph (2003) 'An Austrian Taxonomy of Deflation – with Applications to the U.S.', Quarterly Journal of Austrian Economics, Vol. 6, No. 4, pp. 81-109.

Sangmeister, Hartmut (1988) Auslandsverschuldung Lateinamerikas: Entwicklungskrise ohne Ausweg? In: Beilage zur Wochenzeitung Das Parlament, B 33/34, Bonn, Germany.

Saul, John Ralston (1999) Democracy & Globalisation, Transcript, Lecture delivered at the University of New South Wales, Sydney, Australia, January 1999, http://www.abc.net.au/specials/saul/default.htm.

Schama, Simon [1987] (1988) The Embarrassment of Riches: an Interpretation of Dutch Culture in the Golden Age, University of California Press, Berkeley.

Schmierer, Susan C. (1979) Industry and Inflation in Germany: 1914-1925, Master Thesis, Department of Finance, St John's University, New York.

Schuker, S.A. (1976) The End of French Predominance in Europe: The Financial Crisis of 1924 and the Adoption of the Dawes Plan, University of North Carolina Press, Chapel Hill, NC.

Selgin, George (1990) 'Monetary Equilibrium and the Productivity Norm of Price-Level Policy', Cato Journal, Vol. 10, No. 1, pp. 265-287.

Selgin, George (1997) 'Less Than Zero: The Case for a Falling Price Level in a Growing Economy', IEA Hobart Paper, No. 132, The Institute of Economic Affairs, London.

Sennholz, Hans F. (1979) Age of Inflation, Appleton, WI 54912, USA.

Simpson, Stephen (1831) The Working Man's Manual: a New Theory of Political Economy, on the Principle of Production the Source of Wealth, Thomas L. Bonsal, Philadelphia.

Sitzung des Reichstages, 132nd Steu.Ber., S. 4469.

Smith, Vera C (1936) The Rationale of Central Banking, P.S. King, London.

Sondergerichts Mannheim, Urteil vom 10.7.1936, Az.: SO Kms 6/36.

Sornette, Didier (2007) Endogenous versus Exogenous Origins of Crises, http://www.ess.ucla.edu/faculty/sornette/essay_endogenous.asp#endogenous.

Sornette, Didier (2009) The Chinese Equity Bubble: Ready to Burst, July 10, 2009; http://arxiv.org/ftp/arxiv/papers/0907/0907.1827.pdf, arXiv, Cornell University, New York, USA.

Southern, David B. (1979) The Revaluation Question in the Weimar Republic, The Journal of Modern History, Vol. 51, No. 1, On Demand Supplement (Mar., 1979), pp. D1029-D1054, Published by: The University of Chicago Press, http://www.jstor.org/stable/1878444

Southern, David B. (1988) German Legal Ideas in the Nineteenth and Twentieth Centuries, The Liverpool Law Review Vol.X (1), pp. 63-83.

Stapelfeldt, Gerhard (1984) Peru – im Namen der Freiheit ins Elend, Frankfurt, Germany.

Stavro, Barry (2006) J.K. Galbraith - A critic of his country's materialism, The Sydney Morning Herald, May 1.

Stryker, James (ed.) (1849) The American Quarterly Register and Magazine, Volume 2, Published by the Proprietor, Philadelphia.

Swan, Peter L. (1987) The Pure Food Laws and Regulations: Burdensome Laws in Search of Meaningful Objectives?, Centre for Independent Studies, St. Leonards (NSW).

Szebenyei, Joseph (1922) The Dollar in Wonderland, The Atlantic Monthly (1857-1932), Mar 1922, pp. 412-419.

Taylor, A.J.P. (1976) The Origins of the Second World War, Penguin, Harmondsworth.

Terhalle, F., (1952) Geschichte der deutsch-öffentlichen Finanzwirtschaft vom Beginn des 19. Jahrhunderts bis zum Schluss des 2. Weltkriegs im Handbuch der Finanzwissenschaften, Bd. 1, Tübingen.

Terry, Chris, Ross, Jones & Braddock, Richard (1988) Australian Microeconomic Policies, 3rd edition, New York, Toronto, London.

The Papers of George Washington (2009) The Mount Vernon Ladies' Association & University of Virginia, viewed 1 March 2010, http://gwpapers.virginia.edu/documents/constitution/1787/bowen.html.

Thomas, H. (1997) The Slave Trade: The Story of the Atlantic Slave Trade, 1440-1870, Simon & Schuster, New York, 804-805.

Tooke, Thomas (1826) Considerations on the State of the Currency, John Murray, London.

Trachtenberg, M. (1980) Reparation in World Politics: France and European Diplomacy, 1916-1923, Columbia University Press, New York.

Tucker, S.C. (1999) The European Powers in the First World War: An Encyclopedia, Garland, New York.

Urlanis, B. (2003) Wars and Population, University Press of the Pacific, Honolulu.

van Horn, A., "War Reparations, End," available Online at: http://www.idebate.org/topic_details.php?topicID=612, website visited on June 2, 2008.

Venzky, Gabriele (1979) Verhungern muesste niemand. In: Die Zeit, Nr. 31, Hamburg, Germany.

Von der Reichsschatzkammer zum Bundesfinanzministerium, herausgegeben vom Bundesminister der Finanzen, Köln.

Voss, R., Johannes Popitz, Jurist, Politiker, Staatsdenker (1884-1945).

Wallich, Henry C. (1978), 'Honest Money', Economic Review, Vol. 64, No. 5, pp. 13-16.

Walker, Francis A. [1878] (2008) Money, Adegi Graphics.

Walker, Francis A. [1899] (2009) Discussions in Economics and Statistics, BiblioBazaar.

Wicksell, Knut [1898] (1965) Interest and Prices: A Study of the Causes Regulating the Value of Money, Augustus M. Kelley, New York.

Wicksell, Knut [1904] 'Ends and Means in Economics', in his Selected Papers on Economic Theory, edited by Lindahl, Erik (1958), Allen & Unwin, London.

Wikipedia, "Article 231 of the Treaty of Versailles," (2008(ii)), available Online at: http://en.wikipedia.org/wiki/Article_231_of_the_Treaty_of_Versailles, website visited on June 4, 2008.

Wikipedia "Bandwagon effect", http://en.wikipedia.org/wiki/Bandwagon_effect.

Wikipedia, "German Hyperinflation", http://en.wikipedia.org/wiki/German_hyperinflation_of_1922 Inflation in the Weimar Republic.

Wikipedia, „German Rentenmark", http://en.wikipedia.org/wiki/German_Rentenmark.

Wikipedia, "Gulf War," (2008(iv)), available Online at: http://en.wikipedia.org/wiki/Gulf_War, website visited on June 4, 2008.

Wikipedia, "Harold James (historian)", http://en.wikipedia.org/wiki/Harold_James_(historian).

Wikipedia, "Heinrich Trinowitz", http://en.wikipedia.org/wiki/Heinrich_Trinowitz.

Wikipedia, "Hyperinflation", http://en.wikipedia.org/wiki/Hyperinflation.

Wikipedia, "Hyperinflation in Zimbabwe" http://en.wikipedia.org/wiki/Hyperinflation_in_Zimbabwe.

Wikipedia, "Inflation in the Weimar Republic" http://en.wikipedia.org/wiki/German_hyperinflation_of_1922.

Wikipedia, "Karl Liebknecht" http://en.wikipedia.org/wiki/Karl_Liebknecht.

Wikipedia, "London Ultimatum 1921", http://en.wikipedia.org/wiki/German_hyperinflation_of_1922.

Wikipedia "Mass hysteria", http://en.wikipedia.org/wiki/Mass_hysteria.

Wikipedia, "Reparations for Slavery," (2008(v)), available Online at: http://en.wikipedia.org/wiki/Reparations_for_slavery, website visited on June 10, 2008

Wikipedia, "Robert Fischer (Unionist)", http://en.wikipedia.org/wiki/Robert_Fischer_(Unionist).

Wikipedia, "War Reparations," (2008(i)), available Online at: http://en.wikipedia.org/wiki/War_reparations, website visited on May 3, 2008.

Wikipedia, "World War I Reparations," (2008(iii)), available Online at: http://en.wikipedia.org/wiki/World_War_I_reparations, website visited on June 4, 2008.

Willis, Henry Parker (1933) 'Is Inflation the Way Out? No', The Rotarian, Vol. 42, No. 4, pp. 18-19, 49-50.

Woolley, John & Peters, Gerhard (2010) The American Presidency Project, Santa Barbara, California, viewed 1 March 2010, http://www.presidency.ucsb.edu/ws/?pid=67087.

Worldpress.org, "Ghanaian President Stirs Controversy over Slave Trade Reparations," (April 12, 2007), available Online at: http://www.worldpress.org/Africa/2750.cfm, website visited on June 9, 2008.

Yu, H. & Guernsey, A., "What is the Rule of Law?", University of Iowa Center for International Finance and Development, available Online at: http://www.uiowa.edu/ifdebook/faq/Rule_of_Law.shtml, website visited on March 15, 2008.

Index

G

H

I

S

T

U

V

W

Y

Z

About the Authors

Wolfgang Chr. Fischer
studied Economics, History and Law at the Universität des Saarlandes, Saarbrücken, and at the Rheinische Friedrich-Wilhelms-Universität Bonn. He was awarded Dr.rer.pol. (Doctorate in Economics) in 1971 from the Faculty of Law & Economics, Rheinische Friedrich-Wilhelms-Universität Bonn, where he had been Academic Assistant at the Institute of Economic Policy. From 1975 until his retirement in 2000 he had been University Professor of Economics, specialised in Consumer Affairs, at the University of Bremen. Professor Fischer was Visiting Professor among other universities at the University of San Francisco and the University of Guelph, Canada. Currently he is Adjunct Professor of Economics in the School of Law at James Cook University, Australia.

Harrison Alexander Amankwah
is a Retired Associate Professor in Law, formerly in the School of Law, James Cook University, Townsville, Australia. He studied Law at the University of Ghana, Legon, Accra, and was awarded Bachelor of Arts (Hons) in 1964 and Bachelor of Laws (LL.B) (Hons) in 1966. As a Fulbright Scholar 1967/68 he was awarded Master of Laws (LL.M) in 1969 at Cornell University, New York, USA. In 1978 he was awarded Doctor of Juridical Science (S.J.D) from New York University, USA. He held, among other positions, Deputy Dean of Law, James Cook University; Dean, Faculty of Law, University of Papua New Guinea; Head of Department of Law, University of Ibadan, Nigeria; Head of Department of Law, University of Science and Technology, Kumasi, Ghana; Visiting Professor, School of Law, Hofstra University, New York; Visiting Senior Fellow, School of Law, University of Zambia, Lusaka. Currently he is Adjunct Professor of Law, School of Law University of South Australia, Adelaide, Australia.

Daniel Jason Goulding
is a senior Client Adviser with RBS Morgans in Townsville. He completed a Bachelor of Economics through James Cook University in 2003 and is currently undertaking post graduate studies through the University of Queensland.

Erich Krausbeck
studied medicine at the Johannes Gutenberg-Universität in Mainz, Germany, where he was awarded Dr.med.(MD) in 1981. Subsequently he took up clinical activities in the department of neuro pathology, University of Mainz, in the Psychiatric Hospital Eichberg at Eltville and in the department of neurology at the State Psychiatric Clinic at Alzey. In 1990 he established his business as Specialist for Neurology and Psychiatry in a practice in Bad Ems, which is now a joint practice for neurology, psychiatry and psychotherapy with two other medical doctors. His scientific work encompasses the psychiatry in the Biedermeier Era, the psychopathology of Adolf Hitler, the psychopathology of Fyodor Mikhaylovich Dostoyevsky and analyses of the psychology in the retail trade.

Kenneth Kaoma Mwenda
A Rhodes Scholar, Prof. Kenneth K. Mwenda is Senior Counsel in the Legal Vice-Presidency of the World Bank, Washington DC. He also serves as Extraordinary Professor of Law at the University of Pretoria, South Africa, as well as Adjunct Professor of Law at

American University Washington College of Law in Washington DC. Prof. Mwenda holds, among many qualifications: the Higher Doctorate Degree of Doctor of Laws (LLD) from Rhodes University, South Africa; a PhD in Corporate Law from the University of Warwick, UK; the graduate degree of Bachelor of Civil Law (BCL/MPhil) from the University of Oxford, UK; a Master of Business Administration degree (MBA) from the University of Hull, UK; and, a Bachelor of Laws (LLB) degree from the University of Zambia. Prof. Mwenda has previously served as a full-time academic at the Faculty of Law of the University of Warwick. In addition, he has been Visiting Professor of Law at the University of Zambia, the University of Miskolc (Hungary), the University of Pretoria (South Africa), and the University of Western Cape (South Africa). He has authored and edited twenty-one (21) scholarly books as well as written over seventy (70) peer-reviewed articles in leading academic journals.

Rainhart Schweigert

Rainhart Schweigert studied Law at the University of Frankfurt on the Main from 1959 to 1961 and then commenced Law studies at the University of Würzburg. In 1963 he finished his studies in Law with the first State Examination (Erstes Juristisches Staatsexamen) and then he was a lawyer (Rechtsreferendar) in his mandatory Law Internship in Bavaria. He finished his Law Internship in 1968 in München. He was awarded Dr.jur. in the field of Labour Law at the University of Würzburg. At the end of 1968 he joined the Taxation Administration of the State of Rheinland-Pfalz and was a Head of a Division (Sachgebietsleiter) at the beginning of his career. From 1972 to 1975 he was the Head of the Taxation Office (Amtsvorsteher) at St. Goarshausen on the Rhine. Since April 1975 until today he is a practising Lawyer and Tax Lawyer in his own legal firm in Bad Ems on the Lahn. In former times he was also a lecturer at the Academy of Administration and Economic Affairs at Koblenz on the Rhine & Moselle. His legal work includes Public Law and in particular Taxation Law.

EINZELSCHRIFTEN

Marcus M. Gillhofer
Teilnehmer-Rekrutierung in der Online-Sozialforschung
Lohmar – Köln 2010 ◆ 160 S. ◆ € 47,- (D) ◆ ISBN 978-3-89936-905-2

Jörn-Axel Meyer (Hrsg.)
Strategien von kleinen und mittleren Unternehmen – Jahrbuch der KMU-Forschung und -Praxis 2010
Lohmar – Köln 2010 ◆ 648 S. ◆ € 83,- (D) ◆ ISBN 978-3-89936-911-3

Christian Kille
Güteraufkommen nach Branchen
Lohmar – Köln 2010 ◆ 272 S. ◆ € 58,- (D) ◆ ISBN 978-3-89936-919-9

Antonio Vera
Krankenhausmanagement in einem wettbewerbsorientierten Umfeld
Lohmar – Köln 2010 ◆ 200 S. ◆ € 49,- (D) ◆ ISBN 978-3-89936-922-9

Georges Ulrich und Rödiger Voss (Hrsg.)
Hochschul Relationship Marketing
Lohmar – Köln 2010 ◆ 180 S. ◆ € 48,- (D) ◆ ISBN 978-3-89936-923-6

Christina Völkl-Wolf
Internetgestützte Untersuchung zu Kompetenzen in der Prozentrechnung bei Erwachsenen und Jugendlichen – Neue Erkenntnisse zur Repräsentativität von Online-Befragungen
Lohmar – Köln 2010 ◆ 292 S. ◆ € 59,- (D) ◆ ISBN 978-3-89936-929-8

Robert Kühn und Tanja Siebert
Key Account Management in global tätigen Logistikkonzernen – Strategie, Planung und Implementierung
Lohmar – Köln 2010 ◆ 88 S. ◆ € 37,- (D) ◆ ISBN 978-3-89936-930-4

Wolfgang Chr. Fischer (Ed.)
German Hyperinflation 1922/23 – A Law and Economics Approach
Lohmar – Köln 2010 ◆ 220 S. ◆ € 59,- (D) ◆ Hardcover ◆ ISBN 978-3-89936-931-1

JOSEF EUL VERLAG